INSTRUCTOR'S MANUAL AND TEST BANK

AMERICA

A NARRATIVE HISTORY

BRIEF SECOND EDITION

GEORGE BROWN TINDALL

DAVID E. SHI

Prepared by

David B. Parker, University of North Carolina

Thomas S. Morgan, Winthrop College

W. W. Norton & Company

New York / London

ISBN 0-393-95703-9

W. W. Norton & Company, Inc.
500 Fifth Avenue, New York, NY 10110

W. W. Norton & Company Ltd.
37 Great Russell Street, London WC1B 3NU

1 2 3 4 5 6 7 8 9 0

CONTENTS

Preface   v
Bibliography of Selected Reference Works in American History   vii

1. Discovery and Settlement   1
2. Colonial Ways of Life   10
3. The Imperial Perspective   19
4. From Empire to Independence   28
5. The American Revolution   39
6. Shaping a Federal Union   48
7. The Federalists: Washington and Adams   58
8. Republicanism: Jefferson and Madison   67
9. Nationalism and Sectionalism   76
10. The Jacksonian Impulse   85
11. The Dynamics of Growth   94
12. An American Renaissance: Romanticism and Reform   102
13. Manifest Destiny   111
14. The Old South: An American Tragedy   120
15. The Crisis of Union   129
16. The War of the Union   139
17. Reconstruction: North and South   148
18. New Frontiers: South and West   159
19. Big Business and Organized Labor   169
20. The Emergence of Modern America   179
21. Gilded Age Politics and Agrarian Revolt   188
22. The Course of Empire   199
23. Progressivism: Roosevelt, Taft, and Wilson   210
24. Wilson and the Great War   220
25. Society and Culture Between the Wars   232
26. Republican Resurgence and Decline, 1920–1932   241
27. Franklin D. Roosevelt and the New Deal   252
28. From Isolation to Global War   262
29. The World at War   272
30. The Fair Deal and Containment   282
31. Through the Picture Window: Society and Culture, 1945–1960   292
32. Conflict and Deadlock: The Eisenhower Years   300
33. Into the Maelstrom: The Sixties   309
34. Rebellion and Reaction: The Nixon Years   318
35. Retrenchment: Ford to Reagan   327

Appendix: Sample Final Examinations   336

PREFACE

This *Instructor's Manual and Test Bank* is meant to assist novice instructors in developing a course around the brief second edition of George B. Tindall's and David E. Shi's *America: A Narrative History*, and to aid more experienced instructors with over 1,200 questions for examinations and an outline of each chapter of the text. While Thomas S. Morgan and David B. Parker worked together on the first edition of this manual, Parker alone did the revisions for the present edition. Still, much of Morgan's work remains, and his contributions are here gratefully acknowledged.

Each chapter of this manual provides several suggested lecture topics, closely related to the text itself, with a brief list of possible sources for the lectures. The manual also includes a Test Bank of over 1,200 questions, both multiple-choice and essay. (Most of the questions are multiple-choice, because this format is often the most useful to instructors of large sections.)

A computerized version of the test-item file is available separately for use on the IBM-PC, the Apple IIE, and compatible systems. A test-generating program (the EXAM system) is provided with the test-file diskettes, allowing instructors to create tests easily, choosing those questions from the test file that they wish to use and adding their own questions if they wish. For those who depend more heavily on computers, a more extensive program—known as DIPLOMA—is available, including utilities for class planning, grading, and constructing student tutorials from the test items provided on the diskette. DIPLOMA also includes the EXAM program, and may be requested as an alternative. EXAM and DIPLOMA are available at no charge to instructors who adopt a minimum number of copies of *America: A Narrative History.*

The manual also contains sample final examinations. These can serve as models for instructors, and instructors are invited to modify them to suit the particular needs of their classes. (Unlike the other test items in this manual, the final examinations do not appear on the floppy disks that contain the computerized test bank.) A short bibliography of reference works in American history, which the beginning instructor especially might find useful, is also included.

Instructors who wish their students to use a self-administered guide for assistance in studying the Tindall/Shi text are urged to consider the *Study Guide* written by Thomas S. Morgan and Charles W. Eagles. That guide contains carefully selected documents and readings, and some instructors will want to use it as a required supplement to the course. Others may wish only to request that the campus bookstore order copies to ensure its availability to students. Instructors who adopt the

Tindall/Shi text may request a set of selected map transparencies for use on overhead projectors.

A few words of acknowledgment. A number of my colleagues at the University of North Carolina at Chapel Hill—among them Gary Freeze, Linda Sellars, and Mark Thomspon—offered advice on the various editions of this manual. Thanks also to Chantal, my wife, for her support, and to Katie Mae, our daughter, who more than once gave me an excuse to put the revisions aside for a while. Finally, George Brown Tindall has been for many years a good friend, an able teacher and adviser, and a constant source of inspiration, not only for me but for historians all over the country. My debts to him can never be repaid; the best I can do is to acknowledge them.

David B. Parker
Chapel Hill, North Carolina

BIBLIOGRAPHY OF SELECTED REFERENCE WORKS IN AMERICAN HISTORY

The following list is intended for the beginning instructor as a convenient guide to the wealth of reference materials available for teachers of American history. The usual disclaimer that one finds on such a list—that it is suggestive rather than exhaustive—certainly applies here.

Perhaps the single most useful reference book for historians is the *Harvard Guide to American History* (2 vols.; rev. ed., 1974), edited by Frank B. Freidel. Besides several stimulating essays on the art and methodology of history, the *Harvard Guide* contains a lengthy bibliography. For biographical information, turn first to the multivolume *Dictionary of American Biography* (1928–1987), edited by Allen Johnson, Dumas Malone, and others, and kept up-to-date with periodic supplements. Richard B. Morris's *Encyclopedia of American History* (6th ed., 1982) contains general and topical chronologies, several hundred biographical sketches, and other useful material. The value of Scribner's *Dictionary of American History* (8 vols.; rev. ed., 1976–1978) is greatly enhanced by its comprehensive index. Other useful books include *Documents of American History* (9th ed., 1973), edited by Henry Steele Commager; the *Atlas of American History* (rev. ed., 1984), edited by Kenneth T. Jackson; and the *Album of American History* (6 vols.; 1981), edited by James Truslow Adams. The last-mentioned book is mainly a pictorial work that includes thousands of illustrations covering American history through the early 1960s; a supplement (1985) brings it up to 1982.

Besides the *Harvard Guide*, two bibliographical guides stand out. *America: History and Life* is regularly updated, and is therefore useful for finding more recent materials. *Goldentree Bibliographies in American History*, under the general editorship of Arthur S. Link, are more specialized guides for various topics; examples include John Shy's volume on the American Revolution, Vincent P. De Santis's on the Gilded Age, and Paul M. Gaston's on the New South.

Historical surveys (some more interpretative than others) of various important topics include Thomas A. Bailey's *A Diplomatic History of the American People* (10th ed., 1980), Winthrop S. Hudson's *Religion in America: An Historical Account of the Development of American Religious Life* (4th ed., 1987), Harold Underwood Faulkner et al., *American Economic History* (9th ed., 1976), Alfred H. Kelly, Winfred Harbison, and Herman Belz's *The American Constitution: Its Origins and Development* (6th ed., 1983), Mary P. Ryan's *Womanhood in America:*

From Colonial Times to the Present (3rd ed., 1983), and John Hope Franklin's *From Slavery to Freedom: A History of Negro Americans* (6th ed., 1988).

For ideas concerning lecture topics, instructors might turn to Carl Degler's *Out of Our Past: The Forces That Shaped Modern America* (3rd ed., 1984). *The Comparative Approach to American History* (1968), edited by C. Vann Woodward, compares various aspects of American history to that of other nations. Also useful are *Myth in American History* (1977), by Nicholas Cords and Patrick Gerster; and Daniel Boorstin's *The Americans* (3 vols., 1958–1973). Three series of volumes—the American Historical Association's *AHA Pamphlets*, D. C. Heath's *Problems in American Civilization*, and Little, Brown's *Critical Issues in American History*—offer historical and historiographical introductions to a number of topics. Harold S. Sharp's *Footnotes to American History: A Bibliographic Source Book* (1977) is a handy guide for information on such "footnotes" as the Norse discovery of America, the Lost Colony, the trial of Anne Hutchinson, on down to the Manson family murders, William Calley, and Patty Hearst.

There are a number of books that discuss history itself and the teaching of history. Lester D. Stephens's *Probing the Past: A Guide to the Study and Teaching of History* (1974) offers a good introduction to both topics. For the students' side, see Norman F. Cantor and Richard I. Schneider's *How to Study History* (1967) and Jules R. Benjamin's *A Student's Guide to History* (4th ed., 1987). While meant for students, these last two books have much to offer instructors as well. Some teachers may wish to assign portions of these books to their students at the beginning of the term.

Instructors designing their first course, or changing an existing one, might look at *American History* (3 vols.; 2nd ed., 1987), a set in the series *Selected Reading Lists and Course Outlines from American Colleges and Universities;* Volume 1 contains materials from survey courses in American history. Finally, instructors should consult *The History Teacher*, a quarterly journal that features reviews of textbooks and reference aids, articles on teaching history, and historiographical essays.

Chapter 1

DISCOVERY AND SETTLEMENT

This chapter covers the origins of Indian civilizations in the New World, the Spanish conquest, and developments in other European countries prior to the first permanent English settlements. It then discusses the settlement of each of the thirteen colonies and the general pattern of settlement and government in the English colonies.

Chapter Outline

   I. Pre-Columbian Indian civilizations
      A. Origins of the American Indian
      B. Indians of Central and South America
         1. Mayas
         2. Aztecs
         3. Incas
      C. Indians of North America
         1. Differences from more southern Indians
         2. Methods of livelihood
         3. Indians and Europeans

  II. Europe and the New World
      A. Modernization of Europe
      B. Voyages of Columbus
         1. Early life
         2. First voyage and "discovery" of America
         3. Columbus and the Indians
         4. Later voyages
      C. America named for Amerigo Vespucci

 III. Great biological exchange
      A. Transfer of animals
      B. Transfer of plant life
      C. Transfer of devices and words
      D. Transfer of illnesses

 IV. John Cabot's explorations

   V. Spanish empire
- A. Hernando Cortés and conquest of the Aztecs
- B. Other *conquistadores*
- C. Patterns of Spanish conquest
- D. Decline in Indian population
- E. Indian advocates
- F. Spanish exploration and settlement of North America

  VI. Impact of Protestant Reformation in Europe
- A. Causes and spread of movement
- B. Impact of Calvinism
- C. The Reformation in England
  - 1. Initial political revolt
  - 2. Elizabethan settlement

 VII. Other early European efforts at colonization
- A. French efforts
  - 1. In Canada
    - a. Giovanni da Verrazzano
    - b. Jacques Cartier
    - c. Samuel de Champlain
  - 2. In Louisiana
    - a. Jacques Marquette
    - b. Sieur de La Salle
- B. Dutch efforts
  - 1. Rebellion against Spain
  - 2. Dutch raiders plunder Spanish ships
- C. English effort
  - 1. "Sea Dogges"
  - 2. Defeat of the Spanish Armada
  - 3. Sir Walter Raleigh's unsuccessful efforts and fate of the Lost Colony

VIII. The colonization of North America
- A. Settlement of the English colonies
  - 1. Virginia
  - 2. Maryland
  - 3. Plymouth
  - 4. Massachusetts Bay
  - 5. Rhode Island
  - 6. Connecticut
  - 7. New Hampshire and Maine
- B. Effects of the English Civil War on the colonies

    C. The Restoration and new proprietary colonies
        1. The Carolinas
        2. New York
        3. New Jersey
        4. Pennsylvania
        5. Delaware
        6. Georgia
    D. The general pattern of English settlement

Suggestions for Lecture Topics

For a lecture on the exchange of animals, plants, and diseases from the Old World to the New and vice versa, see Alfred W. Crosby, Jr.'s *The Columbian Exchange* (1972).

John H. Parry's *The Age of Reconnaissance* (1963) has several chapters on the various technical factors that stimulated exploration and made it possible. This would inform a good introductory lecture for the European voyages of discovery.

Good lectures can be developed on the settlement of any of the colonies. A good comparison between Virginia and Massachusetts can be found in Timothy H. Breen's *Puritans and Adventurers: Change and Persistence in Early America* (1980).

An interesting lecture might be based on the differences between Spanish and English colonization in the New World. Merrill Jensen's "The Colonial Phase," in *The Comparative Approach to American History*, edited by C. Vann Woodward (1968), compares the two experiences; for additional details, see James Lang's *Conquest and Commerce* (1975).

Multiple-Choice Questions

    1. It is now generally agreed that the Indians came to the American continent
        A. by developing here as Homo sapiens at the same time that the species was developing in other parts of the world.
        B. by floating across the Pacific Ocean from China.
   * C. by walking across a land bridge to Alaska.
        D. by swimming across the Bering Strait.

2. The Aztecs
   A. were a peaceful people who built gigantic pyramids and temple complexes.
 * B. had an empire of about five million people in Mexico.
   C. absorbed the Mayas around 1325.
   D. lived mainly in the Andes Mountains.

3. Which of the following plants were *not* found in the New World until the Europeans came?
   A. maize (corn) and potatoes
   B. tomatoes and peanuts
   C. tobacco and chicle (for chewing gum)
 * D. rice and oats

4. Which of the following animals were *not* found in the New World before the Europeans came?
   A. flying squirrels and catfish
   B. bison and opossum
 * C. sheep and pigs
   D. armadillos and rattlesnakes

5. In their cultural interaction with the peoples of the New World, the Spanish
   A. tended dogmatically to uproot any existing culture in favor of their own.
 * B. overlaid their own culture without uprooting the native culture they found.
   C. insisted on converting the Indians to Protestantism.
   D. were not concerned with spreading Christianity to the Indians.

6. Christopher Columbus
   A. believed he had discovered a quick route to the Orient.
   B. miscalculated the circumference of the world, believing that it was smaller than it was.
   C. never realized that he had discovered a new continent.
 * D. is correctly described by all the above.

7. Amerigo Vespucci
   A. named the New World after himself.
   B. was the first sailor to circumnavigate the world.
 * C. helped outfit some of Columbus's voyages.
   D. was the first European botanist to classify New World plants.

8. Roger Williams's mistrust of the purity of others eventually led him to the belief that
    A. only he and his relatives were true believers.
  * B. the state should not impose any authority in matters of faith.
    C. the government must direct actions of the church to assure its purity.
    D. only those people who believed exactly as he did could be saved.

9. Cortés was able to subdue the Aztecs because he was aided by *all but which one* of the following?
    A. He was able to ally with other tribes fighting the spread of Aztec power.
    B. He was a gifted diplomat as well as military leader.
    C. He was able to make Montezuma his puppet.
  * D. He had a force of men that greatly outnumbered the Aztecs.

10. The Fundamental Constitution of Carolina
    A. was ignored by Gov. Gentry Wright after the English Restoration.
    B. guaranteed the rights of the Magna Carta to all settlers
  * C. created a formal class of nobility.
    D. created such political controversy that the colony was divided in two.

11. Delaware was at first part of
    A. Maryland.
    B. New Jersey.
    C. New York.
  * D. Pennsylvania.

12. By the seventeenth century, the Indian population in Spain's New World empire had decreased by about
    A. 10 percent.
    B. 25 percent.
    C. 50 percent.
  * D. 90 percent.

13. The defeat of the Spanish Armada in 1588
  * A. led to English supremacy on the sea.
    B. was assisted by Sir Richard Grenville, who destroyed part of the fleet before it sailed.

    C. gave France virtual control of Brazil.

    D. was King Henry VIII's greatest military achievement.

14. Most of the thirteen North American English colonies
    A. were founded on the roots of colonies first developed by other countries.
  * B. were founded in the years of Stuart rule and conflict in England.
    C. were founded after the "Glorious Revolution."
    D. were originally established as royal colonies.

15. One of the important factors aiding the survival of the earliest English colonists was
    A. the large sums of money that were used to bring additional supplies to them regularly.
    B. the absolute control of the seas possessed by the English navy.
  * C. the forest lore and assistance that they gained from the Indians.
    D. the lack of the diseases and hardships that afflicted the earliest colonies.

16. The earliest major French attempts at colonization in the New World were in what is now
    A. Florida.
  * B. Canada.
    C. Cuba.
    D. California.

17. Cecilius Calvert founded the colony of Maryland
    A. after his father, the first Lord Baltimore, fell out of favor with Charles I.
    B. as part of the Chesapeake Stock Company.
  * C. as one of the first proprietary colonies.
    D. as a refuge for French Huguenots.

18. General James E. Oglethorpe founded Georgia
  * A. as a colonial refuge for the poor and the persecuted.
    B. in order to launch military attacks against the French in Florida.
    C. as a Quaker commonwealth, a southern counterpart to William Penn's "Holy Experiment."
    D. as a sanctuary for religious dissenters from Florida.

19. The colony of New York
    A. was formed to serve as a buffer against the French in Canada.
* B. was built upon the conquest of an original Dutch settlement in the area.
    C. was started as a royal colony by the king.
    D. had all the land divided into feudal manors consisting of 1,000 acres each.

20. Which of the following statements was true of the Jamestown colony?
    A. The colonists had to depend on the women among them to do the farming.
* B. The settlement was developed in an area beset by mosquitos.
    C. Captain John Smith was growing tobacco there as early as 1606.
    D. The colonists were repeatedly attacked by Indians during their first year.

21. The headright system adopted in the Virginia colony consisted of
* A. giving fifty acres of land to anyone who would transport himself to the colony.
    B. selling fifty acres of land for 12 1/2 shillings to anyone who would transport himself to the colony.
    C. giving fifty acres of land to each family that came to the colony.
    D. giving free land to all servants who came to the colony.

22. The Plymouth colony
    A. absorbed the Massachusetts Bay colony.
* B. was absorbed by the Massachusetts Bay colony.
    C. was led by John Winthrop.
    D. was led by John Endecott.

23. The Protestant Reformation in England
* A. occurred more for political reasons than because of disagreement about religious doctrine.
    B. was almost undone when Elizabeth tried to reimpose Catholicism.
    C. developed because King Henry VIII wanted to follow the teachings of Calvin.
    D. occurred prior to the Reformation in Germany.

24. Which of the following was *not* true of Pennsylvania?
    A. The colonists had good relations with the Indians.
    B. There was general toleration for other religious groups in the colony.
    * C. The colony grew slowly because of the difficulty in cultivating the land.
    D. The colony was based on a proprietary grant to William Penn.

25. Religious dissenters Anne Hutchinson and Roger Williams left Massachusetts to begin the colony of
    A. Connecticut.
    * B. Rhode Island.
    C. New Hampshire.
    D. Maine.

26. Which of the following was *not* true of the Quaker religion?
    A. It was based on individual inspiration.
    B. The Quakers refused to take oaths.
    * C. The only formal parts of the service were the pastor's sermon and the communion.
    D. The Quakers believed in equality between the sexes and full participation of women in religious affairs.

27. Which of the following was *not* one of the ways in which the English colonies differed from the Spanish?
    A. There was less centralized control in the English colonies than in the Spanish.
    B. The English colonies were developed with private investment funds rather than royal money.
    * C. Most of the settlers in the English colonies came from the mother country, so there was less variety among the views of the settlers.
    D. The English colonies were settled in a compact geographical area.

28. Sir Walter Raleigh's colony at Roanoke
    A. grew to become the present state of North Carolina.
    B. was the first English colony in the New World.
    C. was established to mine the gold that Indians claimed was there.
    * D. was left on its own for three years because of England's war with Spain.

29. The explorer who landed at Newfoundland in 1497 and thus gave England the basis for a claim to North America was
    A. John White.
    * B. John Cabot.
    C. Arthur Barlowe.
    D. Sir Humphrey Gilbert.

30. Which of the following lists of colonies is given in correct chronological order of settlement?
    A. Pennsylvania, Georgia, Virginia, Massachusetts
    B. Virginia, Carolinas, Maryland, Georgia
    C. Massachusetts, Virginia, Pennsylvania, Georgia
    * D. Virginia, Maryland, Pennsylvania, Georgia

Suggested Essay Questions

1. Compare the English pattern of colonization to that of the Spanish.

2. In 1600, which European nation seemed to have the best chance at eventually controlling what is now the United States? Why?

3. Compare the settlement of Virginia and Massachusetts in regard to their founding religion, form of government, and landholding patterns.

4. What were the various effects of the English Civil War on the American colonies?

5. Explain how settlement patterns, family life, and population growth differed in New England and the southern colonies in the seventeenth century.

Chapter 2

COLONIAL WAYS OF LIFE

This chapter deals with major social developments in the colonies in the seventeenth and eighteenth centuries. Among other topics it treats population patterns, regional differences, land and labor systems, class groupings, social stratification, urban life, and the impact of the Enlightenment and the Great Awakening.

Chapter Outline

I. The shape of early America
   A. Overview of colonists
   B. Ecology of the New World
   C. Population patterns in the New World compared to the Old
      1. Cheaper land
      2. Earlier marriage age
      3. Lower death rates
      4. Impact of the frontier
      5. Role and status of women

II. Society and economy in the southern colonies
   A. Advantages of the warm climate
   B. Tobacco, lumber, and naval stores
   C. Headright system
   D. Trend toward large-scale production
   E. Indentured servants solved some labor problems
   F. Slavery developed in the southern colonies
      1. Importation of slaves
      2. Ethnic diversity of slaves
      3. Slave culture
      4. Effect of color
   G. The gentry
   H. Religion
      1. Church of England established in the South
      2. Lack of clergy and bishops placed much control in the hands of laymen

III. Society and economy in New England
  A. Transformation of English village into New England town
    1. No headrights or quitrents
    2. System of land division used
  B. Exports developed in lieu of farm products
  C. Methods used to offset an unfavorable balance of trade
    1. Use of own ships
    2. Finding new markets
  D. Effects of chronic shortage of hard money
  E. Puritan religion
    1. Nature of Puritan reaction to worldly pleasure
    2. Form of church organization
    3. Covenant theory of government
    4. Nature of church-state relationship
  F. Strains in Puritan community in the late-seventeenth century
    1. Economic strains developed as available land diminished
    2. Frequent challenges to authority
    3. The Halfway Covenant
    4. Witchcraft hysteria demonstrated social strains
  C. Society and economy in the middle colonies
    1. Reflected elements of both the southern and New England colonies
    2. Products for export
    3. Land system used
    4. Ethnic elements represented in the population

V. Other social and intellectual features of the colonies
  A. Urban class groupings and stratification
  B. Nature of town and city governments
  C. Transportation and postal service
  D. Early newspapers and editorial freedom
  E. Impact of the Enlightenment
    1. Nature of the Enlightenment
    2. Evidences of the "new sciences"
  F. Developments in education
  G. Impact of the Great Awakening
    1. Causes of the movement
    2. Major figures
      a. Jonathan Edwards
      b. George Whitefield
    3. Impact of the movement on churches and schools

4. Long-range impact of the Great Awakening and the Enlightenment

Suggestions for Lecture Topics

A fascinating lecture on family life in New England could be drawn from John Demos's *A Little Commonwealth* (1970), which focuses on Plymouth. Lois Green Carr and Lorena S. Walsh's "The Planter's Wife: The Experiences of White Women in Seventeenth-Century Maryland" (*William and Mary Quarterly*, 3rd ser., 34 [1970]: 542–571) would be useful for a comparison with the southern colonies. See also Joy Buel and Richard Buel's *The Way of Duty* (1984) on the eighteenth century.

For a lecture on the early history of American slavery, Winthrop D. Jordan's *White over Black* (1968) would be useful. Daniel P. Mannix's *Black Cargoes* (1960) offers information on the Atlantic slave trade.

Paul Boyer and Stephen Nissenbaum, in *Salem Possessed* (1974), explain the witchcraft hysteria there as the result of growing social and economic tensions. Their findings, along with background on the story, are summarized well in *After the Fact*, edited by James West Davidson and Mark Hamilton Lytle (2nd ed., 1986).

A number of good lectures could be derived from John M. McCusker and Russell R. Menard's *The Economy of British America, 1607–1789* (1985). One large section of this useful book is arranged by topic (labor, agriculture, wealth, consumption, manufacturing, etc.). Another section is arranged by region, which allows comparisons among the various colonies.

Multiple-Choice Questions

1. Which of the following statements about the early American colonial population is true?
   A. The birth rate was lower than that in Europe.
   B. The death rate was higher than that in Europe.
   C. Most colonists were female.
 * D. Most colonists were under 25 years of age.

2. Which of the following was *not* one of the ways in which the colonies differed from Europe?
   A. Land was plentiful and cheap.
   B. The population was sparsely distributed.

     * C. Labor was readily available and inexpensive.
         D. A greater proportion of colonial women married.

3. The most culturally diverse of the American colonies were
         A. in the South.
   * B. the middle colonies.
         C. in New England.
         D. none; the colonies were roughly equal in this respect.

4. The slaves who came to the thirteen colonies
         A. were from South Africa.
   * B. had a better chance to survive than those shipped to other New World destinations.
         C. were forced to learn English on the ships.
         D. gave up all their African religious customs.

5. After the English, the next largest ethnic groups in the colonies were the
   * A. Germans and Scotch-Irish.
         B. Irish and Scandinavians.
         C. French and Spanish.
         D. French and German.

6. Women in America found that they were
         A. treated less well than they had been in Europe.
         B. always expected to perform the same lowly jobs they had in Europe.
         C. often given much higher standing before the law than they were in Europe.
   * D. sometimes more highly valued than in Europe.

7. Which colonies produced goods most compatible with the needs of the mother country?
   * A. Southern
         B. Middle
         C. New England
         D. The colonies were roughly equal in this respect.

8. Which of the following was *not* one of the important exports of the southern colonies?
         A. indigo
         B. lumber and naval stores
   * C. fish
         D. tobacco

9. The headright land system
    A. required the head of each household to obtain all the land for that family.
  * B. allowed each person who paid his way to America to have fifty acres of free land.
    C. provided special grants of land to each male who served in the armed forces of the colony.
    D. is correctly represented by all the above statements.

10. George Whitefield
    A. was a British customs agent.
    B. led the witch hunt in Salem, Massachusetts.
  * C. was the major figure in the Great Awakening.
    D. founded the Philadelphia Academy in 1754.

11. Indentured servants were
    A. persons who were captured in England and forced to go to the colonies.
    B. prisoners who were sent to the colonies instead of to jail.
  * C. usually persons who volunteered to work to pay for their transportation to the colonies.
    D. persons bound to a lifetime of service in the colonies.

12. The Pennsylvania Dutch
    A. were Dutch settlers in the backcountry of New York and Pennsylvania.
    B. migrated to Virginia and North Carolina in the late-seventeenth century to escape religious persecution.
    C. were almost wiped out because of a genetic intolerance to New World viruses.
  * D. were a mixture of Mennonites, Lutherans, Moravians, Dunkers, and others.

13. It seems likely that an important factor in the enslavement of Negroes rather than whites was that
    A. the Negroes' different language made them more susceptible to being kept in bondage.
    B. Negroes were lazier and less intelligent than whites.
  * C. the Negroes' black color was associated with darkness and evil by Englishmen.
    D. Negroes clearly preferred the difficult work in rice fields and other areas for which whites were not physically well suited.

14. Of all the slaves brought to the New World from Africa about what percentage came to the colonies of British North America?

    * A. about 5 percent
      B. about 33 percent
      C. about 50 percent
      D. about 90 percent

15. The middle colonies
    * A. followed the headright system of the South.
      B. lacked a suitable base for commerce.
      C. were constantly threatened by attacks from unfriendly Indians, especially in the backcountry.
      D. are correctly represented by all the above statements.

16. The Halfway Covenant involved
      A. full church membership for the children of any member.
    * B. baptism for any children of church members, but not the right for them to vote or take communion.
      C. the right for nonmembers to vote, but not to take communion.
      D. agreement that church membership did not require a true conversion experience.

17. In the southern colonies the established church was
      A. the Anglican in some colonies, but the Catholic or Quaker in others.
      B. carefully controlled by royal governors.
    * C. often almost as much controlled by the laity as the Congregational Puritan churches of New England.
      D. in financial trouble because of the need to depend on voluntary offerings for support.

18. Colonial cities were marked by all the following except
      A. sharp class stratification.
    * B. the lack of public assistance for the poor.
      C. problems of traffic, fire, and crime.
      D. relative isolation from each other.

19. Land policy in New England provided for
      A. giving fifty acres of land to each new settler.
      B. giving no land to people who were not members of the church.
    * C. distributing land on the basis of family size or the number of shares held in the joint-stock company, not on the basis of strict equality.
      D. charging quitrents on all land with the proceeds going to township treasuries.

20. The important staple for export that came from New England was
    A. corn.
    B. molasses.
  * C. fish.
    D. turkeys.

21. Which of the following was *not* true of Puritan beliefs?
    A. The Bible was the ultimate source of religious authority.
    B. Because men were depraved, sinful creatures, government was necessary to control them.
    C. The voluntary union of men in a church for worship was like God's voluntary contract with men for their salvation.
  * D. No one in a Christian community should have any special control or authority over others.

22. The covenant theory from which the Puritans drew their ideas of government
  * A. was analogous to the notion that God had entered into a voluntary compact with man to offer him salvation.
    B. was based on the notion that the king replaced God as the head of the government of the people.
    C. included the notion that men were capable of governing themselves well because they had been absolved of all sin when they entered the church.
    D. included the belief that the church was the ultimate source of authority for the Christian.

23. New England trade
    A. was in most respects the same as that of the southern colonies.
    B. was usually conducted along lines of the "triangle" between New England, Newfoundland, and Cuba.
  * C. was generally unbalanced, since people bought more from England than they sold there.
    D. was based on the great quantities of machinery and paint shipped to Europe.

24. In 1790, about what proportion of the colonial population could trace its origin to England?
    A. 10 percent
  * B. 50 percent
    C. 85 percent
    D. 95 percent

25. Benjamin Franklin
    A. epitomized the Great Awakening.
    B. wrote "Essay on Human Understanding."
    C. built the first telescope in America, classified the plants for Philadelphia's botanical garden, and introduced calculus to the colonies.
    * D. was a publisher.

26. Education in the colonies
    A. was most advanced in the South.
    B. stressed the natural sciences.
    * C. was usually seen as the responsibility of family and church.
    D. was usually reserved for men planning on entering the legal or medical professions.

27. The largest city in the colonies at the end of the colonial period had a population of about
    A. 1,000,000.
    B. 300,000.
    * C. 30,000.
    D. 3,000.

28. The trial of John Peter Zenger
    A. found Zenger guilty of libel for having criticized the governor of New York.
    B. declared unconstitutional all laws that hampered freedom of the press.
    * C. encouraged editors to be more critical of public officials in the future.
    D. denied the principle of trial by jury.

29. The Great Awakening developed in reaction to
    * A. the deism and skepticism associated with the Enlightenment.
    B. the increasing education and sophistication of backwoods settlers.
    C. the increasing role of emotionalism in religion.
    D. splits in established churches into "Old" and "New" factions.

30. Which of the following is *not* a long-range result of the Great Awakening?
    A. the special American style of evangelism and revivalism
    B. the weakening of habits of deference

    C. the encouragement of church members exercising their own individual judgment

* D. an emphasis in American life on conformity and acceptance of established groups

Suggested Essay Questions

1. Discuss the problem of the shortage of labor in the American colonies. What were the implications of this labor shortage and of the colonists' solutions?

2. Compare the development of the Anglican churches in the South with the Puritan churches in New England. Point out and explain their similarities and differences.

3. How did the land policies adopted in New England and the southern colonies affect the development of these regions in the colonial period?

4. Which had the more far-reaching consequences for American culture: the Enlightenment or the Great Awakening? Why?

5. In what ways were the colonies tied to each other? In what ways were they tied to England? Which of these bonds was stronger?

Chapter 3

THE IMPERIAL PERSPECTIVE

This chapter begins with an overview of England's colonial policy. It covers instruments of government in England and in the colonies, as well as economic and political policies. Relations with the Indians are explored, as is the development of French settlements in America. The wars for empire between Britain and France are traced and the chapter concludes with Britain's triumph in the French and Indian War.

Chapter Outline

I. English agencies of colonial policy
    A. Overall policy not coherent or efficient
    B. Consolidation and extension of Navigation Acts by Restoration government
        1. Theory of mercantilism
        2. Navigation Acts of the Restoration
        3. Lords of Trade created by Charles II
        4. Customs collections tightened
    C. Dominion of New England
        1. Andros established as governor
        2. Resentment to his measures
    D. Impact of the Glorious Revolution
        1. Dominion of New England broken up
        2. Leisler's rebellion in New York
        3. Influence of John Locke
        4. Refinement of the Navigation Acts
        5. Creation of the Board of Trade
    E. Period of salutary neglect

II. Governments in the colonies
    A. Role of the governor
        1. Method of election in different colonies
        2. Veto power
        3. Control over convening the assembly
        4. Selection of council members

        5. Role in the courts
        6. Other authority
    B. Role of the assemblies
        1. Restrictions on voting for assemblies
        2. Conflict with governors
        3. Power to approve taxes and initiate legislation
        4. Efforts to gain control over governors

III. Troubled neighbors
    A. Displacing the Indians
        1. Troubles in Virginia and Connecticut
        2. King Philip's War
    B. Bacon's Rebellion
        1. Relation to Indian troubles
        2. Rebellion as class conflict
        3. Outcome of rebellion
    C. New France and Louisiana
        1. Beginnings in Québec
        2. Exploration and settlement of Louisiana and Mississippi
        3. French and English settlements compared

IV. The colonial wars
    A. Nature of the wars
    B. Effect of the wars on colonies
    C. Rivalry over Ohio Valley
    D. Albany Congress
    E. French and Indian War
        1. Pitt's role
        2. Use of English sea power
        3. Battle of Québec
        4. Results of the war

Suggestions for Lecture Topics

For a lecture on colonial government, see Jack Greene's careful examination of colonial assemblies in the early eighteenth century in his *The Quest for Power: Lower Houses of Assembly in the Southern Royal Colonies, 1689–1776* (1963).

Early Navigation Acts are discussed in Oliver M. Dickerson's *The Navigation Acts and the American Revolution* (1951). A lecture based on this book would help prepare students for developments in the following chapter.

Bacon's Rebellion is an interesting episode that illustrates many important themes in American colonial history. Information for a lecture on the topic can be found in Wilcomb E. Washburn's *The Governor and the Rebel* (1957), Edmund S. Morgan's *American Slavery, American Freedom* (1975), and Stephen S. Webb's *1676: The End of American Independence* (1984).

Multiple-Choice Questions

1. The supreme governmental authority in the American colonies was
   A. parliament.
   * B. the king.
   C. the Lords of Trade.
   D. the people of England.

2. Reforms of the colonial system under William and Mary in 1696 included all of the following *except*
   A. allowing accused violators to be tried in Admiralty Courts.
   * B. greatly lowering duties on most items imported.
   C. establishing the Board of Trade.
   D. allowing the use of writs of assistance.

3. Which of the following principles *was not true* of mercantilism as a policy?
   A. A wealthy nation should increase its store of gold and silver.
   B. A nation should limit foreign imports and encourage the development of domestic manufacturing.
   * C. A nation should seek to specialize in the economic goods it produces best, and then trade these with other nations.
   D. Colonies should serve the mother country as a source of raw materials and a market for finished goods.

4. Under the Navigation Acts the enumerated articles could be
   * A. shipped only to England or other English colonies.
   B. purchased only from England.
   C. purchased from any nation.
   D. sold to whomever the colonists wished.

5. The enumerated articles included *all but which* of the following?
   A. tobacco, cotton, and indigo
   B. sugar, rice, and naval stores

      C. hemp, ship masts, and furs
*   D. iron, fish, and molasses

6. By the time of the American Revolution, most of the colonies
  * A. had become royal colonies.
  B. remained proprietary.
  C. were independent in the selection of their governors.
  D. had been absorbed into two large administrative units.

7. The Navigation Acts eventually required that
  * A. all goods imported by the colonies come through England.
  B. the colonies carry on trade only with non-Catholic nations.
  C. all goods sold by the colonies be sold to England.
  D. the colonists pay cash for all goods purchased.

8. The Dominion of New England
  A. was created under King James II.
  B. included all northern colonies down to New Jersey.
  C. was ruled by the governor without any elected assembly.
  * D. is correctly represented by all three statements above.

9. Jacob Leisler is significant in New York history because
  A. he was the lieutenant in charge of New York under Andros's Dominion of New England.
  B. he tried to convince the governor to lead an army against the Indians in the western part of New York.
  * C. after the Glorious Revolution he seized control of the colony and kept it for two years.
  D. he was responsible for the Admiralty Courts and the collection of Customs in the colony.

10. Sir Edmond Andros created hostility through his rule of the Dominion of New England by *all but which one* of the following annoyances?
  A. He suppressed town governments.
  B. He rigidly enforced trade laws and subdued smuggling.
  C. He took over a Puritan church in Boston to use it for Anglican worship.
  * D. He ended the purchase of slaves from abroad.

11. One change brought to the colonies after the Glorious Revolution in England was that
  A. an effort was made to extend the concept of the Dominion of New England to the southern colonies.

    B. the colonies were inspired by Locke's writings to lead a revolt against King William.

    C. the new monarch showed little interest in the colonies because of his desire to force the French out of North America.

* D. Massachusetts and Plymouth were united as Massachusetts Bay.

12. King Philip's War
    A. is also known as the War of the Spanish Succession.
    B. is also known as the War of Jenkins' Ear.
* C. pitted formerly friendly Indians against the New World colonists.
    D. pitted British colonists for the first time against French colonists in a major battle.

13. William Berkeley
    A. was deposed in New York by Jacob Leisler.
    B. was a leading member of the Board of Trade under George I and George II.
* C. was governor of Virginia.
    D. was governor of North Carolina.

14. Which of the following is *not* one of the principles of Locke's contract theory of government?
    A. Men have certain rights in the state of nature which include the right to life, liberty, and property.
* B. Governments were formed when strong men seized authority as kings to protect natural rights.
    C. Kings have a right to stay in power so long as they protect the rights of the people.
    D. If the king violates the rights of the people, the people have the right to overthrow the monarch.

15. During the period of salutary neglect,
* A. the British government took less of a role in governing the American colonies.
    B. new and efficient trade regulations were introduced.
    C. every royal governor fell out of favor with the crown.
    D. a new trade board, the Lords of Trade and Plantations, was introduced.

16. Someone looking for a primary explanation of the development of self-government in the American colonies should examine
    A. the theoretical principles of John Locke.
    B. the theory of the divine right of kings.

C. the role of the council in colonial governments.
* D. the expansion of power and prerogative of the colonial assemblies.

17. In King George's War in the 1740s,
    A. the British pushed the French out of Canada.
    B. Indians refused to take sides in the white man's fights.
    C. the British and the French temporarily allied to put down the Spanish threat.
    * D. the New England colonies were hurt more than the middle colonies.

18. Which of the following was *not* a power of the governor of a colony?
    A. to nominate for life appointment members of his council, which also served as the upper house of the legislature
    B. to command the militia and naval forces of the colony
    * C. to order the search and seizure of any property in the colony
    D. to dissolve the assembly until new elections were held or to postpone elections until he wanted them

19. Which of the following were the two key powers of the colonial assemblies?
    * A. the power to vote taxes and expenditures and the power to initiate legislation
    B. the power to approve appointments of the governor and the power to override his vetoes
    C. the power to approve taxes and the power to approve the appointments of the governor
    D. the power to set times of elections and the power to grant pardons

20. The right to vote for members of the colonial assemblies
    A. was highly restricted because of high property qualifications.
    B. was open to women in most of the colonies.
    * C. was extended to a greater proportion of the population than anywhere else in the world of the eighteenth century.
    D. was based on the same property qualifications as required to vote for Parliament in England.

21. From the perspective of their own welfare, the greatest mistake that the Indians made in relation to the English was

    A. the decision to make war against them when they first landed.

    B. the decision to ally themselves with the French rather than the English.

* C. not opposing the English until they were too entrenched to be pushed back into the ocean.

    D. their refusal to enter into treaties with the English.

22. Which of the following is a correct statement about Bacon's Rebellion?

    A. Bacon was executed by the governor for treason.

* B. Bacon led repeated, indiscriminate attacks on various groups of Indians.

    C. Bacon wanted the governor to stop fighting the Indians and agree to make peace with them.

    D. Bacon was a poor man from the frontier who led other poor men in their opposition to the rich rulers of the Tidewater area.

23. The Plan of Union (1754), drafted in part as a response to problems with the French, was written by a committee headed by

    A. George Washington.

    B. James Wolfe.

* C. Benjamin Franklin.

    D. Jeffrey Amherst.

24. Which of the following was *not* an advantage that the French had in their settlements in North America?

    A. Their claims gave them access to the interior river systems.

    B. They had better relations with the Indians because they wanted only to trade and not to take Indian lands.

    C. Their government was more efficient and responsive to orders from the governors because there were no representative assemblies.

* D. The population that had settled in their lands exhibited greater ethnic diversity.

25. The center of British-French conflict on the North American continent was

* A. the Ohio River valley.

    B. the Great Lakes.

    C. the Mississippi River.

    D. the mouth of the Mississippi and New Orleans.

26. The conflict that became the French and Indian War, or the Great War for Empire, began
    * A. with the surrender of British forces led by George Washington.
    B. in a conflict with the Indians in upper New York State.
    C. in a conflict in India, but rapidly spread to the American continent.
    D. on the border between Georgia and Florida.

27. In 1750
    A. the French population in the New World outnumbered the British.
    * B. the French controlled New Orleans.
    C. the French controlled Florida.
    D. all the above statements are true.

28. The Cajuns of Louisiana were
    A. French Protestants driven from their homeland in southern France.
    * B. French settlers who escaped from the British forces when England took over Nova Scotia.
    C. a group of English people who obtained permission from the French to settle in Louisiana.
    D. a group of Indians who assimilated with French customs and language.

29. The Albany Congress of 1754
    A. was the first official body to consider independence from Great Britain.
    B. signed the Peace of Utrecht, thus ending Queen Anne's War.
    C. was called by Charles II.
    * D. met to consider precautions against the French threat.

30. As a result of the Peace of Paris,
    * A. Spain won control of the Louisiana Territory.
    B. France gave up Florida to England.
    C. England increased her holdings in the New World by nearly 10 percent.
    D. France was pushed back to what is now Oregon and Washington.

Suggested Essay Questions

1. Discuss the evolution of agencies and other means in Britain to control the colonies, and point out the weaknesses of the system which evolved before 1763.

2. Compare the relative roles played in colonial governments by the governor, the council, and the assembly. In which of these did the most power appear to reside? Explain.

3. What significance did the Indians have in the domestic policies of the colonies? What was their significance in the imperial policy of Great Britain?

4. Explain the nature of French colonial policy in America and show how conflict grew between the French and English.

5. Discuss Britain's mercantilist policies toward the colonies. How did the Navigation Acts implement these policies?

Chapter 4

FROM EMPIRE TO INDEPENDENCE

This chapter opens with an assessment of the impact of the Great War for Empire, examines political actions under George III, treats the British plans to raise revenue in the colonies, then traces the counter-play between British actions and colonial reactions up to the opening of the Revolution, at which point the various causes of the revolt are assessed.

Chapter Outline

   I. Heritage of war
      A. Rumblings of American nationalism
      B. New problems facing England

  II. British politics
      A. Nature of the government
      B. Instability of ministers

 III. Problem of western lands acquired in 1763
      A. Indian uprisings in the Ohio region
      B. Proclamation of 1763 to keep out British settlers
         1. Kept British settlers out of lands beyond the Appalachians
         2. Québec created in the western area
      C. Many settlers ignored Proclamation Line

  IV. Grenville's colonial policy
      A. Efforts to raise revenue
         1. Tightened customs collections
         2. New vice-admirality court in Halifax had jurisdiction over all the colonies
         3. Sugar Act of 1764 cut molasses taxes in half
         4. Currency Act of 1764 extended prohibition of paper money to all the colonies
         5. Stamp Tax, 1765
         6. Quartering Act

    B. Colonial reaction
        1. Imbued with Whiggery
        2. Grenville program appeared to herald tyranny
        3. Cry of no taxation without representation
        4. British response of "virtual representation"
        5. Impact on the most articulate colonists
        6. Actions in colonies
            a. Intimidation of stamp agents to encourage their resignation
            b. Adoption of nonimportation agreements
            c. Stamp Act Congress, October 1765
        7. Grenville ministry replaced by Rockingham, July 1765
        8. Repeal of the tax and passage of the Declaratory Act, March 1766

  V. Townshend's colonial policy
    A. Musical chairs in the ministry
    B. Townshend's acts
        1. Suspended New York Assembly
        2. Revenue Act
        3. Set up Board of Customs Commissioners
        4. Creation of additional vice-admiralty courts
        5. Use made of duties collected
    C. Colonial reaction
        1. *Letters from a Farmer in Pennsylvania*
        2. Circular letter of Samuel Adams and James Otis, 1768
        3. Boston Massacre
        4. Parliament repealed all Townshend duties except tax on tea, April 1770
        5. Two years of relative peace

  VI. Backcountry dissent
    A. Creation of state of Vermont
    B. Paxton boys of Pennsylvania took revenge on Indians
    C. South Carolina Regulators demanded protection from the Indians
    D. North Carolina people protested abuses and extortion of easterners

  VII. Other protest acts
    A. *Gaspee* burned
    B. Committees of Correspondence formed

    C. Lord North's Tea Act of 1773
      1. Terms of the act
      2. Colonials refused to accept the tea
      3. Boston Tea Party

VIII. British responded with Coercive Acts
    A. Closed port of Boston
    B. Allowed trials of government officials to be transferred to England
    C. New quartering act for soldiers
    D. Massachusetts Council and law-enforcement officers made appointive
    E. No town meetings
    F. Québec Act also fueled movement for colonial unity

IX. First Continental Congress, September 1774
    A. Make-up of Congress
    B. Endorsed Suffolk Resolves
    C. Adopted Declaration of American Rights
    D. Adopted Continental Association
    E. Called another congress for May 1775

X. British response
    A. Declared Massachusetts in rebellion
    B. Royal authorities losing control
    C. Gage moved to confiscate supplies in Concord
    D. Battle of Lexington

XI. Other acts of protest
    A. Second Continental Congress
    B. Seizures in New York
    C. Congress adopted Continental Army
    D. Battle of Bunker Hill
    E. Olive Branch Petition and Declaration for Taking Up Arms
    F. Congress gradually assumed functions of general government
    G. Thomas Paine's *Common Sense*, January 1776
    H. Declaration of Independence, July 1776

XII. Assessment of the causes of the Revolution

Suggestions for Lecture Topics

For a lecture on the Declaration of Independence, have students read the document ahead of time in the Appendix of the textbook. Carl Becker's classic *The Declaration of Independence* (1922) discusses the political ideas behind the Declaration. Julian P. Boyd's *The Declaration of Independence: The Evolution of the Text* (1945) shows how the document changed from Jefferson's rough draft to the version passed by Congress. Much of this material, plus other background information, is nicely summarized in *After the Fact*, edited by James West Davidson and Mark Hamilton Lytle (2nd ed., 1986).

The connection between the French and Indian War and the Revolution would be the subject of an instructive lecture. Two good sources are Lawrence Henry Gipson's "The American Revolution Considered as an Aftermath of the Great War for Empire" (*Political Science Quarterly* 65 [1950]: 86–104) and Jack P. Greene's "The Seven Years' War and the American Revolution: The Causal Relationship Reconsidered" (*Journal of Imperial and Commonwealth History* 8 [January 1980]: 85–105).

Students may find it difficult to understand how Tom Paine's pamphlet could cause such an uproar in the colonies. For a good discussion of this topic, see Bernard Bailyn's "Common Sense: The Most Uncommon Pamphlet of the Revolution," in *American Heritage* (December 1973). More information can be found in Eric Foner's *Tom Paine and Revolutionary America* (1976).

For a lecture that ties together the various causes of the Revolution, see Jack P. Greene's "An Uneasy Connection: An Analysis of the Preconditions of the American Revolution," in *Essays on the American Revolution*, edited by Stephen G. Kurtz and James H. Hutson (1973).

Multiple-Choice Questions

1. The Proclamation Line of 1763 was drawn to keep the colonists out of the territory acquired from France primarily because
    A. the British government did not want colonists to become too wealthy.
  * B. Indian uprisings in this area were a threat to settlers.

    C. the British government wanted to reward the French settlers with this territory in order to win their support.

    D. the land over the mountains was, according to legend, a "Great Desert."

2. The Sugar Act of 1764
    A. increased taxes on molasses imported into the colonies.
    B. prohibited any trade with the French West Indies.
    C. was primarily designed to regulate trade rather than to raise revenue.
  * D. reduced the tax on molasses in order to make sure the tax was collected.

3. The term "Whig" in British politics meant
    A. those persons who had supported James II on the throne.
  * B. the champions of liberty and parlimentary supremacy.
    C. the leaders from the towns who sought to have the government give more consideration to the needs of the cities.
    D. the people in Parliament who wanted to give independence to the African colonies.

4. The reaction of England to the Boston Tea Party was
    A. the Declaratory Act.
  * B. the Coercive Acts.
    C. the clash with the colonists at Lexington.
    D. the dissolving of the colonial legislatures.

5. All the following were factors in the repeal of the Stamp Act *except*
    A. a change in ministry in England, from Grenville to Rockingham.
    B. issuance of a Declaration of the Rights and Grievances of the Colonies.
    C. the activities of the Sons of Liberty.
  * D. passage of the Olive Branch Petition.

6. As George Grenville surveyed the taxation of the American colonists in 1763, he discovered that
    A. much money was being spent annually to collect a much smaller amount in taxes.
    B. colonists had a lighter tax burden than people in England.
    C. the Americans were smuggling illegal goods rather than pay taxes on them.
  * D. all the above were true.

7. The writings of the "Real Whigs"
   A. implicitly supported the divine right of kings.
 * B. argued that human nature is corruptible and lusts after power.
   C. refuted the Whig polemics of John Locke.
   D. supported the idea of virtual representation.

8. With the Declaratory Act, Parliament
   A. announced that it would no longer attempt internal taxation in the colonies.
   B. announced its findings that the colonists bore "full and total responsibility" for the Boston Massacre.
 * C. asserted its power to make laws for the colonies.
   D. repealed the Quartering Act.

9. Which of the following statements about the Virginia Resolves is *not* true?
   A. They said that Virginians had the rights of Englishmen, including the right to be taxed only by their own representatives.
   B. Patrick Henry supported them in the House of Burgesses.
 * C. They led to the eventual repeal of the Townshend Acts.
   D. Assemblies in other colonies passed similar resolutions.

10. When Americans objected to the Stamp Act with the cry of "no taxation without representation," the British reply was
   A. that Americans would be permitted to vote on the measure in each of the colonial assemblies.
 * B. that, by means of virtual representation, the interests of Americans had been considered in Parliament.
   C. an agreement that the funds collected from the taxes would be used to improve roads in the colonies.
   D. that because this was an internal tax, no approval from the Americans was needed.

11. The Continental Association referred to
   A. an organization of post offices and libraries in the colonies of North America.
   B. a network of correspondents in the colonies that kept all informed of the actions of the British.
 * C. local committees of patriots charged with enforcing the boycotts of British goods.
   D. the meeting of representatives from all colonies for the purpose of taking action against England.

12. Which sequence of British ministers is in correct chronological order regarding the periods of their major influence on colonial trade policy?
    A. Townshend, North, Grenville
    B. North, Grenville, Rockingham
    C. Townshend, Grenville, Rockingham
    * D. Grenville, Townshend, North

13. One of the special objections of the colonials to the taxes raised by the Townshend Acts was that
    A. the taxes were internal rather than external.
    B. the taxes did not raise enough revenue to pay the debts of the war.
    * C. the revenue raised could be used to pay governors and other colonial officials and thus release those officials from dependence on the colonial assemblies.
    D. the taxes would include a tax on tea, which was considered the national drink and was not supposed to be subject to taxation.

14. The Townshend Acts included *all but which one* of the following?
    * A. refusal to permit any of the colonial governors to make new appointments without the approval of Parliament
    B. suspension of the New York Assembly until it agreed to provide quarters for the British troops stationed in the colony
    C. a special tax on imports of lead, tea, glass, paints, and paper
    D. establishment of a Board of Customs Commissioners in Boston to prevent smuggling

15. Among the colonial responses to the Stamp Act was
    * A. a boycott of British goods.
    B. the Suffolk Resolves.
    C. the formation of Committees of Correspondence.
    D. all the above.

16. *Letters from a Farmer in Pennsylvania*
    A. was written by James Otis.
    * B. argued that Parliament had no right to levy taxes for revenue.
    C. was a protest against the Tea Act of 1773.
    D. was a major factor in the repeal of the Stamp Act.

17. The Boston Massacre
    A. developed in protest to the Boston Tea Party.
    B. involved the slaughter of slaves in Boston by British troops.
    * C. grew out of crowd reaction and heckling of British soldiers in Boston.
    D. was the unprovoked slaughter of dozens of Boston patriots by the Hessian soldiers hired by Britain.

18. The so-called Regulator movement of the backcountry involved
    A. efforts of the backcountry patriots to begin the war of independence against the British.
    B. refusal of the people of the Piedmont to pay taxes to support the government of England.
    * C. demands by the backcountry people for more effective government in their areas.
    D. efforts of the Scotch-Irish to defeat the Indians.

19. John Dickinson
    A. was the only colonist convicted of destruction of property as a result of the Boston Tea Party.
    B. was an able and fair British minister who, unfortunately for the colonists, died three months after taking office.
    C. vehemently argued in a 1767 essay that Parliment had no right to regulate colonial commerce.
    * D. wrote the Olive Branch Petition.

20. Colonists opposed the Tea Act of 1773 because
    A. it almost doubled the price of tea.
    * B. it gave Lord North's friends a virtual monopoly on the tea trade.
    C. it was internal rather than external taxation.
    D. it forbade them from reexporting surplus stocks of tea.

21. The Declaration of American Rights
    A. declared the Intolerable Acts null and void.
    B. was proposed by Joseph Galloway.
    C. was rejected by a small margin in the First Continental Congress.
    * D. conceded Parliament's right to regulate commerce.

22. Which of the following was *not* a result of the Coercive Acts?
    * A. Town meetings were called by the governor in each community to raise taxes to pay for the tea tossed into Boston Harbor.
    B. The port of Boston was closed to commerce.

    C. The governor was permitted to transfer trials of Massachusetts officials to England.

    D. Law enforcement officers in the colony were made appointive.

23. The reaction of the other colonies to the closing of the port of Boston was

    A. sending armed forces from each colony to attack the British troops stationed in New York.

  * B. demanding a meeting of representatives from all the colonies to discuss action.

    C. making efforts to persuade the Indians to come together and attack the British.

    D. sending George Washington to London to plead with Parliament to open the port.

24. The man most responsible for organizing the Sons of Liberty was

  * A. Sam Adams.

    B. Thomas Hutchinson.

    C. Thomas Jefferson.

    D. John Pitcairn.

25. At the Battle of Bunker Hill,

  * A. the British lost about half their troops.

    B. the colonists held their position on Breed's Hill.

    C. British Gen. William Howe was killed.

    D. the Green Mountain Boys under Ethan Allen defeated a larger British army.

26. The firing of shots at Lexington and Concord occurred because

    A. the patriot armies sought to march on Boston by going through those towns.

  * B. General Gage sent patrols out from Boston to take the supplies of the patriots located at Concord.

    C. General Gage sent patrols to arrest all patriots who would not swear allegiance to the king.

    D. the patriots lined up to oppose the British and fired when the British moved against them.

27. At the meeting of the Second Continental Congress

  * A. the Massachusetts militia which surrounded Boston was adopted as the Continental Army.

    B. General Washington was authorized to begin a tour of the colonies to recruit an American army.

    C. Boston was surrounded by British forces that were trying to bring about the surrender of the city.

    D. all American ships were ordered to become part of an American navy under John Paul Jones's command.

28. Thomas Paine, in *Common Sense*, brought what important new element into the debate with Britain?
    A. He emphasized that neither internal nor external taxes could be imposed on the colonies.
    B. He attacked Parliament as not being fit to rule the colonies.
 * C. He directed an attack on the king, rather than simply Parliament.
    D. He argued that the concepts developed by John Locke proved that the colonies were already free of British rule.

29. The Declaration of Independence based its argument for freedom of the colonies primarily on
    A. "the rights of Englishmen."
 * B. "laws of Nature and Nature's God."
    C. Thomas Jefferson's theory of the dominion status of the colonies.
    D. the concept of judicial review which allowed the courts of England to declare America free.

30. Which of the following series of events is listed in the correct chronological order?
 * A. Navigation Acts, Stamp Act, Coercive Acts, Declaration of Independence
    B. Stamp Act, creation of the Continental Association, Declaration of Independence, Battles of Lexington and Concord
    C. Stamp Act, Declaratory Act, Declaration of Independence, Coercive Acts
    D. Stamp Act, Declaratory Act, Intolerable Acts, Townshend duties

Suggested Essay Questions

1. Which was more important in the coming of the Revolution: the development of a set of intellectual assumptions in the American colonies regarding liberty, equality, and so forth, or changes in British imperial policy?

2. In what way did the French and Indian War pave the way for the Revolution?

3. Explain the meaning of Levi Preston's words at the end of this chapter: "Young man, what we meant in going for those redcoats was this: we always had governed ourselves, and we always meant to. They didn't mean we should." How accurate is his statement in explaining the causes of the Revolution?

4. At what point (if any) did the Revolution become inevitable? Why?

5. Summarize the argument for independence presented in the Declaration of Independence and explain how that argument followed from earlier colonial arguments regarding the government of the colonies.

Chapter 5

THE AMERICAN REVOLUTION

This chapter treats the principal battles of the Revolution by chronology and region, investigates loyalist and patriot strengths, surveys problems of the Continental Army and the financing of the war, examines the degree to which a revolution occurred at home, covers the technical moves for independence at state and national levels, and discusses in some detail the impact of the Revolution on social status, slavery, women, landholding, and religion. It closes with a discussion of nationalism in the new nation, as expressed in painting, literature, education, and other cultural forms.

Chapter Outline

I. The campaigns of 1776
   A. Howe assembled largest British army ever
   B. Battle of Long Island
   C. Thomas Paine's *The American Crisis*
   D. Washington attacks on Trenton and Princeton

II. Division of support in the colonies
   A. Three groups: Patriots, Tories, and an indifferent middle group
   B. Elements of civil war
   C. Tories' cause was hurt by licentiousness of British troops
   D. Patriot groups materialized when troops were needed, then vanished

III. Analysis of the colonial war effort
   A. Nature of the Continental Army
   B. Supplies obtained directly from farmers
   C. Financing of the war

IV. Setbacks for the British in 1777
   A. Problems of the British war effort
   B. Howe's three-pronged attack

   C. Saratoga
      1. Howe's strategy
      2. British defeat
   D. Alliance with France
      1. Terms of the French-American agreements
      2. Spain entered war as France's ally
   E. A world war

V. Regrouping in 1778
   A. Parliament's efforts toward reconciliation
   B. British decision to fight in the South
   C. Washington's winter of despair gave way to a spring of renewal
   D. Actions on the frontier
      1. George Rogers Clark
      2. Colonist-Indian relations
         a. Sullivan and the Iroquois
         b. Later effects of battles with Indians

VI. Southern campaign
   A. Reasons for the move south
   B. Savannah captured
   C. Clinton took Charleston
   D. Cornwallis routed Gates's forces at Camden, S.C.
   E. Tarleton and Ferguson defeated at Kings Mountain by overmountain men
   F. Greene placed in command of colonials in the South
   G. Pyrrhic victory over Cornwallis at Guilford Courthouse
   H. Cornwallis defeated at Yorktown
      1. Nature of the Yorktown campaign
      2. Results and their significance

VII. Peace negotiations
   A. Negotiators
   B. Problems with France and Spain
   C. American initiatives with Britain
   D. Terms of Peace of Paris

VIII. The Revolution at home
   A. Revolutionary concepts developed in America
      1. American Revolution unique
      2. Nature of republican governmental ideas
   B. Changes in state governments
      1. Concept of written constitutions
      2. Other principles in new state governments

    C. Articles of Confederation
      1. Need for a central government
      2. Powers of central government under Articles

IX. Social impact of the Revolution in the colonies
    A. Equality and its limits
      1. Less deference
      2. Greater suffrage and fairer representation
      3. More democratic land tenure
    B. Impact of the revolution on slavery
      1. States' control of slave trade
      2. Role of blacks in the war
      3. Efforts of states toward emancipation
    C. Impact of the Revolution on women
      1. Involvement in prewar boycotts and in providing wartime supplies
      2. Limited gains in law for women
    D. Impact of the Revolution on religion
      1. Disestablishment of church
      2. National church organizations

X. Sense of nationalism inspired by the Revolution
    A. First generation of native artists and writers
      1. John Trumbull
      2. Charles Willson Peale
    B. Impact of nationalism on education
      1. Development of state universities
      2. Development of general systems of education
    C. General impact of nationalism

Suggestions for Lecture Topics

The first two chapters of Russell F. Weigley's *The American Way of War* (1973) would be useful for a lecture on the strategy of the Revolution and why Americans fought as they did. These chapters are also good for comparing the northern and southern campaigns.

For a lecture on the social effects of the Revolution, begin with J. Franklin Jameson's *The American Revolution Considered as a Social Movement* (1926). Frederick B. Tolles revises some of Jameson's findings in "The American Revolution Considered as a Social Movement: A Re-Evaluation" (*American Historical Review* 60 [1954]: 1–12). See also Charles Royster's *A Revolutionary People at War* (1982).

A discussion of the loyalists—who they were and why they remained loyal to England—can be based on the pertinent chapters in Wallace Brown's *The American Tory* (1961). See also Bernard Bailyn's fine biography of the controversial Massachusetts governor, *The Ordeal of Thomas Hutchinson* (1974). Mary Beth Norton's "The Loyalist Critique of the Revolution," in the Library of Congress's *The Development of a Revolutionary Mentality* (1972), argues that the loyalists, like the revolutionaries, were motivated by Whig thought.

Multiple-Choice Questions

1. Washington's surprise move on Christmas night, 1776, was at
   A. Québec.
   * B. Trenton.
   C. Morristown.
   D. Harlem Heights.

2. *The American Crisis*
   A. was a pamphlet written by Benjamin Franklin.
   B. concerned slavery in the American colonies, which the author said could "ignite a terrible and bloody moral war."
   * C. inspired the declining morale of the American troops.
   D. encouraged the Americans to compromise their principles and return to the control by the mother country.

3. The Battle of Long Island
   * A. was a result of Washington's unwise attempt to defend New York.
   B. was the first major win for the Americans.
   C. saw the use of 9,000 Hessians on the colonial side.
   D. came immediately after Washington's surprise win at Princeton, N.J.

4. American Tories
   A. numbered no more than 5 percent of the colonial population.
   * B. made up roughly a third of the colonial population.
   C. were also known in the colonies as Whigs.
   D. were seldom found in seaport cities.

5. The state militia units
   A. were joined with the Continental Army for the duration of the Revolution.

      * B. often seemed to appear at crucial moments and then mysteriously disappear.

      C. provided the most seasoned troops of the war because of their past experience fighting the Indians.

      D. were highly successful as organized units even though they refused to wear uniforms.

6. Before the American Revolution was over, it had become a world war with the British fighting
   A. the Spanish, French, and Dutch as well as the Americans.
   B. in the Mediterranean, Africa, and India as well as North America.
   C. against powerful navies as well as land armies.
   * D. all the above.

7. Which of the following was *not* one of the British generals in charge of forces in America?
   A. William Howe
   B. Henry Clinton
   C. Charles Cornwallis
   * D. Nathanael Greene

8. "The Swamp Fox" was
   A. Banastre Tarleton.
   * B. Francis Marion.
   C. John Sullivan.
   D. Charles Cornwallis.

9. The final result of the three-pronged British attack on New York State was
   * A. Burgoyne's surrender at Saratoga.
   B. the capture of Howe's army in New York City.
   C. the successful splitting of New England from the rest of the states.
   D. the defeat of a British army by the Indians at Fort Ticonderoga.

10. The victory at Saratoga was important for the Americans because it
    A. made the British resolve to fight with greater determination.
    * B. brought the French into the war against Britain.
    C. opened the way for the Americans to enter the Great Lakes.
    D. convinced the Indians to join the American side against the British.

11. A problem with the Spanish entry into the Revolution against Britain was that Spain
    * A. entered as an ally of France rather than of the United States.
    B. demanded that the United States surrender Georgia as a price for its help.
    C. agreed to fight the British but only on the open seas.
    D. said that it would attack only the British colonies in South America.

12. Most of the Americans' funding for the Revolution was obtained
    A. through issuing bonds to foreign countries.
    B. by requisitions on the states.
    * C. from printing paper money.
    D. from selling bonds to the American people.

13. After 1778, most of the fighting in the Revolution was done
    A. in the West.
    * B. in the South.
    C. by regular Continental Army troops rather than militia.
    D. in large pitched battles.

14. The great exploit of George Rogers Clark was the
    A. conquest of the Great Lakes for the United States.
    * B. capture of the western area around the present state of Illinois.
    C. destruction of the Iroquois federation in New York State.
    D. destruction of the Cherokees on the frontiers of Virginia and the Carolinas.

15. A major reason for the British shift to campaigns in the southern colonies late in the war was
    * A. the expectation of significant Tory help in the South.
    B. the need to protect the South from conquest by the Spanish.
    C. that the British had already conquered all the northern colonies.
    D. the extremely harsh winter of 1778–1779, which made major troop movements north of Virginia impossible.

16. An important American victory in the South was
    A. Savannah.
    B. Camden.
    * C. Kings Mountain.
    D. Charleston.

17. The victory over the British at Yorktown was made possible by
    A. the prompt arrival of the French infantry.
    B. the American navy commanded by John Paul Jones.
    C. the Spanish forces waiting in the Chesapeake.
 * D. the French navy.

18. An important factor in the conclusion of peace negotiations with Britain was
 * A. the American decision to negotiate separately with the British.
    B. the decision to abandon claims to western lands.
    C. the support that the French gave to the Americans in the peace negotiations.
    D. the Spanish decision to trade their claim to Gibraltar for American independence.

19. Which of the following was *not* one of the provisions of the Peace of Paris?
    A. Americans could fish off the coast of Newfoundland and dry their catch on the shore.
    B. Congress would not prevent the British merchants from collecting debts owed to them by Americans.
    C. Great Britain recognized the independence of the United States.
 * D. Congress would restore all property confiscated from loyalists during the war.

20. The British campaign in the South
 * A. was more brutal than that in the North.
    B. was led by Patrick Ferguson and Barry St. Leger.
    C. began immediately after Howe took Philadelphia in September 1777.
    D. led to the fall of Atlanta and Columbia.

21. The Articles of Confederation were ratified by the states
 * A. in 1781.
    B. in 1784.
    C. despite the opposition of John Dickinson.
    D. because most people wanted a strong central government.

22. The Peace of Paris was signed in
    A. 1779.
    B. 1781.
 * C. 1783.
    D. 1785.

23. Which of the following was *not* a power granted to the national government under the Articles of Confederation?
    A. full power over foreign affairs
  * B. the right to levy taxes on trade and commerce
    C. control of government in the western territories
    D. authority to coin money, run a postal service, and direct Indian affairs

24. Under the government of the Articles of Confederation
    A. an amendment required the approval of all the states.
    B. most important actions required approval of nine of the thirteen states.
    C. there was no executive or judicial branch.
  * D. all the above were true.

25. The chief contribution of the Revolution to women's equality was
    A. the securing of the right to vote in most new state constitutions.
    B. the admission of women to all public schools.
  * C. a challenge to many old concepts, which helped lay the groundwork for the future.
    D. the admission of women to the military on an equal status with men.

26. The Revolution brought changes in religion by
  * A. removal of tax support for the Anglican church.
    B. complete separation of church and state in New England Congregational churches.
    C. the development of northern and southern church organizations among some denominations.
    D. the complete elimination of religious tests for holding government offices.

27. Among the social effects of the Revolution were all the following *except* that
    A. property qualifications for voting were lowered.
    B. opportunities for higher education were greatly increased.
  * C. lands confiscated from Tories were returned.
    D. western lands were opened for settlement.

28. Early art works in the United States
  * A. tended to glorify the American nation and its heroes.
    B. reflected an interest in classical subjects presented in Roman and Greek scenes.

    C. were often scenes of Indians and the wilderness that represented the promise of America.

    D. were usually in the form of abstract designs for flags or stamps.

29. The effects of the Revolution on slavery included all the following *except*

    A. the British army was the greatest instrument of emancipation.

    B. slaves who fought for the colonies were given their freedom.

    C. several northern states forbade slavery.

  * D. a reopening of the Atlantic slave trade.

30. Charles Willson Peale

    A. published the first arithmetic in America.

    B. wrote *History of the American Revolution* in 1789.

    C. was the influential president of Princeton University.

  * D. was known for his portraits of George Washington.

Suggested Essay Questions

1. Compare the militia and the Continental Army in the colonists' war effort.

2. In what ways were the campaigns in the North different from those in the South?

3. Discuss the validity of the following assertion: "Without the cooperation of the French, American victory in the Revolution would not have been possible."

4. Discuss the social effects of the Revolution. In what areas was the revolutionary promise or spirit most fulfilled? In what areas was it least fulfilled?

5. What were the key factors in America's surprise victory over the British in the Revolution?

Chapter 6

SHAPING A FEDERAL UNION

This chapter covers the accomplishments and weaknesses of the Confederation government, the movement for a new constitution, the key developments in the convention, a brief analysis of the historiographical controversy over the writing of the Constitution, and the movement for the ratification of the Constitution. The chapter closes as plans are laid for inauguration of the new government.

Chapter Outline

I. Government of the Confederation period
   A. Called the "critical period"
   B. Authority given to Congress by the Articles of Confederation
   C. Basic accomplishments of the Confederation government
   D. Nature of congressional administration during the war
   E. Financial problems of the government
      1. Robert Morris, secretary of finance
      2. Scheme for a national bank failed to receive unanimous approval
      3. Failure of Morris's plan
   F. Development of a land policy
      1. Direct congressional authority prevailed
      2. Geographic areas covered by the policy
      3. Land ordinances set precedents for future treatment of territories
         a. Ordinance of 1785
         b. Ordinance of 1787
         c. Western lands south of the Ohio River
         d. Indian treaties made to gain claim to western lands
   G. Effects of the war on farming
      1. Fighting seldom affected farming except to bring price increases

      2. Slaves taken from tidewater areas

      3. Lost British bounties on indigo and naval stores

   H. Effects of the war on merchants

      1. New outlets needed for trade

      2. Sentiment for free trade

      3. Exclusion of Americans from British West Indies

      4. Commerce and exports in "critical period" compared to colonial era

   I. Diplomatic problems

      1. Problems with Britain

         a. British retained forts in the North

         b. Treatment of loyalists

         c. Exchange of diplomatic representatives

      2. Problems with Spain

         a. Southern boundary

         b. Right of U.S. to navigate to mouth of Mississippi River

   J. Efforts of states to exclude imperial trade

   K. Effects of shortage of cash

      1. Demands for legal paper currency

      2. Depreciation of paper currency varied

   L. Impact of Shays's rebellion

      1. Farmers demanded paper money to pay off taxes

      2. Militia scattered "Shays's Army"

      3. Legislature lowered taxes for the next year

   M. Demands grow for stronger government

II. Adopting the Constitution

   A. Preliminary steps to the convention

      1. Mount Vernon meeting of 1785

      2. Annapolis meeting of 1786

      3. Call for the constitutional convention

   B. Nature of the convention

      1. Nature of the delegates

      2. Political philosophy represented at the convention

      3. Secrecy of the proceedings

   C. Conflict of the Virginia and New Jersey plans

      1. Terms of the Virginia plan

      2. Terms of the New Jersey plan

      3. Convention chose to create a new government

   D. Major issues of dispute in drafting the Constitution

      1. Basis for representation of the states

    2. Disputes between North and South over counting of slaves
    3. No discussion of women's rights
   E. Separation of powers
    1. Nature of legislature
    2. Nature of the office of president
    3. Nature of the judicial branch
    4. Examples of countervailing forces in the government
   F. Ratification provisions

 III. The fight for ratification
   A. Nationalists vs. Antifederalists
   B. Charles Beard's argument for economic motivation of the delegates
    1. Personalty interests vs. realty interests
    2. Concept of localist vs. cosmopolitan elements
    3. Other factional considerations among the population
   C. Arguments of *The Federalist* for ratification
   D. Views of Federalists and Antifederalists
   E. The pattern of ratification
    1. Smaller states acted first
    2. New Hampshire was ninth state
    3. The effort to convince Virginia and New York
    4. Rhode Island held out until 1790
   F. Plans for transition to a new government

Suggestions for Lecture Topics

An interesting lecture for this period might cover the historiography of Beard's economic interpretation of the Constitution. A quick review of key interpretations can be found in *Essays on the Making of the Constitution*, edited by Leonard W. Levy (1969). Also useful here would be Henry Steele Commager's "The Economic Interpretation of the Constitution Reconsidered," in his *The Search for a Usable Past* (1967).

A lecture on the Constitutional Convention itself could use information found in Catherine Drinker Bowen's *Miracle at Philadelphia*(1966), recently reissued to mark the bicentennial of the Constitution.

You may wish to open a discussion on how the Constitution has fared over its 200-year history. Consult the collection of essays, *A Workable Government? The Constitution after 200 Years*, edited by Burke Marshall (1987).

Multiple-Choice Questions

1. The major source of wealth from which the Confederation could pay its debts was
     A. the gold deposits in the West.
   * B. the sale of western land.
     C. trade with European countries.
     D. Indian furs which could be obtained by trade.

2. Although separate branches of government were not formed in the Confederation period, four departments of government were established. They were:
     A. State, Defense and Interior.
     B. Finance, War, and Interior.
     C. Treasury, Agriculture, and Navy.
   * D. Foreign Affairs, Finance and War.

3. Of the following, the one that gave the Confederation government the most trouble was
   * A. finances.
     B. Indian affairs.
     C. land policy.
     D. postal service.

4. The Confederation government came closest to having a head of government in the person of
     A. George Washington.
     B. John Hancock.
     C. Alexander Hamilton.
   * D. Robert Morris.

5. In the lands south of the Ohio River,
     A. settlement proceeded more slowly than in the Northwest.
     B. the Scioto Company was given a grant for a large area.
   * C. Georgia, North Carolina, and Virginia kept their titles to the western lands for the time being.
     D. Indians were given a huge reservation in an area that is now New York and Pennsylvania.

6. Perhaps the most difficult problem to overcome in the Confederate government—and the most glaring defect in the Articles of Confederation—was
     A. the government's inability to negotiate treaties.
   * B. the requirement that all states had to approve any amendment to the Articles.

    C. the government's inability to regulate commerce.

    D. the lack of a legislative branch.

7. The United States departed from the colonial policies of Great Britain by

 * A. promising statehood to all the unsettled western territory.

   B. prohibiting national control of trade with other nations.

   C. promising freedom for all western Indians.

   D. prohibiting the movement of slaves between states, except for sale.

8. The system for administering western lands in the United States, which was developed in the Land Ordinance of 1785, favored

   A. people from existing states who wanted to settle in the new lands.

 * B. speculators, who could afford to purchase large blocks of land.

   C. Indians, who were not forced to vacate any lands.

   D. Revolutionary War veterans, who were given first choice of all lands.

9. Which of the following does *not* describe the provisions of the Northwest Ordinance?

   A. Slavery was prohibited in the territory above the Ohio River.

   B. Statehood was allowed when a territory had a population of 60,000 people.

   C. Religious freedom was guaranteed in a "bill of rights."

 * D. Title to the lands of the territories remained with New York and Pennsylvania until states were formed.

10. After the Revolutionary War, American trade

   A. was officially prohibited to the British West Indies.

   B. began to follow more the free trade writings of Adam Smith.

   C. resumed with Great Britain after 1783.

 * D. is correctly described by all the above.

11. Diplomatic disagreements continued with Britain after the peace treaty of 1783 over *all but which one* of the following issues?

   a. Britain's refusal to vacate forts along the northern boundary

 * b. Britain's refusal to receive a U.S. ambassador

    c. Britain's refusal to lift certain trade restrictions

    d. rights of loyalists to regain property taken from them during the war

12. The nation with which the United States had a major diplomatic dispute over navigation of the Mississippi River was

    A. France.

    B. Great Britain.

    C. Canada.

  * D. Spain.

13. Who said, "The tree of liberty must be refreshed from time to time with the blood of patriots and tyrants"?

  * A. Thomas Jefferson

    B. George Washington

    C. Abigail Adams

    D. Gouverneur Morris

14. Which of the following statements about trade and the economy in the new nation is *not* true?

    A. Merchants had suffered more in the Revolution than had farmers.

    B. Congress had little to do with the economic depression of the period.

    C. Farm exports doubled after the war.

  * D. American indigo and naval stores benefited by separation from the British Empire.

15. The movement for the Constitution grew out of

    A. a resolution from the Confederation Congress to develop a stronger government.

    B. a need to solve problems between the government and the Indians in the West.

  * C. meetings called to develop interstate cooperation on rivers.

    D. a movement to open trade with British territory.

16. A severe shortage of paper money

    A. alleviated the Confederation's financial problems in 1787.

  * B. led to Shays's Rebellion in Massachusetts.

    C. led creditors to demand that more be printed.

    D. led debtors to demand that only hard money be accepted for debts.

17. Which of the following prominent early leaders was not present at the Constitutional Convention because of his diplomatic responsibilities in Europe?
    A. William Paterson
    B. Benjamin Franklin
    C. Roger Sherman
    * D. Thomas Jefferson

18. The differences in political philosophy among the delegates to the Constitutional Convention
    A. were great because few had done extensive reading in law, history, or philosophy.
    B. resulted in a two-year delay before agreement could be reached.
    * C. were narrow; on many fundamentals they agreed.
    D. were evident mostly in the debates over the judiciary.

19. The Virginia Plan presented at the Constitutional Convention
    * A. was drafted mainly by James Madison.
    B. proposed a unified government with executive, legislative, and judicial functions contained in one branch.
    C. proposed equal representation in the legislature for each of the states.
    D. made no provisions for a judicial branch.

20. One of the chief differences between the Virginia and New Jersey plans was
    A. whether the national or state governments would control western lands.
    B. whether the national government would have the authority to levy taxes directly on the people.
    * C. whether representation in Congress would be apportioned by state or by population.
    D. whether Congress would be given the power to regulate commerce between the states.

21. In the discussions at the Constitutional Convention concerning slavery,
    A. most northern delegates demanded immediate abolition.
    * B. it was decided that each slave would count as three-fifths of a person for purposes of taxation and representation.
    C. it was decided to ban the Atlantic slave trade immediately.
    D. southerners wanted slaves to count for purposes of taxation, but not for representation.

22. The Constitutional Convention met
    A. in New York.
    B. in Washington, D.C.
    C. in 1785.
  * D. in 1787.

23. Which of the following was *not* given to the president in the Constitution?
    A. the right to veto laws passed by Congress, unless a two-thirds vote in each House of Congress overruled his veto
  * B. the right to set aside any law temporarily if he felt that to do so was in the national interest
    C. the right to appoint diplomats, judges, and other officers with the consent of the Senate
    D. his role as commander-in-chief of the armed forces

24. The part of government most answerable to the people under the original Constitution was
    A. the executive.
    B. the judiciary.
    C. the Senate.
  * D. the House of Representatives.

25. The Constitution was to be considered ratified as soon as it had been approved by
    A. all thirteen states.
    B. three-quarters of the states.
  * C. nine of the states.
    D. a majority of the states.

26. The Constitution
    A. had checks and balances corresponding to those in the English government.
    B. was written, according to Charles Beard, by men whose wealth was largely in land and slaves.
    C. specifically authorized judicial review and *ex post facto* laws.
  * D. did not allow the direct popular election of the chief executive.

27. Which of the following was *not* one of the writers of *The Federalist*?
    A. Alexander Hamilton
  * B. Patrick Henry
    C. John Jay
    D. James Madison

28. *The Federalist* argued that
    * A. diversity of the nation would make it impossible for any one faction to control the government.
    B. the Constitution was necessary to prevent one faction from taking control of the nation.
    C. a republican form of government could not work in a nation as large as the United States, and therefore the Constitution was necessary.
    D. the Constitution would promote control of the government by one faction, which would be good for the nation.

29. Which of the following is *not* true of the Antifederalist leaders?
    A. They contended that the writing and ratification of the Constitution was an illegal action under the Articles of Confederation.
    B. They were often men whose careers had been established well before the Revolution.
    * C. They had been the chief proponents of a stronger central government at the Constitutional Convention.
    D. They demanded a Bill of Rights to protect individuals from the new government.

30. The last of the thirteen original states to ratify the Constitution was
    A. Delaware.
    B. New Hampshire.
    C. New York.
    * D. Rhode Island.

Suggested Essay Questions

1. Discuss the following assertion in light of the facts and the arguments between the Federalists and the Antifederalists: "The Articles of Confederation framed a weak government which, if it had been allowed to continue to operate, would have been swallowed up by Britain or Spain, thus ending the independence of the United States."

2. Describe the system of checks and balances in the Constitution.

3. What were the effects of the Revolutionary War on the agriculture, trade, diplomacy, and finances of the new nation?

4. Discuss the conflict between Federalists and Antifederalists in the writing and ratification of the Constitution and show how the arguments of each group reflected its own economic self-interest.

5. What major compromises were made at the Constitutional Convention, and what issues did they settle? What issues remained unsettled?

Chapter 7

THE FEDERALISTS: WASHINGTON AND ADAMS

This chapter covers the major developments of the first two presidential administrations of the new government. Significant attention is given to Hamilton's proposals for the economic development of the new nation and to the clash of philosophies between Hamilton and Jefferson. Diplomatic problems with Britain, France, and Spain are treated in some detail. Land policy through 1804 is summarized, and there is a summary of Washington's farewell address. The focus of the treatment of the Adams administration is on the conflict with France and its domestic ramifications in the Alien and Sedition Acts. The elections of 1796 and 1800 are both explained. The chapter closes with the outgoing Federalist administration packing the judiciary.

Chapter Outline

1. Organizing the new government
   A. The convening of Congress
   B. Washington's procession
   C. Symbols of authority
   D. Cabinet posts and appointments
   E. Bill of Rights added to the Constitution
   F. Revenue for the government

II. Hamilton's vision of America
   A. Hamilton's background and character
   B. Establishing the public credit
      1. Provisions of the Report on Public Credit
      2. Reactions to Hamilton's credit proposals
         a. Concern about rewarding speculators
         b. Sectional differences
         c. Compromise solution
   C. Hamilton's plan for a national bank
      1. Advantages of a bank
      2. Controversy over the constitutionality of the bank
   D. Hamilton's *Report on Manufactures*

      1. Advantages of governmental development of manu-
facturing
      2. Proposed tariff
      3. Some tariff proposals enacted
   E. Overall assessment of Hamiltons contribution
      1. Brilliant administrator
      2. Promoted class and sectional interests
      3. Tied government to the wealthy
      4. Antagonized others in the South and backcountry

III. Development of political parties
   A. The eighteenth-century view of parties
   B. Madison's and Jefferson's general reactions
   C. Jefferson's background
   D. Jefferson's and Hamilton's views compared

IV. Crises foreign and domestic
   A. Foreign affairs
      1. Impact of the French Revolution
      2. Washington's neutrality proclamation
      3. Actions of Citizen Genêt
      4. Polarization of American opinion and parties
      5. Jay's negotiations with Great Britain
         a. Jay's instructions
         b. Terms accepted by Jay
         c. Public reactions to the treaty
         d. Congressional reaction
   B. Frontier problems
      1. Indian uprisings
      2. Treaty of Greenville
   C. Whiskey Rebellion
      1. Basis for the rebellion
      2. Army sent to disperse the rebellion
      3. Effects of the incident
   D. Treaty with Spain
      1. Spanish intrigues in the West
      2. Terms of the Treaty of San Lorenzo
   E. Development of land policy
      1. Conflict over basic principles of land policy
      2. Relationship of land policy to the political parties
      3. Congressional changes in land policy from 1796 to
1804
   F. Washington's Farewell Address
      1. Summary of his achievements as president
      2. General principles of the address

V. The Adams administration
   A. Election of 1796
      1. Candidates
      2. Hamilton's scheme
      3. Outcome of the election
   B. Adams's life and character
   C. Troubles with France
      1. Reasons for trouble
      2. The XYZ Affair
      3. Creation of a navy
      4. Organization of a new army
      5. Peace and convention of 1800
   D. Alien and Sedition Acts
      1. Terms of the acts
      2. Arrests and prosecutions under the acts
      3. Kentucky and Virginia Resolutions

VI. Election of 1800
   A. Candidates
   B. Outcome of the election
   C. Packing the judiciary

Suggestions for Lecture Topics

For a lecture on how citizens of the new nation viewed George Washington, see Marcus Cunliffe's *George Washington, Man and Monument* (1958) and Wendy C. Wick's *George Washington: An American Icon* (1982).

The first two chapters of Seymour Martin Lipset's *The First New Nation* (1963) provide a good basis for a lecture comparing the American experience with that of other new nations.

For a lecture comparing the Federalists and the Jeffersonians, see Richard Buel, Jr.'s *Securing the Revolution* (1972). Buel shows how each group drew on and transformed the Revolutionary ideology of republicanism.

Have students read *The Federalist* number 10, available from many sources, before class. Your lecture on the topic could use Garry Wills's *Explaining America* (1981); Douglass Adair's two essays on the Tenth Federalist in his *Fame and the Founding Fathers* (1974) are also useful.

Multiple-Choice Questions

1. George Washington
   A. won 65 of 95 electoral votes to become the first president.
   * B. was an awkward speaker.
   C. opposed all pomp and circumstance.
   D. is correctly represented by all the above.

2. Washington's secretary of state was
   * A. Thomas Jefferson.
   B. John M. Thompson.
   C. John Jay.
   D. Edmund Randolph.

3. The Bill of Rights
   A. was strongly supported by Alexander Hamilton.
   B. contained twelve amendments to the Constitution that for the most part concerned the relationship between states and the national government.
   * C. did not become effective until Dec. 1791.
   D. was opposed by most Antifederalists.

4. Which of the following is *not* a correct description of Alexander Hamilton?
   A. He came from a background of illegitimacy and poverty.
   B. He sought to tie the wealthy class to the government.
   C. He paid little attention to the needs of small farmers and people on the frontier.
   * D. He was critical of the British on most issues.

5. America's first vice-president was
   A. Alexander Hamilton.
   * B. John Adams.
   C. Thomas Pinckney.
   D. Aaron Burr.

6. The question of assumption of the public debt
   A. received little debate in Congress.
   B. was divided along sectional lines, eastern seaboard against western backcountry.
   C. was the subject of Hamilton's *Report on Manufactures*.
   * D. was resolved in a compromise involving the location of the national capital.

7. The objections to paying off the debt at full value included
   - A. the unfairness of allowing speculators to make money on bonds that they had bought at reduced prices.
   - B. the great cost that such action would entail.
   - C. the great percentage of the debt that was held by people in the North.
   - * D. all the above.

8. Hamilton supported establishing a national bank for all the following reasons *except*
   - A. it would provide a uniform circulating currency.
   - B. it would provide a source of credit for the new nation.
   - * C. it would provide a source of many jobs for the nation's citizens.
   - D. it would provide a means to handle many bookkeeping chores of the national government.

9. Madison and Jefferson objected to the national bank primarily because
   - * A. they believed in a strict interpretation of the Constitution.
   - B. Article 1, Section 8 of the Constitution reserved to the states powers not delegated to Congress.
   - C. it would cost the government too much money.
   - D. it would be located in New York instead of Virginia.

10. Hamilton's plan to encourage manufacturing included all but which one of the following?
    - A. protective tariffs
    - B. bounties and premiums to encourage industry
    - * C. national government loans to new industries
    - D. encouragement of new inventions

11. The largest department of the national government during Washington's administrations was the
    - A. State Department.
    - B. War Department.
    - * C. Treasury Department.
    - D. Justice Department.

12. The Hamiltonian program
    - * A. led to the first national political parties.
    - B. was based on Hamilton's desire for personal financial gain.
    - C. arose naturally from his wealthy family background.
    - D. is correctly represented by all the above statements.

13. Which of the following is *not* a correct description of Thomas Jefferson?
    A. He was born and reared in a family of wealth.
    * B. He supported tradition and respected institutions like the established church.
    C. He had wide-ranging intellectual interests that included agriculture and engineering.
    D. He favored a government that catered to yeoman farmers.

14. In the Convention of 1800,
    A. America and Spain agreed on the Florida boundary.
    B. France and England agreed to end their fighting.
    * C. France agreed to end its military alliance with America.
    D. America and England agreed on the Canadian boundary.

15. Regarding the warfare that developed between Britain and France as a result of the French Revolution, Washington took the position of
    A. support for Britain because of its conservative government.
    B. support for France because of its assistance in the American Revolution.
    * C. neutrality, remaining "friendly and impartial" toward both sides.
    D. allying with other nations to oppose both Britain and France.

16. Citizen Genêt
    A. was murdered during his tour of America.
    * B. encouraged Americans to attack foreign territory on the frontiers.
    C. came to the United States because of his friendship with Alexander Hamilton.
    D. is correctly described by all the above.

17. As a result of Jay's Treaty,
    * A. the British agreed to evacuate their northwest posts by 1799.
    B. the border with Canada was adjusted in favor of America.
    C. all American trade with the British West Indies was legalized.
    D. duties on most items imported from England were cut in half.

18. A key factor in encouraging the Whiskey Rebellion was
    A. the opposition to drinking alcohol prevalent in the United States at the time.

    * B. the limited means of transportation for moving bulky grain from the frontier to market.
    C. Hamilton's support of small farmers on the frontier.
    D. the development of improved rifles which gave the frontiersmen an advantage over the army.

19. The Whiskey Rebellion ended when
    A. Congress removed the tax on whiskey.
    B. the Republicans sent funds and ammunition to the disgruntled farmers.
    * C. Washington sent an army larger than any he had ever commanded in the Revolution to put down the revolt.
    D. a compromise was reached in which the leaders were executed and the tax was gradually lowered.

20. Pinckney's Treaty
    * A. gave the United States the right to navigate the Mississippi River and deposit goods at New Orleans.
    B. settled the boundary dispute between Spanish Louisiana and the United States.
    C. was only narrowly approved by the Senate.
    D. brought an alliance of the United States and Spain against the Indians.

21. On the issue of land policy,
    A. the Federalists and the Republicans agreed.
    B. Republicans won out in the Land Act of 1796.
    C. Federalists pushed for the sale of small parcels of land to settlers, rather than large parcels to speculators.
    * D. influential Federalists wanted to build the population of the East before the West, to protect their political influence.

22. In his Farewell Address, Washington
    A. decried the spirit of sectionalism that was developing.
    B. discouraged the idea of political parties.
    C. urged the United States never to become involved in permanent alliances with foreign nations.
    * D. supported all the above sentiments.

23. In the election of 1796,
    A. John Adams defeated George Washington.
    * B. Alexander Hamilton's scheming against John Adams allowed Thomas Jefferson to win the vice-presidency.
    C. the nation experimented for the first time with the direct election of the president.

  D. George Washington announced his support for Thomas
   Jefferson.

24. *Notes on Virginia* was written
  A. by America's second president.
 * B. by America's third president.
  C. in support of the Virginia Resolves.
  D. in opposition to the Virginia Resolves.

25. The XYZ Affair
 * A. became an excuse for Congress to raise an army and prepare
   for war.
  B. involved American diplomats in England who refused to
   give their names.
  C. led to a declaration of war by the United States on France.
  D. led to a major appropriation to pay for bribes rather than
   bullets.

26. The XYZ Affair led to all but which one of the following?
  A. the establishment of an American navy in 1798
  B. the call-up of Washington from his retirement to com-
   mand an army
  C. an undeclared naval war with France in the West Indies
 * D. an American effort to break political ties with the
   British

27. The Alien and Sedition Acts
  A. were aimed against the British.
  B. were a partisan attempt to stifle the Federalists.
 * C. resulted in ten convictions.
  D. were ruled unconstitutional by the Supreme Court in 1798.

28. The Virginia and Kentucky Resolutions asserted
 * A. that states could decide if laws were unconstitutional.
  B. that the taxes imposed by Congress were unconstitutional.
  C. that immigrants should be expelled from the country if
   they were not loyal to the American cause.
  D. that freedom of speech was an unlimited right guaranteed
   to all Americans.

29. Jefferson's election in 1800
  A. continued the Federalist domination of the United States
   government.
 * B. had to be settled by the House of Representatives.
  C. came because Aaron Burr agreed to withdraw as a
   candidate for president.

     D. was almost assured when George Washington announced his support of Jefferson just three weeks before the election.

30. The Judiciary Act of 1801
    A. created three new positions on the Supreme Court.
    B. was the first act passed by the Republicans in power.
    C. allowed federal judges to be impeached under the Sedition Act.
*   D. was the legacy of the Federalists as they left office.

Suggested Essay Questions

1. Compare the arguments of Jefferson and Hamilton for and against the constitutionality of the Bank of the United States.

2. Explain each of Hamilton's three major economic programs and how they collectively promoted the economic growth of the United States. Which of Hamilton's proposals were enacted into law?

3. What were the major points of the Federalists' foreign policy? What factors influenced that policy?

4. What was George Washington's greatest achievement as president? What was his worst failure? Overall, was his administration a success for the nation? Was it a success for the Federalists?

5. Account for the development of political parties in the Washington administration and show the alignments that developed among the two parties.

Chapter 8

REPUBLICANISM: JEFFERSON AND MADISON

This chapter focuses on the political events of the years 1801–1815, including the War of 1812. Beginning with a description of the new city of Washington, the chapter covers in some detail Jefferson's two terms in office, the *Marbury v. Madison* decision, the Louisiana Purchase, and the Burr Conspiracy. The history and historiography of the War of 1812 is traced. The major battles of the war are covered. The chapter concludes with the peace that ended the war and a brief reflection on the immediate aftermath of the war.

Chapter Outline

I. Jefferson in office
  A. The inauguration
  B. Evidences of the simple style
  C. The "Revolution of 1800"
    1. An orderly transfer of power
    2. Jefferson's role as party leader
  D. Jefferson and the judiciary
    1. Repeal of the Judiciary Act of 1801
    2. Importance of the *Marbury v. Madison* ruling
  E. Conflicts with Federalist policies
    1. Repeal of excise taxes
    2. Land policies
    3. Treatment of army and navy
    4. Slave trade outlawed
  F. Conflict with the Barbary pirates
    1. Causes for conflict
    2. United States actions
  G. The Louisiana Purchase
    1. Interest in the territory
    2. Negotiating the purchase
    3. Republican reaction to constitutional issues
    4. Explorations of Lewis and Clark
  H. Political schemes of the Federalist camp

       1. Thomas Pickering and the Essex Junto considered secession
       2. Burr's duel ended his political career

II. Divisions within the Republican Party
    A. Emergence of John Randolph and the *Tertium Quids*
       1. John Randolph's philosophy
       2. Randolph's final break with Jefferson
    B. The Burr conspiracy
       1. Burr's background and character
       2. Burr's excursion
       3. Disposition of the charge of treason
          a. Jefferson's use of "executive privilege"
          b. Rigid definition of treason adopted

III. War in Europe
    A. Napoleon's victories
    B. Harassment of shipping by Britain and France
       1. Mutual blockades
       2. Impressment of sailors
    C. The Jefferson Embargo
       1. Nature of the act
       2. Impact of the embargo
    D. Madison and Clinton elected in 1808
    E. The drift toward war
       1. Non-Intercourse Act
       2. Macon's Bill No. 2
       3. Intrigues with Britain and France over the trade restrictions
    F. Madison's request for war

IV. The War of 1812
    A. Causes of the war
       1. Demand for neutral rights
       2. Geographical distribution of war sentiment
          a. Farming regions and shippers
          b. Concern for the Indians
          c. Desire for new land in Florida and Canada
       3. Indian uprisings
       4. National honor
    B. Preparations for war
       1. Banking problems affecting financing of the war
       2. Problems with building an army
       3. State of the navy
    C. War in the North

      1. Three-pronged strategy failed
      2. Detroit forces surrendered
      3. Niagara contingent refused to fight in Canada
      4. Champlain group would not march to Canada
      5. Perry's exploits on Lake Erie
      6. Harrison won victory at Battle of the Thames
   D. Jackson's raid into Florida
   E. British threefold plan of 1814
      1. Invasion via Niagara and Lake Champlain
      2. Extension of coastal blockade to New England
      3. Seizure of New Orleans
   F. Invasions at Washington and Baltimore
   G. Battle of New Orleans
   H. Treaty of Ghent
   I. The Hartford Convention
      1. Composition
      2. Actions taken
      3. Consequences of the gathering
   J. Aftermath of the war
      1. Inspired patriotism and nationalism
      2. Action against the pirates of the Barbary Coast
      3. Reversal of roles by Republicans and Federalists

Suggestions for Lecture Topics

For a lecture on how the Republicans functioned once in power—the mechanics of their day-to-day operations—see Leonard D. White's *The Jeffersonians* (1951), an interesting administrative history of the party. White's *The Federalists* (1948) would make for a useful contrast.

Another useful lecture might use Merrill D. Peterson's *The Jeffersonian Image in the American Mind* (1960) to show something of the tremendously influential shadow Jefferson has cast over the years.

For an interesting lecture on the Burr conspiracy, see Thomas P. Abernethy's *The Burr Conspiracy* (1954) or, perhaps more useful, Chapter 11 of his *The South in the New Nation* (1961). A more recent source is the second volume of Milton Lomask's *Aaron Burr* (1982).

For a lecture on the historiography of the causes of the War of 1812, use *The Causes of the War of 1812*, edited by Bradford Perkins (1962), or *The War of 1812*, edited by George R. Taylor (1963). A more recent good work on the causes of the war is J.C.A. Stagg's *Mr. Madison's War* (1983).

Multiple-Choice Questions

1. The Louisiana Purchase was made from
   A. England.
   * B. France.
   C. the Netherlands.
   D. Spain.

2. Thomas Jefferson's inaugural address reflected
   A. his strong partisan desire to oppose the Federalists now that he was in office.
   * B. a tone of simplicity and conciliation.
   C. his desire to adopt Federalist principles now that he was in office.
   D. an affirmation of educational elitism and commitment to continued governmental formality.

3. Probably the most revolutionary thing about Jefferson's presidency was
   A. his commitment to acquire new land.
   B. the change in the style of entertainment in the White House.
   C. his stand against the judicial branch of the government.
   * D. the orderly transfer of power and offices from one party to another.

4. In the case of *Marbury v. Madison,*
   A. Jefferson was forbidden to change appointments made to the Supreme Court.
   * B. a law of Congress was declared unconstitutional.
   C. the Supreme Court acknowledged that it had no power over the president.
   D. the Federalists won the assurance that they would keep their appointments in the judicial branch of government.

5. James Wilkinson
   * A. was Burr's accomplice in Burr's western intrigues.
   B. was Jefferson's first vice-president.
   C. was Jefferson's second vice-president.
   D. led the daring raid on Tripoli.

6. Jefferson's domestic reforms
   * A. included an act in 1807 which outlawed the foreign slave trade.
   B. included the dismantling of most of Hamilton's programs.

    C. included raising the excise tax on whiskey.

    D. included decreasing the sale of western lands for revenue.

7. Jefferson's problems with the Barbary States

    A. began when American smugglers killed the captain of an Algerian frigate.

   * B. gave Jefferson second thoughts about cutting the size of the navy.

    C. led to a short but extremely costly war for the United States.

    D. were over issues involving fishing rights in the North Atlantic.

8. The Louisiana Purchase

    A. was favored by New England Federalists.

    B. cost the United States $3 million plus the assumption of French debts owed to Americans.

   * C. more than doubled the territory of the United States.

    D. for the first time gave Americans a strip of land from the Atlantic Ocean to the Pacific.

9. The Louisiana Purchase was a problem for Jefferson because

    A. the cost was too high for the United States to pay.

    B. acquisition of new Indian lands was contrary to his principles and beliefs.

    C. the territory was ideal for slavery, which he opposed.

   * D. he believed that the Constitution did not give authority to acquire new land.

10. The primary aim of the Lewis and Clark expedition was

    A. to develop plans for fortifying the newly acquired Louisiana Territory.

   * B. to explore the land and wildlife of Louisiana.

    C. to survey a route to China through the American Northwest.

    D. to survey the exact boundary of the Louisiana Purchase.

11. The Essex Junto

    A. was a group of New Englanders who supported the Louisiana Purchase against Federalist opposition.

    B. was the name given to Republican supporters of Aaron Burr.

   * C. was an extremist group of Federalists in New England who developed the idea of secession from the Union.

    D. was the primary supporter of Jefferson's Embargo.

12. The "Old Republicans"
    A. believed in a strong central government.
    B. supported the Louisiana Purchase.
    C. opposed Jefferson because he refused to compromise his Republican principles, no matter what the circumstances.
  * D. were led by John Taylor.

13. The overwhelming electoral success of Jefferson and the Republicans in 1804 led to
  * A. splits in the Republican Party.
    B. an almost equal party division in the new Congress.
    C. riots by disgruntled Federalists in South Carolina.
    D. rejuvenation of the Federalist Party.

14. Aaron Burr
  * A. was found innocent of treason because John Marshall adopted a strict definition of treason.
    B. was killed in a duel with Alexander Hamilton.
    C. argued *Marbury v. Madison* before the Supreme Court.
    D. was vice-president under both John Adams and Thomas Jefferson.

15. The Chesapeake incident involved
    A. an American ship sunk by the British.
  * B. British seizure and search of an American ship.
    C. Americans seizure of a British ship.
    D. American harassment of a British merchant ship.

16. American shipping after 1805 was hampered by
    A. the British claim that goods from the French and Spanish West Indies were liable to seizure anywhere.
    B. the British Orders in Council that created a blockade of continental Europe.
    C. the French blockade of the British Isles.
  * D. all the above.

17. Timothy Pickering
    A. was the American negotiator for the Louisiana Purchase.
    B. said "Don't give up the ship" when a British ship attacked his vessel.
    C. led the American victory at Detroit.
  * D. was a Federalist.

18. Jefferson's response to British and French interference with U.S. shipping was
    A. an effort to woo France into an alliance.

       * B. what he called a policy of "peaceful coercion."
         C. an effort to woo Britain into an alliance.
         D. to ignore the matter and continue trading with both.

19. The Embargo Act of 1807
         A. was passed over Jefferson's veto.
         B. was not a success because too many items were exempted.
       * C. did not hurt the French very much.
         D. was a response to England's "Continental System."

20. Macon's Bill No. 2
         A. opened trade with all countries except France and England.
       * B. opened trade with both France and England.
         C. authorized the president to reopen trade with England or France whenever these countries dropped their trade restrictions against America.
         D. failed to pass Congress by a small margin.

21. The greatest support for the declaration of war in 1812 came from
         A. the New England area.
         B. the areas where commerce and international trade were a primary occupation.
         C. the manufacturing center of the United States.
       * D. the agricultural regions of the South and West.

22. Which of the following was *not* one of the important causes of the War of 1812?
         A. British restriction of U.S. neutral rights at sea
       * B. the British invasion of Florida
         C. a desire of western states to obtain more land from Britain
         D. fear of British aid to Indians who attacked frontier settlements

23. During the War of 1812 the most effective victories for the United States occurred
         A. at sea, with attacks on the British navy in the English Channel.
         B. on land, with the effective invasions of Canada.
         C. along the eastern seaboard, where British efforts to invade were repeatedly repelled.
       * D. on the Great Lakes, where the small American navy repeatedly raised morale with victories over British ships.

24. The greatest humiliation to the United States in the War of 1812 occurred when
    A. the British won victories over the small American navy on the Great Lakes.
    * B. the capital city of Washington was invaded and burned.
    C. the British captured Fort McHenry and Baltimore.
    D. the British attacked New Orleans two weeks after the war ended.

25. The treaty ending the War of 1812 provided
    * A. for the restoration of the same boundaries as before the war started.
    B. for British evacuation of their forts in the Northwest Territory.
    C. that the British would stop violating American neutral rights at sea.
    D. for removal of American warships from the Great Lakes and British access to the Mississippi River.

26. At the Hartford Convention, delegates from the New England states
    A. voted to secede from the union.
    * B. proposed a series of constitutional amendments to limit Republican influence in government.
    C. denounced New England merchants who had traded with the British during the war.
    D. voted to join the Republican Party.

27. One of the greatest hindrances to American success in the War of 1812 was
    A. the lack of western enthusiasm for the war.
    B. the lack of nearby British territory which could be attacked.
    * C. the lack of military preparation for war during the Jefferson and Madison administrations.
    D. the action of William Hull, an American who spied for the British.

28. The Treaty of Ghent
    A. was signed on Christmas Eve, 1816.
    B. was never ratified by the Senate.
    * C. was signed two weeks before the Battle of New Orleans.
    D. is correctly represented by all the above.

29. Following the War of 1812,
    A. Federalists and Republicans returned to their prewar positions.
    B. Federalists argued for a broad construction of the Constitution.
    * C. Republicans argued for a national bank and a peacetime army.
    D. both parties opposed spending money on internal improvements.

30. The Jeffersonian approach to dealing with foreign challenges was
    A. ignoring them and relying on strict neutrality.
    * B. the use of economic policy to gain our goals.
    C. reliance on military force to achieve results.
    D. a search for new patterns of alliance with foreign nations.

Suggested Essay Questions

1. Assess the degree to which Jefferson's election as president can accurately be called the "Revolution of 1800."

2. In what ways did the Federalists and Republicans seem to reverse their positions during the early nineteenth century? What might explain these reversals?

3. Political dissension seemed to be an important factor in the era of Jefferson. This can be seen in the appearance of, among other things, the "Old Republicans," the Burr Conspiracy, the Essex Junto, and the Hartford Convention. How can you account for these examples, and what generalizations can you draw from them?

4. Why did the United States go to war with England in 1812? Which groups of people supported and opposed the war? Why?

5. "The War of 1812 was an unnecessary conflict which solved nothing and brought no benefit to either side." Discuss the validity of this assertion.

Chapter 9

NATIONALISM AND SECTIONALISM

This chapter focuses on the effects of nationalism following the War of 1812 on the economy, on government centralization, on diplomacy, on Supreme Court decisions, and on politics, as well as the expressions of sectionalism in the era. It follows the shifting political party patterns, while narrating key developments of the administrations of Monroe and Adams. The chapter concludes with the election of Andrew Jackson in 1828.

Chapter Outline

   I. Action for economic nationalism
      A. National bank
          1. Effects of the expiration of the national bank in 1811
          2. Proposal for a new national bank
          3. The support and opposition to the bank characterized
      B. Protective tariff
          1. Tariff of 1816
          2. Changing sectional attitudes
      C. Internal improvements
          1. Early efforts
          2. Calhoun's bill and its fate

  II. An era of political harmony
      A. James Monroe characterized
      B. Monroe's cabinet
      C. Election of 1820 and demise of the first party system

 III. Diplomatic developments
      A. Rush-Bagot Agreement of 1817 to limit naval forces on the Great Lakes
      B. Convention of 1818
          1. Northern boundary of Louisiana Purchase
          2. Joint occupation of Oregon
          3. Fishing rights off Newfoundland
      C. Acquisition of Florida
          1. Spain's powerlessness in Florida

      2. Jackson sent on campaign against the Seminoles
      3. Reactions to Jackson's campaign
      4. Adams made treaty with Spain to acquire Florida

IV. Portents of diminishing political harmony
    A. Panic of 1818
      1. Cotton prices fell in England
      2. Easy credit
      3. State banks lent beyond their means
      4. Bank of the U.S. added to speculative mania
      5. State banks forced to maintain specie reserves
    B. The Missouri Compromise
      1. Accidental balance of slave and free states
      2. Tallmadge resolution relating to Missouri slavery
      3. Arguments for and against slavery
      4. Compromise to admit Missouri
        a. Maine and Missouri balanced together
        b. Amendment to exclude slavery in northern Louisiana Purchase

V. Judicial nationalism
    A. John Marshall
    B. Cases asserting judicial review
      1. *Marbury v. Madison* (1803)
      2. *Fletcher v. Peck* (1810)
    C. Protection of contract rights in *Dartmouth College v. Woodward* (1819)
    D. Curbing state powers in *McCulloch v. Maryland* (1819)
    E. National supremacy in commerce in *Gibbons v. Ogden* (1824)

VI. Nationalist diplomacy
    A. Negotiating Russia out of Oregon
    B. The Monroe Doctrine
      1. Impact of Napoleonic Wars on Latin America
      2. British efforts to protect Latin America
      3. The Monroe Doctrine asserted
      4. Reactions to the doctrine

VII. One-party politics
    A. The candidates
    B. The system for nomination
    C. The issues
    D. Outcome of the race
    E. Charges of "Corrupt Bargain"

VIII. Presidency of John Quincy Adams
    A. Adams's character and plans
    B. Adams's mistakes
       1. Demeaning voters
       2. Conjuring notions of a royal family
       3. Tariff of 1828
          a. Failure of high tariff of 1820
          b. Provisions of 1824
          c. Calhoun's proposal to defeat a tariff increase
          d. Calhoun's protest

IX. Election of 1828
    A. Opposition to Jackson
    B. His appeal to different groups
    C. Extensions of suffrage in the states
    D. Other domestic trends
    E. Outcome of the election

Suggestions for Lecture Topics

For a lecture on the important topic of the nationalism of the Supreme Court, see Alfred H. Kelly, Winfred A. Harbinson, and Herman Belz's *The American Constitution: Its Origins and Development* (6th ed., 1983). More specific is William F. Swindler's *The Court and Chief Justice Marshall* (1978). Interesting details on the major cases discussed in the text can be found in *Quarrels That Have Shaped the Constitution*, edited by John A. Garraty (1964). Excerpts from the cases themselves are in *The Supreme Court and the Constitution*, edited by Stanley I. Kutler (3rd ed., 1984).

Glover Moore's *The Missouri Compromise, 1819–1821* (1953) is the standard source for a lecture on that important topic.

For a lecture on the formation of the Monroe Doctrine, see Dexter Perkins's *A History of the Monroe Doctrine* (1955). Ernest R. May's *The Making of the Monroe Doctrine* (1975), an interesting revisionist account, shows how domestic policies and personal ambitions governed foreign policy.

Multiple-Choice Questions

   1. Who wrote the "South Carolina Exposition and Protest"?
     A. John Q. Adams
     B. Henry Clay

* C. John C. Calhoun
  D. Daniel Webster

2. The lack of a national bank during the War of 1812
   * A. led to muddling of the nation's finances.
     B. restricted the lending ability of state-chartered banks.
     C. increased the value of state banknotes.
     D. helped regulate the amount of currency in circulation.

3. Support for a national bank in 1816 came from *all but which one of the following?*
   A. John C. Calhoun
   * B. Daniel Webster
   C. Henry Clay
   D. James Madison

4. The Tariff of 1816
   * A. was the first intended more for protection than for revenue.
     B. was opposed in the Old Northwest.
     C. passed only by a narrow margin.
     D. came at a time when sources of cheap British imports were drying up.

5. Support for the Tariff of 1816 came from
   A. the South.
   B. New England.
   * C. the middle states.
   D. all areas of the country.

6. Internal improvements in the first half of the nineteenth century
   A. included the National Road from Maryland to Illinois.
   B. generally proceeded in a very unsystematic fashion.
   C. were usually the responsibility of the states and private enterprise.
   * D. are correctly represented by all the above statements.

7. Construction of new roads to the West after the War of 1812
   * A. was vetoed by Madison because he thought the Constitution did not permit it.
     B. was opposed by Calhoun because he thought it would hurt South Carolina.
     C. was supported by New England, which wanted ready access to the West.
     D. was opposed by westerners who preferred the isolation of the frontier.

8. James Monroe
    A. opposed a constitutional amendment concerning internal improvements.
  * B. continued the "Virginia Dynasty."
    C. coined the phrase "Era of Good Feelings."
    D. pushed for economic nationalism harder than any of his predecessors.

9. Monroe's election as president in 1820 was
    A. a resounding triumph over his Federalist opponent.
  * B. without opposition.
    C. unanimous; he won every electoral vote.
    D. opposed only by the New England states.

10. The Rush-Bagot Agreement
    A. renewed diplomatic ties between the United States and Great Britain.
    B. was a formal treaty dealing with trade with the British West Indies.
  * C. ended naval competition on the Great Lakes by limiting naval forces there.
    D. dealt with fishing rights off Newfoundland.

11. Most of the U.S.–Canadian boundary was settled in
    A. the Peace of Ghent.
    B. 1823.
  * C. the Convention of 1818.
    D. two Supreme Court cases concerning slavery in the Louisiana territory.

12. In 1825 Florida belonged to
  * A. the United States.
    B. Spain.
    C. France.
    D. the Seminole and Creek Indians.

13. In 1824 the United States signed a treaty with Russia concerning
    A. Louisiana.
    B. Florida.
  * C. Oregon.
    D. Minnesota.

14. Although Secretary of State Adams had ready claim to Florida in 1818, he delayed a treaty on the issue until
  * A. he could also gain agreement on the western boundary of Louisiana.

     B. 1827.

     C. Spanish forces also gave up their claim to Cuba.

     D. Spain agreed to give up Florida without any payment.

15. The panic of 1819
    - A. was started by a collapse of the second Bank of the United States.
    - B. led most Americans to appreciate the national bank.
  - * C. was brought on by a severe drop in cotton prices.
    - D. demonstrated the financial soundness of government land-sale policies.

16. The controversy over admitting Missouri as a state arose because
    - A. there were more slave states than free states.
    - B. there were more free states than slave states.
    - C. in the Convention of 1818 the United States had, in part, agreed to exclude slavery in the western territories.
  - * D. a New York congressman tried to exclude slavery from Missouri.

17. The Missouri Compromise
    - A. was debated almost wholly on moral grounds.
    - B. brought Vermont into the Union as a free state.
    - C. allowed for the freedom of all slaves in Missouri at the age of 25.
  - * D. kept a balance between slave and free states in the Senate, but not in the House of Representatives.

18. A principle affirmed in *Fletcher v. Peck* was
  - * A. the right of the U.S. Supreme Court to examine the constitutionality of state laws.
    - B. the right of citizens to petition Congress for redress of grievances.
    - C. the lack of authority which the federal courts had over state courts.
    - D. the right of free trade between states.

19. The Supreme Court ruled that congressional power to regulate commerce "is complete in itself" and "may be exercised to its utmost extent" in
    - A. *Marbury v. Madison.*
  - * B. *Gibbons v. Ogden.*
    - C. *Comer v. Woodward.*
    - D. *Cohens v. Virginia.*

20. In the case of *McCulloch v. Maryland*, the Supreme Court ruled in favor of
    A. strict and limited construction of the U.S. Constitution.
  * B. the constitutionality of the Bank of the United States.
    C. the right of the national bank to issue currency.
    D. the right of states to tax federal property.

21. The Supreme Court ruled against the right of a state to impair private contracts in
    A. *Marbury v. Madison.*
    B. *Cohens v. Virginia.*
  * C. *Dartmouth College v. Woodward.*
    D. *Martin v. Hunter's Lessee.*

22. The decisions of the Marshall Supreme Court were generally
  * A. strongly in favor of national authority over the states.
    B. protective of the rights of state government.
    C. balanced and based on a literal and strict interpretation of the Constitution.
    D. hostile to the development of business.

23. Andrew Jackson
    A. opposed American intrusions into Florida.
  * B. was known as "Old Hickory."
    C. opposed slavery and supported the national bank.
    D. is correctly represented by all the above.

24. John Quincy Adams
  * A. promoted internal improvements, a national university, scientific explorations, and a department of the interior.
    B. was accused of collaborating with Andrew Jackson in a "corrupt bargain" in the election of 1824.
    C. had replaced Langdon Cheves as director of the second Bank of the United States.
    D. is correctly represented by all the above.

25. *All but which one* of the following were part of the Monroe Doctrine?
    A. The American continents were closed to further European colonization.
    B. Any attempt to extend the European political system in this hemisphere would be considered dangerous to U.S. peace and safety.
  * C. The United States would work for the independence of any remaining European colonies in this hemisphere.

    D. The United States would stay out of the internal affairs of European nations.

26. All the following were presidential candidates in 1824 *except*
    A. John Quincy Adams.
    * B. John C. Calhoun.
    C. Henry Clay.
    D. Andrew Jackson.

27. The presidential election of 1824
    A. was a victory for nationalism and the American system.
    * B. was lost by the candidate with the most popular and electoral votes.
    C. was decided in the Senate since no candidate received a majority of the popular vote.
    D. was one of the first to turn more on issues of substance rather than on personalities or sectional allegiance.

28. In the presidential election of 1828,
    A. John C. Calhoun won the South but lost in New England.
    B. the vote was mainly on the issue of the tariff.
    C. the vote was mainly on the issue of the national bank.
    * D. Andrew Jackson won almost all the electoral votes in the states west and south of Pennsylvania.

29. The tariff of 1828
    A. included outrageously high duties on raw materials.
    B. was intended to promote the ambitions of Jackson by killing the tariff increases.
    C. led to a reversal of positions by Webster and Calhoun.
    * D. is correctly described by all the above.

30. The Monroe Doctrine was
    A. a treaty between the United States and Britain.
    B. a joint declaration among the United States, Britain, and France.
    * C. part of Monroe's annual message to the Congress.
    D. immediately praised by most European nations.

Suggested Essay Questions

1. Contrast the expressions of nationalism and sectionalism in the period 1815–1828 and explain which force was dominant in that period.

2. In what ways might the foreign policy of this period be called nationalistic?

3. How might one account for the victory of Andrew Jackson in the election of 1828?

4. In what ways did the Supreme Court act as a force for nationalism in this period?

5. Explain the causes and consequences of the Panic of 1819.

Chapter 10

THE JACKSONIAN IMPULSE

This chapter focuses on the controversies of Jackson's presidency and the emergence of a new party system. It narrates and explains the nullification controversy, the bank war, and Indian policy. The economic issues of the Van Buren administration and the emergence of a second party system are treated. There is a final historiographical assessment of the Jacksonian period.

Chapter Outline

  I. The Jacksonian presidency
    A. Inauguration
    B. Nature of appointments
    C. Political rivalry between Van Buren and Calhoun
    D. The Peggy Eaton affair

 II. Policies of conflict with Calhoun
    A. Internal improvements
        1. Justification of Jackson's veto of the Maysville Road Bill, 1830
        2. Attitude toward other internal improvements
    B. The nullification issue
        1. Basis for South Carolina's concern about the tariff
        2. Calhoun's theory of nullification
        3. The Webster-Hayne Debate
            a. Original issue of the debate
            b. Views of Hayne and Webster
        4. Jackson's toast at the Jefferson Day Dinner
    C. The final break with Calhoun
        1. Crawford's letter relating to Calhoun's disciplining of Jackson
        2. Cabinet shake-up
        3. Van Buren's appointment to England killed by Calhoun

III. The nullification crisis
    A. South Carolina's actions of nullification

      B. Jackson's firm response
         1. Nullification Proclamation
         2. Troop reinforcements
         3. Force Bill
         4. Lowering the tariff
      C. Resolution of the crisis

IV. Jackson's Indian policy
      A. Jackson's attitude
      B. Indian Removal Act and treaties
      C. Black Hawk War
      D. Seminole War
      E. Cherokees' Trail of Tears
         1. Georgia's legal actions against the Indians
         2. Supreme Court rulings
         3. Jackson's reaction
         4. Cherokee removal

V. The bank controversy
      A. Jackson's views
      B. The bank's opponents
      C. Biddle's effort to recharter
      D. Jackson's grounds for veto
      E. The election of 1832
         1. Innovations of the Anti-Masonic party
         2. National conventions of the National Republicans and the Democrats
         3. Results of the election
      F. Jackson's removal of deposits
         1. Basis for his actions
         2. Changes in the Treasury
         3. Removals to pet banks
      G. Economic reaction to the removal
         1. Contraction of credit in Biddle's bank
         2. Speculative binge
         3. Increase in land sales
         4. State indebtedness
      H. Bursting the bubble
         1. Distribution Act
         2. Specie Circular
         3. International complications
            a. Specie from England, France, and Mexico
            b. Decrease in British investments

    VI. Van Buren and the new party system
        A. Emergence of the Whigs
            1. Sources of support
            2. Whig philosophy
        B. Democratic nominees
        C. Whig coalitions
        D. Results of the election

   VII. Van Buren's administration
        A. Van Buren characterized
        B. The Panic of 1837
            1. Causes and effects
            2. Government reaction
        C. Proposal for an independent treasury
            1. Basis for the concept
            2. Passage in 1840
        D. Other issues of the times
            1. Slavery in the District of Columbia
            2. The northern boundary

  VIII. The election of 1840
        A. Democratic nominees
        B. Whig nominees
        C. Nature of the campaign
        D. Results of the election

    IX. Assessing the Jacksonian years
        A. Mass political parties and increased voter participation
        B. Jackson a compound of contradictions

Suggestions for Lecture Topics

For a lecture on Jacksonian America, a handy source is Edward Pessen's *Jacksonian America: Society, Personality, and Politics* (rev. ed., 1978).

For a lecture on Jackson's character, see the several interpretations presented in *After the Fact*, edited by James West Davidson and Mark Hamilton Lytle (2nd ed., 1986). Also, see the two chapters on "The President Who Walked in the Shadow of Death," in John B. Moses and Wilbur Cross's *Presidential Courage* (1980).

Construct a lecture around the major issues of the Jacksonian period: nullification, the bank, Indian removal, and so forth. A good, comprehensive source is Glyndon Van Deusen's *The Jacksonian Era, 1828–1848* (1959).

Another good topic for a lecture is the formation of the second party system. See Richard P. McCormick's *The Second Party System* (1966) and Richard Hofstadter's *The Idea of a Party System* (1969). Leonard D. White's *The Jacksonians* (1954), a continuation of his two earlier studies, might also be useful here.

Multiple-Choice Questions

1. In his 1829 inaugural address Andrew Jackson announced that he favored all the following *except*
   A. retirement of the national debt.
   B. a proper regard for states' rights.
   C. rotation in office.
   * D. lowering the tariff rates.

2. The spoils system
   A. involved congressional approval for federal spending in the various congressional districts.
   B. reached its peak during Jackson's first year in office.
   * C. was a way of rewarding political supporters.
   D. was another name for "pork barrel" legislation.

3. Who was elected Jackson's vice-president in 1828?
   * A. John C. Calhoun
   B. Martin Van Buren
   C. John Randolph
   D. Henry Clay

4. Peggy Eaton
   A. was the White House hostess who arranged parties for the "common man" during Jackson's administration.
   * B. was involved in a scandal that rocked Jackson's administration.
   C. was the first female reporter for a major Washington newspaper.
   D. was the first woman appointed to the cabinet.

5. Jackson's opposition to internal improvements
   * A. was based on constitutional scruples
   B. reflected his tremendous respect for Henry Clay.
   C. reflected his concern for the size of the national debt.

    D. meant that no interstate projects received federal aid during his administration.

6. The "South Carolina Exposition and Protest" (1828)
   A. argued that southern states had the right to take drastic actions to prevent slave insurrections.
   B. condemned the appointment of women to the cabinet.
   C. was written by Senator Samuel A. Foot.
 * D. was written in response to the so-called Tariff of Abominations.

7. The theory of nullification
   A. allowed the U.S. Congress to nullify laws passed by the state legislatures.
   B. was first raised in the congressional debates over the sale of public lands.
   C. is usually associated with the name of Daniel Webster.
 * D. was argued by advocates of states' rights.

8. In the Hayne-Webster debate, Robert Y. Hayne argued that
   A. the Supreme Court's authority was "full and complete" in its jurisdiction.
 * B. the Union was created by a compact of the states.
   C. Congress had no right to pass laws.
   D. the northern and southern states had to unite against the West on issues involving public lands.

9. In the Hayne-Webster debate, Daniel Webster argued that
   A. each section of the country had to stand up and fight, if necessary, for its rights.
   B. states had the right to nullify national laws.
   C. the Union was made up of sovereign states.
 * D. final jurisdiction on all questions of constitutionality rested in the nation's Supreme Court.

10. John C. Calhoun
 * A. resigned the vice-presidency in order to defend nullification.
   B. would have been appointed minister to England except for Van Buren's negative vote.
   C. was an extreme states'-rights sectionalist during all his political career.
   D. is correctly represented by all the above.

11. The Nullification Proclamation
   A. was issued in response to the Force Bill.

    * B. was issued in response to the South Carolina Ordinance.
      C. condemned Georgia, Alabama, and Mississippi for their stands on nullification.
      D. condemned Daniel Webster's proposal as an "impractical absurdity."

12. The South Carolina Ordinance
      A. was written in response to Jackson's Nullification Proclamation.
      B. was written in response to Jackson's Force Bill.
    * C. forbade the collection of tariff duties in South Carolina.
      D. was secretly written by Martin Van Buren.

13. The Indian Removal Act of 1830
      A. allowed Indians who wished to become U.S. citizens to remain on their homeland.
      B. was vetoed by Jackson.
    * C. proposed moving Indian tribes to areas west of the Mississippi River.
      D. contained many loopholes designed to exclude peaceful Indians from the application of the act.

14. Which Indian tribe was forced westward on the route that came to be known as the Trail of Tears?
    * A. Cherokee
      B. Chickasaw
      C. Choctaw
      D. Creek

15. President Jackson's attitude toward the Supreme Court's decision in *Worcester v. Georgia* was one of
      A. elation.
      B. sadness.
      C. acquiescence.
    * D. defiance.

16. Nicholas Biddle
      A. was the leading member of Jackson's cabinet after Calhoun moved to London.
    * B. managed the Bank of the United States.
      C. opposed the Bank of the United States because it seemed to favor business and the wealthy.
      D. opposed the Bank of the United States because it allowed local and state banks to expand their issue of notes.

17. President Jackson vetoed the bill to recharter the Bank of the United States in 1832
    A. but the veto was overturned by the Senate.
    B. although most laborers and westerners supported it.
  * C. in part because he questioned the bank's constitutionality.
    D. All the above are true.

18. The Anti-Masonic Party
    A. was the first national third party.
    B. was the first party to hold a national nominating convention.
    C. nominated William Wirt for president.
  * D. is correctly represented by all the above.

19. "Pet banks" were
  * A. those state banks that received government deposits.
    B. allowed to issue notes that were not covered by specie reserves.
    C. those established by Jackson's executive order in 1829.
    D. chartered in 1832 for the express purpose of handling foreign investments.

20. As a result of Jackson's bank policies,
  * A. sales of public land rose tremendously.
    B. credit became much tighter after 1835.
    C. total state indebtedness decreased by $170 million.
    D. the national debt rose by $7 million in 1835.

21. The Specie Circular of July 1836
    A. distributed the federal surplus to the states.
    B. ordered banks to issue notes only up to the amount that could be covered by their specie reserves.
  * C. ordered that payments for public lands be made in gold or silver.
    D. was an attempt to increase private investments.

22. The one thing that united all members of the new Whig Party was
    A. opposition to the Bank of the United States.
  * B. opposition to Andrew Jackson.
    C. support for internal improvements.
    D. support for a higher protective tariff.

23. Which of the following men was *not* a Whig candidate in 1828?
    A. Daniel Webster
    B. William Henry Harrison

    C. Hugh Lawson White
* D. William T. Duane

24. All the following factors contributed to the Panic of 1837 *except*
    A. the withdrawal of European investments and loans.
    B. an economic depression in England.
* C. the tariff of 1833, which had raised duties to dangerous levels.
    D. the great increase in financial speculation during Jackson's administration.

25. Discontent during Van Buren's administration
* A. was brought on in part by a depressed economy.
    B. cost him the Democratic presidential nomination in 1840.
    C. started when the Bank of the United States went bankrupt in 1837.
    D. is correctly represented by all the above.

26. The Whigs in 1840
* A. feared splitting their party and hence had no platform.
    B. nominated Winfield Scott for president.
    C. campaigned for a program similar to Clay's American system.
    D. tried to play down their candidate's war record.

27. In the election of 1840,
    A. William Henry Harrison won by the smallest margin of anyone in nineteenth-century presidential elections.
* B. voter turnout was high.
    C. Martin Van Buren became the first president in the second party system to win reelection.
    D. both parties alienated many voters by their stands on controversial issues.

28. Osceola
    A. led the Sauk and Fox Indians against the United States during the Black Hawk War.
    B. invented the written language of the Cherokees.
* C. led the Seminole resistance in Florida.
    D. persuaded his Creek Indians to move peacefully to the West.

29. The proposal for an Independent Treasury
* A. would allow the government to stop risking its deposits in shaky banks.
    B. was vetoed by Van Buren.

   C. was supported by most Whigs.

   D. was never passed by Congress.

30. The irony of Jackson's political philosophy is that

   A. the special privileges he urged for business led to wide-scale abuse.

   B. his opposition to an Independent Treasury was based on his belief in centralizing the functions of government.

 * C. his laissez-faire rationale for republican simplicity became the justification for the unregulated growth of centralized economic power.

   D. his concern for the common man came at a time of extremely low voter participation.

Suggested Essay Questions

1. Discuss the presidential elections of 1832, 1836, and 1840, describing the candidates, major issues, voting patterns, and so forth.

2. What was Jackson's most important accomplishment as president? What was his greatest failure?

3. Why was the banking controversy so important in the 1830s? What actions did Jackson take against the bank?

4. In the Hayne-Webster debate, what were the main arguments of each man?

5. Describe the new party system that emerged in the 1830s.

Chapter 11

THE DYNAMICS OF GROWTH

This chapter traces economic and social developments from about 1800 to 1860, including developments in agriculture, transportation, technology, industrial production, corporate organization, urbanization, immigration, labor unions, land policy, and the distribution of wealth.

Chapter Outline

I. Agriculture
    A. The importance of cotton to the economy
        1. Invention of the cotton gin
        2. Revolutionary impact of the gin
            a. Impact on slavery
            b. Encouragement of westward migration
            c. Cotton became an important export
    B. The westward movement
        1. Changes in land laws
            a. Land law of 1820
            b. Preemption Act of 1830
            c. Graduation Act of 1854
        2. Development of improved iron plows

II. Improvements in transportation
    A. Opening new roads
        1. Turnpikes
        2. National Road
    B. River transportation
        1. Steamboats
        2. Flatboats
        3. Growth of canals
    C. Development of railroads
        1. Early roads
        2. Railroads surpass canals
        3. "Spark arrester" and coal
        4. Water travel compared to rail

D. Ocean transport
1. Transatlantic packet service
2. Clipper ships
E. Financing internal improvements
1. Railroads first came from private investment
2. Federal railroad assistance

III. Industrialization
A. The growth of industry
1. Persistence of the handicraft system
2. Britain's lead in industrial production
3. Impact of War of 1812 on early textile manufacturing
B. Advances in technology
1. Steam engines
2. Examples of the impact of inventions
C. Emergence of the factory system
1. Waltham plan
2. Family system

IV. Urbanization
A. Relation to commerce and industry
B. Leading cities of the antebellum period

V. Immigration
A. Continuing need for labor
B. Ebb and flow of immigration
C. Characteristics of ethnic groups
1. Irish
2. Germans
3. British
4. Scandinavians
5. Chinese
D. Nativist reaction to immigrants
1. Reasons for antagonism toward immigrants
2. Nativist organizations
a. Early associations
b. Know-Nothing party formed in 1854
E. Ethnic labor groups

VI. Labor organization
A. Early social organizations among urban artisans
B. Importance of *Commonwealth v. Hunt* decision, 1842
C. Efforts to create national trade unions
D. Urban labor politics
1. Their rise
2. Reasons for decline

          3. Factionalization of labor unions
          4. Locofocos in New York
          5. Impact of labor parties
      E. Producers' and consumers' cooperatives
      F. Continuing activities of unions

VII. Jacksonian inequality
      A. Examples of self-made men
      B. Distribution of wealth
      C. Increasing social rigidity in the age of the common man

Suggestions for Lecture Topics

George R. Taylor's *The Transportation Revolution, 1815–1860* (1951) would be a good source for lectures on several topics. The work is best known for its chapters on roads, canals, railroads, steamboats, and so forth, but the book is also a general economic history of the period, and its chapters on manufacturing, labor, the role of government in economic development, etc., are also good.

For a lecture on America's early industrialization, see Thomas C. Cochran's *Frontiers of Change* (1981).

An interesting and instructive lecture on urbanization might use Edward K. Spann's *The New Metropolis* (1981), a study of New York City in the 1840s and 1850s. Spann's book is big, but its organization will allow the reader to pick topics to emphasize.

For a lecture on the immigration of the period, two good sources are Marcus Lee Hansen's *The Atlantic Migration, 1607–1860* (1940) and the relevant chapters in Maldwyn A. Jones's *American Immigration* (1960).

Multiple-Choice Questions

1. The inventor of the cotton gin was
      A. Samuel Slater.
   * B. Eli Whitney.
      C. Phineas Miller.
      D. John Kay.

2. The widespread use of the cotton gin
    A. made millions of dollars for the inventor.
    B. made cotton easier to pick.
    C. resulted in the rapid decline of the South's slave population.
 * D. made cotton a major export commodity.

3. By 1860
 * A. more than half of the nation's population lived west of the Appalachian Mountains.
    B. cotton accounted for almost 15 percent of the nation's exports.
    C. railroad mileage had finally caught up with that of canals.
    D. iron plows had begun to replace wooden ones.

4. The Preemption Acts of 1830
    A. greatly lowered the price of unsold public lands.
 * B. allowed squatters to stake out claims ahead of the land surveys.
    C. limited the amount of cotton exported per year.
    D. set guidelines for the construction of new roads.

5. The Wilderness Road
    A. was opened in 1832.
 * B. followed the trail blazed by Daniel Boone.
    C. was in the Deep South.
    D. ran to Valdalia, Illinois.

6. Which of the following statements about steamboats is *not* true?
    A. Steamboats carried bulk commodities more cheaply than did Conestoga wagons.
    B. Robert Fulton and Robert Livingston's improvements made commercially successful steamboats possible.
 * C. Since most steamboats had at least eight-foot drafts, they were useful only on large, deep rivers.
    D. The steamboat was a major factor in the development of the Mississippi Valley.

7. The Erie Canal
    A. was completed in 1849.
    B. connected St. Louis and Lake Erie.
    C. and its branches soon put most of Ohio and Indiana within reach of water transportation.
 * D. carried the trade of the Great Lakes region east to New York City.

8 The advantages of water travel over railroads in 1860 included
* A. comfort.
 B. cost.
 C. speed.
 D. all the above.

9. Clipper ships
 A. were slower than the steamships.
 B. had more cargo space than steamships.
* C. were first built in 1845.
 D. quickly became the standard method of ocean transport and remained so until World War I.

10. Elias Howe invented
 A. the grain reaper.
 B. a process for vulcanizing rubber.
 C. the telegraph.
* D. the sewing machine.

11. Jefferson's embargo in 1807 and the War of 1812
 A. almost destroyed American manufacturing.
 B. had surprisingly little effect on the growth of textile manufacturing in America.
* C. encouraged rapid growth in American manufacturing.
 D. restricted exports and thereby hurt the growth of American manufacturing.

12. The Rhode Island system
* A. often used whole families in the mills.
 B. was also known as the Merrimack plan.
 C. emphasized nighttime production.
 D. was most common in textile manufactures outside of northern New England.

13. The Know-Nothing Party
* A. was established in 1854.
 B. was especially unsuccessful in Massachusetts.
 C. was based on prejudice against the Negro.
 D. is correctly represented by all the above.

14. The factory system, where all the manufacturing processes were brought under one roof,
 A. did not develop in America until after the Civil War.
* B. was developed in Massachusetts.

    C. was more important in the southern states.

    D. produced most of American textiles by 1820.

15. The workers at Lowell
  * A. were often young women.
    B. were often widows or older unmarried women.
    C. were usually hired in family units.
    D. were usually immigrants who could speak little English.

16. What percentage of Americans lived in urban areas in 1860?
    A. 1.5.
    B. 3.3.
  * C. 16.1.
    D. 29.8.

17. The first American city to have a population of more than a 1,000,000 was
    A. Baltimore.
    B. Boston.
  * C. New York.
    D. Philadelphia.

18. The "Locofocos" were
  * A. members of the Equal Rights Party.
    B. railroad workers who went on strike in 1844 for higher wages.
    C. special detectives hired to break up the early unions.
    D. Irish factory workers.

19. The largest group of immigrants living in America in 1860 was
    A. British.
    B. Chinese.
  * C. Irish.
    D. Scandinavian.

20. Chinese immigrants in the nineteenth century
    A. usually moved to Wisconsin and Minnesota.
    B. were usually skilled artisans.
    C. came for the most part before 1850.
  * D. often were employed for heavy construction work.

21. Most nineteenth-century Irish immigrants
  * A. came to America to escape famine.
    B. were Protestants.
    C. were skilled artisans.
    D. moved to the South.

22. The German migration to the United States
    A. included few skilled workers or independent farmers.
    B. peaked in 1831.
    C. was in most respects similar to that of the Irish.
    * D. often ended in St. Louis, San Antonio, or Milwaukee.

23. Americans were hostile toward the immigrants in large part because of differences in
    * A. religious practices.
    B. political philosophies.
    C. languages.
    D. family traditions.

24. The greatest proportionate influx of immigrants in American history came in which of the following decades?
    A. 1815–1824
    B. 1825–1834
    C. 1835–1844
    * D. 1845–1854

25. Immigrants in the middle-nineteenth century
    A. created such a surplus of labor that wages fell drastically.
    * B. made up around half the labor force in New England mills.
    C. slowed America's economic growth.
    D. usually worked for just over half the wages formerly paid to women and children.

26. In the case of *Commonwealth v. Hunt* (1842), the Massachusetts Supreme Court decided that
    A. the Graduation Act of 1854 was unconstitutional.
    B. the Graduation Act of 1854 was constitutional.
    * C. forming a trade union was not illegal.
    D. Catholics were ineligible for office.

27. The various workingmen's parties failed for all the following reasons *except* that
    A. they often splintered into factions.
    B. labor politicians were inexperienced.
    C. they were vulnerable to charges of radicalism.
    * D. the major parties refused to adopt any of their causes.

28. The shoemakers' strike at Lynn and Natick, Massachusetts,
    * A. was one of the few of this period that the workers won.
    B. was successful because it remained a local issue, affecting only those two towns.

      C. spelled the end of the New England Protective Union.
      D. is correctly represented by all the above.

29. The trade unions of the 1840s and 1850s
      A. were unusually successful in their ability to achieve higher wages and better working conditions through strikes.
      B. were mostly affiliates of the National Trades Union.
 * C. were mostly local and weak.
      D. were mainly concerned with immigration reform.

30. Recent studies have shown that social mobility
      A. was probably higher in the 1830s than at any time before or since.
 * B. was probably highest in the late-eighteenth century.
      C. decreased over time as new lands opened up.
      D. increased over time as the frontier disappeared.

Suggested Essay Questions

1. Why is "the age of the common man" or "the age of Jacksonian Democracy" an ironic name for this period?

2. Compare the growth of roads, river transportation, and railroads through 1860. What were the advantages and disadvantages of each means of transport?

3. Describe the Lowell and Rhode Island (or Fall River) system of labor. What did each offer its workers?

4. Describe the situation for labor during this period. How successful were laborers at reform?

5. Describe the general immigration trends of the period. What forms did the nativist response to this immigration take?

Chapter 12

AN AMERICAN RENAISSANCE: ROMANTICISM AND REFORM

This chapter explores intellectual currents prior to the Civil War. It reviews the important literary accomplishments of the first half of the nineteenth century, the developments in religion and education, and major reform movements including temperance, prison reform, aid to the insane, women's rights, and utopian communities. Antislavery is discussed in Chapter 14 on slavery and the Old South.

Chapter Outline

I. The impact of the Enlightenment on nineteenth-century America
    A. The concept of mission in the American character
    B. The development of deism
        1. Roots in rationalism and Calvinism
        2. Nature of the beliefs
    C. The development of Unitarianism
        1. Nature of the beliefs
        2. Role of William Ellery Channing
        3. Creation of American Unitarian Association, 1826
    D. The development of Universalism
        1. Nature of the beliefs
        2. Comparison with Unitarianism

II. The Second Great Awakening
    A. Origins of the revival movement
    B. The frontier phase of revivalism
        1. Role of the Baptists
        2. The Methodists' impact
        3. Camp meetings
    C. Revivals
        1. Role of Charles Grandison Finney
        2. Nature of Oberlin College
    D. Rise of the Mormon church
        1. Role of Joseph Smith, Jr.
        2. Characteristics of the church

       3. Persecution of Mormons
       4. The move to Utah

III. Romanticism in America
    A. Nature of the Romantic revolt
    B. Transcendentalism as a Romantic expression
       1. Nature of Transcendentalism
       2. Roots of Transcendentalism
       3. Ralph Waldo Emerson
       4. Henry David Thoreau
       5. The impact of Transcendentalism

IV. The flowering of American literature
    A. Emily Dickinson
    B. Nathaniel Hawthorne
    C. Edgar Allan Poe
    D. Herman Melville
    E. Walt Whitman
    F. The popular press
       1. Impact of advances in printing technology
       2. Sensational New York daily papers
       3. New York *Tribune* (1841)

V. Education
    A. Level of literacy
    B. Rising demand for public schools in the 1830s
    C. Role of Horace Mann
    D. Developments in higher education
       1. Post-Revolutionary surge in college formation
       2. Conflicts over offering broader levels of education
    E. Education for women

VI. Movements for reform
    A. Roots of reform
    B. Temperance
       1. Heavy consumption of alcohol in the United States
       2. Arguments for temperance
       3. Early efforts at reform
       4. Development of the American Temperance Union (1833)
    C. Prison reform
       1. Growth of public institutions to treat social ills
       2. Prevention and rehabilitation versus punishment for crime
       3. Auburn prison system (1816)

    D. Reform in treatment of the insane
        1. Early state institutions for the insane
        2. Work of Dorothea Lynde Dix
    E. Crusade for women's rights
        1. Catharine Beecher and the "cult of domesticity"
        2. Advantages of domestic role for women
        3. Status of women in the antebellum period
        4. Seneca Falls Conference (1848)
        5. Hindrances to success
        6. Evidence of success of the movement
        7. Women in education and other professions
        8. Work of Margaret Fuller
    F. Utopian communities
        1. Proliferation of utopian communities
        2. Nature of the Shaker communities
        3. Development and contributions of the Oneida Community
        4. Concept of New Harmony
        5. The importance of Brook Farm
        6. The impact of the utopian communities

Suggestions for Lecture Topics

Irving H. Bartlett's *The American Mind in the Mid-Nineteenth Century* (1967) covers many of the topics discussed in this chapter. The book would be especially useful for a lecture on the American literary renaissance.

For a lecture (or lectures) on the major reform movements, see Ronald G. Walters's *American Reformers, 1815–1860* (1978) and Alice F. Tyler's older but still valuable *Freedom's Ferment* (1944).

For a discussion of the religious movements of the period, see Part 4 of Sydney Ahlstrom's *A Religious History of the American People* (1972).

Keith Melder's *Beginnings of Sisterhood* (1977) would be a good source for a lecture on the women's movement of the first half of the nineteenth century.

Multiple-Choice Questions

    1. Which of the following attracted mainly workers and poor people?

    A. Calvinism
    B. Deism
    C. Unitarianism
* D. Universalism

2. Unitarianism stressed
   * A. reason and conscience.
    B. creeds and confessions.
    C. belief in the Holy Trinity.
    D. ritualistic practices.

3. Which of the following emphasized the image of God as "the Master Clockmaker"?
    A. Calvinism
   * B. Deism
    C. Universalism
    D. Unitarianism

4. Thomas Jefferson and Benjamin Franklin became followers of
    A. Calvinism.
   * B. Deism.
    C. Unitarianism.
    D. Universalism.

5. One of the most successful of the Methodist circuit riders was
    A. Austin Hamilton.
    B. William Ellery Channing.
    C. Charles Grandison Finney.
   * D. Peter Cartwright.

6. Brigham Young
    A. founded the Mormon faith.
    B. was shot and killed in 1844 by an anti-Mormon lynch mob in Illinois.
   * C. led the Mormons to their settlement near the Great Salt Lake in Utah.
    D. was unable to make the Mormons' settlement at Salt Lake, Utah, a success.

7. The "Burned-Over District" was
    A. the southern frontier.
    B. the coastal areas of the Carolinas.
   * C. western New York.
    D. the Appalachians.

8. Transcendentalism
   * A. stressed intuition over experience or reason.
   B. was a phenomenon that spread mainly in the American South.
   C. expressed a strong belief in science and reason.
   D. grew directly out of the Enlightenment.

9. The author of "Civil Disobedience" (1849)
   A. was Ralph Waldo Emerson.
   B. was Margaret Fuller.
   * C. emphasized the Transcendentalist theme that men must follow their consciences.
   D. argued that violent resistance to an unjust law was justified.

10. Romanticism in America
    A. was a reaction to the Transcendental excesses of the Enlightenment.
    * B. stressed individualism and emotions over conformity and reason.
    C. opposed, among other things, the Quaker doctrine of the inner light.
    D. was supported by Benjamin Franklin and Thomas Paine.

11. Nathaniel Hawthorne
    * A. used the themes of guilt and evil in many of his stories.
    B. became a writer on a bet with his wife.
    C. wrote "Rip Van Winkle" and "The Legend of Sleepy Hollow," which relied extensively on German folk tales.
    D. began the American literary renaissance with his poem "Thanatopsis."

12. Which of the following statements about Emily Dickinson is *not* true?
    A. Only two of her poems were published before her death.
    * B. She was better known as a Boston socialite.
    C. She wrote on the elemental themes of life, death, fear, and, above all else, God.
    D. She lived in Massachusetts.

13. Edgar Allan Poe wrote
    A. *Typee.*
    * B. "The Raven."
    C. *The Scarlet Letter.*
    D. "Drum Taps."

14. Who wrote *Leaves of Grass*?
    * A. Walt Whitman
      B. Emily Dickinson
      C. Henry Wadsworth Longfellow
      D. John Greenleaf Whittier

15. Which of the following statements about Herman Melville's *Moby Dick* is *not* true?
      A. On one level, it is an allegory of obsession.
      B. The setting for the book was based in part on Melville's own seafaring experiences.
    * C. The book sold well, becoming an almost instant classic.
      D. In it, Melville explored the darker recesses of the human soul.

16. Walt Whitman
      A. was a strong defender of slavery.
      B. wrote several essays attacking "the excesses of Emerson."
    * C. shocked many people with the sexual frankness of some of his works.
      D. first gained fame with the publication of his "The Tell-Tale Heart."

17. Horace Greenley
    * A. was editor of the New York *Tribune*.
      B. was editor of the New York *Herald*.
      C. promoted sensationalism in journalism.
      D. developed a rotary press capable of printing 20,000 sheets an hour.

18. The first American college to admit both blacks and women was
      A. the University of Virginia.
    * B. Oberlin.
      C. Vassar.
      D. William and Mary.

19. The literacy rate for Americans in 1840
      A. was lower than anywhere else in the western world.
      B. was high because every state had modern public school systems.
      C. was higher for blacks than for whites.
    * D. was about 80 percent.

20. The greatest dietary reformer of the age was
      A. William Cobbett.
    * B. Sylvester Graham.

     C. Emma Willard.

     D. Mary Lyon.

21. Most of the institutions of higher education founded in the 1830s
     A. were coeducational.
*   B. were church-supported.
     C. were agricultural and mechanical colleges.
     D. were in the West.

22. The American Temperance Union lost many members in 1836 when it
     A. supported Hugh L. White for president.
*   B. called for abstinence from all alcoholic beverages.
     C. allowed members to drink beer and wine.
     D. began to ask each member to put by his signature a "T" for "Total Abstinence."

23. The Auburn Penitentiary
     A. was the first to house insane prisoners with sane prisoners.
     B. was designed by Calvin H. Wiley.
*   C. stressed penitence and rehabilitation, rather than punishment.
     D. showed that lax discipline and inmate fraternization were not incompatible with rehabilitation.

24. Dorothea Lynde Dix directed her reform efforts at
*   A. asylums for the insane.
     B. institutions for the blind and deaf.
     C. prisons.
     D. almshouses.

25. The Declaration of Sentiments of the Seneca Falls Convention said that
     A. institutions for the blind and deaf should be improved.
     B. excessive drinking destroyed many families.
     C. women should be ashamed of their domestic duties.
*   D. "all men and women are created equal."

26. The woman who argued that "woman's sphere" was the home was
*   A. Catharine Beecher.
     B. Harriet Hunt.
     C. Lucretia Mott.
     D. Elizabeth Cady Stanton.

27. Elizabeth Blackwell
    A. wrote *Women in the Nineteenth Century*.
    B. rewrote the Bible removing all references to God as "He" and "Father."
    C. led a revolt at a Massachusetts jail to free women convicted of prostitution.
  * D. was an early woman doctor.

28. Margaret Fuller
  * A. edited *The Dial*.
    B. was the first female member of the American Bar Association.
    C. founded the Shakers (the United Society of Believers).
    D. wrote *The Blithedale Romance*.

29. New Harmony was a utopian community based on
    A. sexual abstinence.
    B. millennialism.
    C. health and diet.
  * D. Enlightenment rationalism and symmetry.

30. The Oneida Community
    A. was founded by Robert Owen.
    B. was founded George Ripley.
    C. was a home for writers, artists, and so forth—an early "think tank."
  * D. practiced "free love."

Suggested Essay Questions

1. Compare the major "rational religions" (Deism, Unitarianism, Universalism) of this era, characterizing the origins and adherents of each.

2. According to the text, "the romantic movement in thought, literature, and the arts" was a "great victory of heart over head." Explain this statement.

3. What were the basic doctrines of the Second Great Awakening? Why did it occur when it did?

4. Discuss the contributions of Catharine Beecher, Elizabeth Cady Stanton, Susan B. Anthony, Elizabeth Blackwell, and Margaret Fuller to women's rights.

5. Using specific examples, discuss the objectives, membership, practices, and success of the nineteenth-century utopian communities.

Chapter 13

MANIFEST DESTINY

This chapter covers the period 1841–1848, focusing on Tyler's domestic problems, the Webster-Ashburton Treaty, the settlement of the Far West, Polk's election, the acquisition of Texas and Oregon, and the Mexican War and its results.

Chapter Outline

I. Harrison's brief term

II. The Tyler years
    A. His position on issues
    B. Domestic affairs
        1. Clay's program
        2. Tyler's actions
        3. Cabinet resignations
        4. Tyler left without a party
    C. Foreign affairs
        1. Problems with Britain needing solution
        2. Compromises of the Webster-Ashburton Treaty
            a. Canada–U.S. borders settled
            b. Joint patrols of Africa

III. Westward expansion
    A. The idea of "manifest destiny"
    B. Movement to Santa Fe
    C. Move to Oregon country
        1. Joint occupation with Britain
        2. Mass migration of Americans by 1843
    D. Eyeing California
        1. Ship trading with the area
        2. Sutter's colony
        3. Frémont's mapping activities
        4. Efforts to acquire California

IV. Annexing Texas
    A. American settlements

1. Role of Stephen F. Austin
2. Mexican edict against immigration

B. Independence for Texas
1. American demands
2. Santa Anna's actions
3. Independence declared

C. War for Texas independence
1. Battle of the Alamo
2. Role of Sam Houston
3. Santa Anna's trade

D. Efforts for annexation
1. Jackson's delayed recognition
2. Secret negotiations
3. Calhoun's treaty rejected

V. The election of 1844
A. Desire to keep the Texas issue out of the campaign
B. Whig refusal to refer to Texas questions
C. Democrats nominate a dark horse—Polk
D. Clay's hedging gives votes to the Liberty Party
E. Polk's victory

VI. Polk's presidency
A. Polk's background
B. Polk's program
C. Annexation of Texas by Tyler
D. Oregon demands
1. Polk's demands
2. British hesitancy about war
3. Compromise treaty

VII. Mexican War
A. Negotiations with Mexico
B. Provocation of an attack
C. The request for war
D. Opposition to the war
1. In various parts of the country
2. In New England
E. Preparation for war
1. Troops compared
2. Comparisons of other factors
3. Selection of a commander
F. Taylor's conquest of northern Mexico
G. Annexation of California
1. Frémont's efforts

  2. Republic of California
  3. The United States claims California
 H. Taylor's battles
  1. Victory at Monterrey
  2. Polk's assumptions and suspicions
  3. Santa Anna's return to power
  4. Battle of Buena Vista
 I. Scott's move to Mexico City
  1. Amphibious attack on Vera Cruz
  2. Troop reinforcements
  3. Attack on Mexico City
 J. Treaty of Guadalupe Hidalgo
  1. Terms of the treaty
  2. Ratification
 K. The war's legacy
  1. Gains and losses
  2. Innovations
  3. Lack of legendary quality for the war

Suggestions for Lecture Topics

Frederick Merk's *Manifest Destiny and Mission in American History* (1963), especially Chapter 1, would be a good source for a lecture on "manifest destiny." Also useful are the first sections of Henry Nash Smith's *Virgin Land* (1950), which shows how the West affected the American imagination.

A good source for a lecture on the overland emigrants themselves is John D. Unruh, Jr.'s *The Plains Across* (1978).

For a lecture on the various historical interpretations of the causes of the Mexican War, see *The Mexican War*, edited by Ramon Eduardo Ruiz (1963).

James K. Polk was, in several ways, one of our most successful presidents. For a discussion of his achievements, see the chapter on Polk in *America's Eleven Greatest Presidents*, edited by Morton Borden (2nd ed., 1971).

Multiple-Choice Questions

1. William Henry Harrison
   A. was the last president elected from the Jacksonian Democratic Party.

       B. developed a close association with Henry Clay during his presidency.
  * C. was elected more on his military record than for his stand on the issues.
       D. was the first president to be assassinated.

2. John Tyler
       A. was elected by the House of Representatives to fill out Harrison's term.
       B. favored Clay's American System.
  * C. favored both a strict construction of the Constitution and states' rights.
       D. took an ambiguous stand on most domestic issues.

3. The program that Henry Clay proposed in 1841
       A. was a success, thus ensuring Clay's leadership of the Whig Party.
       B. was a failure, thus ending Clay's leadership of the Democratic Party.
       C. included a lower tariff and the establishment of an Independent Treasury.
  * D. included the establishment of a third Bank of the United States and distribution to the states of proceeds from public-land sales.

4. The "Creole" incident
       A. strained relations between the United States and France.
  * B. involved a slave mutiny on an American ship, after which the British freed the slaves.
       C. involved the seizure and destruction of an American steamboat at Niagara Falls.
       D. was solved almost singlehandedly by Henry Clay.

5. As a result of the Webster-Ashburton Treaty (1842),
       A. the United States and Britain each banned the African slave trade.
       B. the British government agreed to pay reparations for the destruction of the "Creole."
  * C. the boundary dispute in Maine was settled.
       D. the United States gave up what is now Newfoundland.

6. The most important issue for Americans in the early 1840s was
       A. the boundary dispute with England.
  * B. westward expansion.
       C. the tariff.
       D. distribution of proceeds from public-land sales.

7. John Louis O'Sullivan
   * A. coined the term "manifest destiny."
   B. was secretary of war under Tyler.
   C. was Tyler's minister to Great Britain.
   D. wrote fanciful letters under the name of "William Walker" urging churches to send missionaries to the western Indians.

8. American emigration to the Oregon country
   * A. began in earnest in the early 1840s.
   B. started as a result of rumors of gold discoveries.
   C. had been considered very dangerous between 1818 and 1843 because Spain and Russia had agreed to "joint occupation" of the area.
   D. was usually along a southern route, through Texas, New Mexico, and California.

9. When Tyler vetoed the establishment of a third Bank of the United States,
   A. Congress easily overrode his veto.
   B. Henry Clay resigned as vice-president.
   C. most people were surprised, because he had promised support of the Bank during his campaign for the presidency.
   * D. most members of his cabinet resigned.

10. One of the most famous—and certainly the most successful—of California's promoters was
    A. John A. Sutter.
    B. Stephen Kearny.
    C. Christopher "Kit" Carson.
    * D. John Charles Frémont.

11. The Mexican ban on American immigration to Texas
    * A. was ineffective.
    B. halted the flood of Americans to the area.
    C. went into effect in 1820.
    D. was necessary since Americans in Texas already numbered almost half the Mexican population there.

12. Stephen F. Austin
    A. was killed at the Battle of the Alamo.
    * B. brought many Americans to Texas in the 1820s.

    C. wrote *The Trail West,* a book he hoped would convince people to move to Oregon and California.

    D. was the first president of the Republic of Texas.

13. American settlers in Texas
    A. seldom stayed more than a year.
    B. usually converted to Catholicism.
* C. were often farmers attracted to the cheap cotton land.
    D. were not allowed to bring their slaves.

14. The Battle of the Alamo
    A. cost 188 American lives with only negligible losses for the Mexicans.
* B. inspired the rest of Texas to fanatical resistance.
    C. claimed the life of Sam Houston.
    D. is correctly represented by all the above.

15. Texas obtained its independence from Mexico
* A. in exchange for releasing General Santa Anna (although the Mexican Congress repudiated the treaty).
    B. in exchange for $5 million and an agreement to pay the debts owed American settlers.
    C. after Congress voted to declare war on Mexico.
    D. in 1844.

16. All the following contributed to the failure of the United States to annex Texas before 1845 *except*
    A. sectional divisions in the Senate.
    B. fear of war with Mexico.
    C. solid Whig opposition.
* D. the reluctance of Texans.

17. The "spot resolutions" were introduced into Congress
    A. to rally support for a war against Mexico.
* B. by Abraham Lincoln.
    C. in 1839.
    D. All the above are true.

18. James K. Polk
    A. was the Whig candidate for president in 1844 for his expansionist stance.
* B. was often called "Young Hickory."

   C. argued that annexation of Oregon was "not called for by any general expression of public opinion."
   D. won the 1844 Democratic presidential after Martin Van Buren died.

19. In the presidential election of 1844,
   A. John C. Calhoun ran against James K. Polk.
 * B. the popular vote was one of the closest in history.
   C. both parties supported expansionism in their platforms.
   D. both parties opposed expansionism in their platforms.

20. On the question of Oregon,
   A. Polk privately favored compromise with the British.
   B. England did not think the issue worth a war.
   C. the border was drawn at the Forty-ninth Parallel.
 * D. all the above are true.

21. The United States annexed Texas
 * A. by a joint resolution of Congress.
   B. on the condition that what was then the Texas Territory be divided up into five smaller states.
   C. following a lopsided (44–8) vote on the treaty in the Senate.
   D. despite Polk's opposition.

22. As president, Polk supported all the following *except*
   A. the reestablishment of the Independent Treasury.
   B. a reduction in the tariff.
 * C. the immediate abolition of slavery.
   D. the acquisition of California.

23. Henry Clay
 * A. first opposed, then slightly supported, the annexation of Texas.
   B. first supported, then slightly opposed, the annexation of Texas.
   C. opposed the annexation of Texas on constitutional grounds.
   D. supported the annexation of Texas as "the manifest destiny of the American republic."

24. Support for the Mexican War
   A. came from John Quincy Adams and many other statesmen.
 * B. was high in the Mississippi Valley.
   C. was greater the farther north one traveled.
   D. was high among Whigs.

25. At the beginning of the Mexican War,
    A. American forces were prepared, since war with Britain had been threatening for over a year.
    B. American forces numbered over 200,000.
  * C. Polk had no plan of action.
    D. Polk named Zachary Taylor as his first commander in Texas.

26. The Republic of California
    A. was never recognized by John C. Frémont.
  * B. lasted less than a month.
    C. sided with Mexico in the Mexican War.
    D. claimed its independence from Mexico before Polk's declaration of war.

27. President Polk
    A. understood the problems of fighting in the desert.
  * B. allowed General Santa Anna to regain control of the Mexican Army.
    C. fully supported General Zachary Taylor.
    D. wanted only Texas, not California, from Mexico.

28. The American capture of Mexico City was led by
    A. John C. Frémont.
    B. Zachary Taylor.
  * C. Winfield Scott.
    D. Jefferson Davis.

29. All the following statements about the Treaty of Guadalupe Hidalgo are true *except*
    A. Mexico gave up all claims to Texas.
    B. Mexico ceded California to the United States.
    C. the United States agreed to pay Mexico $15 million.
  * D. the treaty never passed the Senate.

30. Which of the following statements about the Mexican War is *not* true?
    A. It was America's first successful offensive war.
  * B. The annexations following the war rounded out the continental United States.
    C. Over 1,700 Americans died in battle and over 11,000 died of disease.
    D. The fighting lasted less than two years.

Suggested Essay Questions

1. Why was Henry Clay and not the incumbent John Tyler nominated by the Whig Party in 1844?

2. Explain the phrase "manifest destiny." What factors were most important in drawing Americans to the West?

3. In which territory—Texas, California, or Oregon—was America's claim best? In which was it worst?

4. Discuss the American movement to annex Texas between 1820 and 1845.

5. Why were many Americans opposed to the Mexican War?

Chapter 14

THE OLD SOUTH: AN AMERICAN TRAGEDY

This chapter discusses the Old South, slavery, and the development of the antislavery movement up to the early 1840s, attempting to sort myth from reality. Included are statistics on the economic development of the South plus descriptions of white society and black slavery in the South, the condition of free blacks in both the South and the North, the growth of antislavery sentiment and action, and the major defenses of slavery.

Chapter Outline

I. Myth and reality in the Old South
  A. Southern mythology
  B. The southern condition
    1. Causal effects of the environment and of human decisions and actions
    2. Factors that contribute a sense of sectional distinction
      a. The weather
      b. A biracial population
      c. Highly native population
      d. Architecture, work ethic, penchant for the military, country-gentleman ideal
      e. Preponderance of farming
  C. Myth of the cotton kingdom
    1. Actual variety of staple crops
    2. Exhaustion of the soil
  D. Causes for southern lag in economic development
    1. The South as a colonial economy
    2. Traditional claims
      a. Claims that blacks were unsuited to factory work
      b. Contention that aristocratic prestige precluded trade ventures
    3. Profitability of slaves
  E. Southern income compared with that of the nation and the world
  F. South's link to the demand for cotton

II. White society in the South
   A. The plantation defined
   B. The planter
      1. Relative ownership of slaves
      2. Style of life
   C. The middle class
      1. Largest group of whites
      2. General style of life
   D. Poor whites
      1. General characteristics
      2. Effects of infections and dietary deficiencies

III. Black society in the South
   A. Free blacks
      1. Methods of obtaining freedom
      2. Occupations for free blacks
   B. Slaves
      1. Statistics of population and value
      2. Standards of care for valuable property
      3. Domestic slave trade replaces foreign slave trade
      4. Plantation slave life
         a. Classes among plantation slaves
         b. Work schedules
         c. Punishment
      5. The nature of slavery as an institution
   C. Forging the slave community
   D. Slave religion and folklore
      1. Nature of the religion
      2. Use of religion as an instrument of white control and black refuge
      3. The uses of folklore
   E. The slave family
      1. Legal status
      2. Importance of the nuclear family
      3. Sexual exploitation of slaves

IV. Antislavery movements
   A. Establishment of the American Colonization Society (1817)
      1. Appeals to different groups of whites
      2. Acquisition of and settlement in Liberia
   B. The movement toward abolition
      1. David Walker's demand for insurrection
      2. William Lloyd Garrison's call for immediate emancipation

      C. Creation of the American Anti-Slavery Society
         1. Predecessor societies
         2. Aims of the organization
         3. Propaganda efforts
      D. The antislavery movement split
         1. Garrison and the radical wing refuse compromise
         2. Others only want to purge American society of slavery
         3. Showdown comes in 1840 over women's rights in the society
         4. Garrisonians win the right of women to participate
         5. New Yorkers break away
      E. Black antislavery advocates
         1. Conflicts over the right of blacks to participate in antislavery activities
         2. Former slaves who became public speakers
      F. The Underground Railroad
      G. Discrimination against blacks in the North

V. Reactions to antislavery agitation
      A. Suppression of abolitionist efforts in the South
      B. The "Gag Rule" in Congress
      C. Development of the Liberty Party (1840)
      D. Defenses of slavery
         1. Virginia's proposed emancipation plan
         2. Biblical arguments
         3. Inferiority of blacks
         4. Practical considerations
         5. George Fitzhugh's comparison of slavery in the South to northern wage slavery

Suggestions for Lecture Topics

Clement Eaton's *The Mind of the Old South* (rev. ed., 1967) would be a good source for a lecture on the class structure of southern white society.

For a lecture on the differences between northern and southern society, see Edward Pessen's "How Different from Each Other Were the Antebellum North and South?" (*American Historical Review* 85 [1980]: 1119–1149) and the comments by other historians (pp. 1150–1166).

A lecture on slavery could take several directions. For the rich literature on slavery, see the books listed in the bibliography for Chapter 14.

For a discussion of how to approach the subject conceptually, see Stanley M. Elkins's *Slavery* (3rd ed., 1976), Chapters 1 and 6. Many of the recent studies have used various types of first-person accounts of slavery, a good selection of which can be found in *Slave Testimony*, edited by John Blassingame (1977). Blassingame's introduction to the book is useful for showing how historians use these accounts, and this would be another good lecture on the broad topic of slavery.

Abolitionists worked against slavery for a number of reasons. For a lecture describing their motivations, consult *The Abolitionists*, edited by Richard O. Curry (1965), and *Antislavery Reconsidered*, edited by Lewis Perry and Michael Fellman (1979).

Multiple-Choice Questions

1. Southerners became conscious that they were a minority, especially around
   - A. 1790.
   - B. 1805.
   - * C. 1820.
   - D. 1840.

2. David Walker
   - A. led the movement for industrialization in the Old South.
   - B. wrote fanciful tales of plantation life in the Old South that promoted many of the myths that still exist today.
   - * C. was a black abolitionist.
   - D. edited *The Liberator*.

3. All of the following might be used to explain the South's distinctiveness *except*
   - A. its climate.
   - * B. the large number of immigrants who came to the South after 1760.
   - C. its biracial population.
   - D. its country-gentlemen ideal.

4. Among the long-term costs of slavery was
   - A. few immigrants.
   - B. few cities.
   - C. more isolation.
   - * D. all the above.

5. In an economic comparison, the South would
   * A. lose to the North.
   B. come out ahead of the North.
   C. lose to most developed nations of the world.
   D. come out ahead only of undeveloped countries.

6. Agricultural diversity in the Old South
   A. was practically nonexistent.
   B. could be found only in the states of the Deep South.
   * C. allowed southerners to feed themselves largely from their own fields.
   D. consisted only of cotton, white potatoes, and wheat.

7. The resolve of whites to maintain white supremacy in the South
   A. led most southerners to try to abolish slavery before 1830.
   * B. muted class conflicts among whites.
   C. stripped slaves of all traces of their Afro-American culture.
   D. led to great divisions among whites.

8. Corn as a crop in the South
   * A. was used mainly for immediate consumption.
   B. went into market.
   C. was found almost exclusively in the upper southern states.
   D. was found almost exclusively in the Deep South.

9. The South's great staple crops
   A. included rice and indigo.
   B. did poorly in the market during the late 1850s.
   * C. tended to exhaust the soil rapidly.
   D. are correctly represented by all the above.

10. Manufacturing in the Old South lagged behind that in the North because
   A. black labor was incompatible with industry.
   B. white leaders in the South were more concerned with prestige than with profits.
   C. the South lacked important natural resources.
   * D. cotton was a more profitable investment.

11. The planter class in the Old South
   A. actually owned only 10 percent of the South's slaves.
   * B. saw its interests as the interests of the entire South.
   C. usually lived lives of splendor and leisure.
   D. numbered under 5,000 in 1860.

12. The South's "poor whites"
    A. were for the most part the descendants of indentured servants or convicts.
    B. were generally the result of genetically dangerous inbreeding.
  * C. provided one of the most prevalent images in Old South mythology.
    D. came into being only after the Civil War.

13. The most numerous white southerners were
    A. the planters.
  * B. the middle-class yeoman farmers.
    C. the "poor whites."
    D. the manufacturers.

14. "Free persons of color"
    A. were not allowed to own slaves.
    B. were usually very wealthy.
    C. lived, for the most part, in the Deep South.
  * D. were often mulattoes.

15. The end of the foreign slave trade
    A. made slaves more valuable.
    B. gave rise to a flourishing domestic trade.
    C. had the unexpected effect of tempering some of slavery's harsher features.
  * D. is correctly represented by all the above.

16. In 1860 about half the slaves
  * A. worked as field hands on plantations.
    B. had run away at least twice.
    C. were severely beaten at least once a week.
    D. had been born in Africa.

17. Nat Turner's slave insurrection
    A. resulted in the death of eight whites in Charleston, South Carolina.
    B. was betrayed by Denmark Vesey.
  * C. was the largest in this country.
    D. never passed the planning stage.

18. The South's "lazy diseases"
  * A. were often caused by dietary deficiencies.
    B. were often caused by infection-carrying rats.
    C. were eliminated by the time of the Civil War.
    D. were usually fatal.

19. Slave religion
    A. was often used by whites to teach humility and obedience.
    B. was often used by blacks to release their emotions and soothe their troubles with the promise of a better life to come.
    C. was a mixture of African and Christian elements.
 * D. is correctly represented by all the above.

20. Slave culture
    A. did not include a strong belief in magic.
    B. existed only where the owners allowed it.
    C. was largely based on the culture of the white South.
 * D. found its most important manifestation in the slaves' religion.

21. All the following statements about William Lloyd Garrison are true *except*
 * A. he was the editor of *The Emancipator*.
    B. slaveholders wrongly accused him of stirring up the unrest that led to Nat Turner's insurrection.
    C. he pushed for immediate emancipation.
    D. he was a pacifist, opposed to the use of physical violence.

22. The slave family
    A. was usually headed by the mother.
    B. was seldom allowed to stay together for more than a year or two at a time.
 * C. often gave slave children some independence from white influence.
    D. is correctly represented by all the above.

23. The American Colonization Society
    A. was organized to colonize freed slaves in South America.
 * B. helped about 12,000 blacks migrate to Africa.
    C. had the support of most black leaders.
    D. was opposed by Henry Clay, John Marshall, Daniel Webster, and James Madison.

24. The American Anti-Slavery Society
    A. was opposed by David Walker because it advocated the violent overthrow of slavery.
 * B. was founded by Arthur and Lewis Tappan.
    C. split in 1840 over the issue of colonization.
    D. is correctly represented by all the above.

25. The Grimké sisters
    A. were freed slaves who became effective speakers for the American Anti-Slavery Society.
    B. argued in several popular books that slavery was beneficial to both races.
  * C. worked for women's rights as well as racial justice.
    D. were antislavery propagandists who hid their gender by using male pseudonyms.

26. Most white abolitionists
    A. favored violent action to free the slaves.
    B. favored greater black involvement in the antislavery movement.
    C. opposed William Lloyd Garrison's advocacy of physical violence.
  * D. favored the formation of separate black antislavery organizations.

27. All the following were reactions to the antislavery campaign *except*
    A. the murder of antislavery editor Elijah P. Lovejoy in Illinois.
  * B. a federal law against delivering abolitionist propaganda through the mails.
    C. a "gag rule" automatically tabling abolitionist petitions presented to the Congress.
    D. a shift in intellectual defenses of slavery, from excusing it as a necessary evil to justifying it as a positive good.

28. The presidential candidate of the Liberty Party in 1840 and 1844 was
    A. Frederick Douglass.
  * B. James G. Birney.
    C. Charles Osborn.
    D. Benjamin Lundy.

29. In the early 1830s a plan of gradual emancipation and colonization was debated and narrowly defeated in the state legislature of
    A. North Carolina.
    B. Georgia.
  * C. Virginia.
    D. Tennessee.

30. George Fitzhugh argued that
    A. slavery was justified in the Bible.
  * B. southern slavery was better for workers than the "wage slavery" of northern industry.
    C. blacks were the product of a separate creation.
    D. blacks and whites could not live together without risk of race war, except for slavery.

Suggested Essay Questions

1. How important was slavery to the economy of the Old South? Discuss its effects on agriculture, industry, and any other relevant aspects of the southern economy.

2. What roles did religion and family life play in the lives of slaves in the South?

3. Evaluate the goals, methods, and leadership of the abolitionist movement. Which of the methods were most effective? Why?

4. How did the Old South's obsessive defense of slavery affect its intellectual life?

5. George Fitzhugh argued that slaves in the South were better off than workers in the North, who he said were subject to "wage slavery." Do you agree or disagree? Explain.

Chapter 15

THE CRISIS OF UNION

This chapter covers political developments from the election of 1848 through the secession of the lower South and the period prior to Lincoln's inauguration. It includes the controversy over the expansion of slavery in western lands, the development of the Compromise of 1850, assertions of manifest destiny on the world scene, the controversy over Kansas, the Lincoln-Douglas debates, the election of 1860, the secession of the lower South, and the events prior to Lincoln's inauguration.

Chapter Outline

I. Quarrels arising from the conquest of Mexican territory in the Southwest
   A. The Wilmot Proviso
   B. Calhoun's resolutions in reaction to the Proviso
   C. Other proposals to deal with slavery in the territories
      1. Extension of the Missouri Compromise line
      2. Popular, or squatter, sovereignty
   D. Controversy over admission of Oregon as a free state

II. Presidential election of 1848
   A. Democrats nominate Lewis Cass (and deny power of Congress to interfere with slavery)
   B. Whigs choose Zachary Taylor (and adopt no platform at all)
   C. Development of the Free Soil Party from the rebellious Democrats, conscience Whigs, and the abolitionist Liberty Party—to nominate Van Buren
   D. Election goes to Taylor

III. The push for California statehood
   A. California gold rush
   B. Zachary Taylor as president
   C. Taylor calls for admission of California as a free state

IV. The development of the Compromise of 1850
   A. Clay's compromise package of eight resolutions

B. Calhoun's response
C. Webster's plea for union
D. Seward's response for the abolitionists
E. The Committee of Thirteen proposes an "Omnibus Bill"
F. Taylor's death
G. Fillmore supports the Clay compromise
H. The Douglas strategy of six (later five) separate bills
I. Terms of the Compromise

V. Reaction to the Compromise
A. The Fugitive Slave Law
1. Terms of the law
2. Northern reaction to the law
B. The effect of *Uncle Tom's Cabin*

VI. The election of 1852
A. The Democrats turn to Franklin Pierce
B. Whigs turn to Winfield Scott and his martial glory
C. Pierce the victor

VII. "Manifest destiny" on the world scene
A. Efforts to expand southward
1. Early efforts to capture Cuba
2. The Ostend Manifesto
B. Achievements of American diplomacy in the Pacific
1. Opening of China to Americans
2. Perry's expedition to Japan
C. The Gadsden Purchase

VIII. The Kansas-Nebraska Crisis
A. Ideas for a transcontinental railroad
B. Douglas's Nebraska bill leads to repeal of the Missouri Compromise
C. Northern reactions to the extension of slavery
D. Strains on the political parties
E. The "battle" for Kansas
1. Efforts to promote settlement of Kansas by Free Soilers and proslavery forces
2. The official proslavery government
3. The countergovernment in Topeka
4. Violence in Lawrence and Pottawatomie
F. The Sumner-Butler-Brooks clash in Congress

IX. The election of 1856
A. The American and Whig parties nominate Fillmore

    B. The Republicans choose John Frémont as their first presidential candidate

    C. The Democrats nominate James Buchanan

    D. The campaign and Buchanan's election

    E. Nature of the Buchanan presidency

X. The Dred Scott decision

    A. Nature of the case

    B. Analysis of the court's decision

XI. Movements for Kansas statehood

    A. The Lecompton Constitution

    B. Buchanan's support for Lecompton

    C. Defeat of the proposal

    D. Postponement of Kansas statehood

XII. Financial panic of 1857

    A. Causes and nature of the economic reversal

    B. Sectional reactions to the economic problems

XIII. The Lincoln-Douglas senatorial contest in Illinois

    A. The candidates and their situation

    B. The Freeport Doctrine

    C. Douglas's efforts to bait Lincoln

    D. Results of the election

XIV. Further sectional problems at the end of the decade

    A. John Brown's raid at Harpers Ferry

    C. The effects of Brown's raid and martyrdom

XV. The election of 1860

    A. The Democratic convention eventually nominates Douglas

    B. The "Rump Democrats" nominate Breckenridge

    C. The Republican convention nominates Lincoln and adopts a platform

    D. The Constitutional Union Party formed to support Bell and the preservation of the Union

    E. Nature of the campaign

    F. Outcome of the election

XVI. Secession begins

    A. Secession of states of the Deep South

    B. Buchanan's reactions to secession

    C. Problems of federal property in the seceded South

    D. Last efforts to compromise

Suggestions for Lecture Topics

For a discussion of the various crises that divided the Union in the 1850s, see David M. Potter's *The Impending Crisis, 1848–1861* (1976).

For a lecture on the various causes of the Civil War, see *The Causes of the American Civil War*, edited by Edwin C. Rozwenc (2nd ed., 1972). David Donald's "An Excess of Democracy," in his *Lincoln Reconsidered* (2nd ed., 1961), offers another interesting interpretation.

Multiple-Choice Questions

1. The Wilmot Proviso sought to
    A. assure protection of slavery in Texas.
    * B. forbid slavery in any of the lands acquired through the Mexican War.
    C. keep slavery out of all territories of the United States.
    D. apply the principle of popular sovereignty to all future territories of the United States.

2. The irony in John C. Calhoun's argument concerning slavery in the territories was that
    A. the Missouri Compromise, which he had earlier opposed, offered the only legitimate solution.
    * B. he used the Bill of Rights as a guarantee for slavery.
    C. he was personally opposed to slavery.
    D. his father, according to family tradition, was black.

3. Which of the following would have been least likely to join the Free Soil Party?
    * A. "Cotton" Whigs
    B. rebellious Democrats
    C. members of the Liberty Party
    D. white farmers in the territories who wanted blacks kept in the South

4. In 1848, the Free Soil Party
    A. gained most of the Whig votes in the South.
    B. forced the Democrats and Whigs to take a definite stand on the issue of slavery.
    * C. split the Democratic vote in New York State.
    D. won electoral votes only in Ohio and Illinois.

5. President Zachary Taylor wanted to admit California as a state immediately because

A. he was antislavery, and California had voted on a free-state constitution.

B. he was pro-slavery, and California had voted on a slave-state constitution.

* C. he wished to by-pass the divisive issue of slavery in the territories.

D. he was afraid Mexico would make new claims on the area since gold had been discovered there.

6. During the debates over the Compromise of 1850, one senator made a conciliatory speech in which he said, "I speak today for the preservation of the Union." That senator was
   A. Henry Clay.
   B. Henry S. Foote.
   C. William H. Seward.
   * D. Daniel Webster.

7. Which of the following was *not* true of popular sovereignty?
   * A. It was first proposed by President Taylor.
   B. It would apparently allow slaveholders to enter any new territory.
   C. It could be used as a compromise between the extreme positions of David Wilmot and John C. Calhoun.
   D. It seemed likely to lead to free-state status for most unorganized western territory in the 1850s.

8. Stephen A. Douglas was more successful than Clay in getting the Compromise of 1850 passed because
   A. he dropped the question of slave trade in the District of Columbia.
   B. he could depend on a sympathy vote from supporters of the deceased President Taylor.
   C. as a result of his support for popular sovereignty, he could gain votes from abolitionist senators.
   * D. he split the issues into five separate bills.

9. Which of the following was *not* one of the terms of the Compromise of 1850?
   A. California was admitted as a free state.
   B. Utah and New Mexico were organized as territories with no reference to slavery in either area.
   * C. Oregon was admitted as a state with the issue of slavery to be decided by popular sovereignty.
   D. The slave trade was prohibited in the District of Columbia.

10. Which one of the following statements was *not* true of the Fugitive Slave Law of 1850?
    - A. It denied a jury trial for alleged fugitives.
    - B. By providing a fee of $10 for each fugitive returned, it was an incentive to capture free Negroes.
    - C. It was often ignored or openly opposed in the North.
    - * D. It brought about the recapture of some 2,500 escaped slaves.

11. Zachary Taylor's death
    - A. lessened the chances for compromise in 1850.
    - B. put proslavery Franklin Pierce in the White House.
    - * C. perhaps saved the nation from civil war in 1850.
    - D. was caused by a heart attack he suffered on the Senate floor.

12. Harriet Beecher Stowe's novel *Uncle Tom's Cabin*
    - * A. was perhaps the most effective piece of antislavery propaganda.
    - B. alerted northerners to the plight of the slave, although the book was a commercial failure.
    - C. was called by Representative Preston S. Brooks "the greatest book of the age."
    - D. is correctly identified by all the above.

13. In the presidential election of 1852
    - * A. Democrats managed to unite the factions within their party.
    - B. the Whigs refused to endorse the Compromise of 1850.
    - C. the Whigs nominated Millard Fillmore for a full term.
    - D. the Free Soil Party won almost a million popular votes.

14. The New England Emigrant Aid Society was formed
    - * A. to send free-soil settlers to Kansas.
    - B. to send settlers to Cuba.
    - C. to send blacks out of the country.
    - D. by Edmund Ruffin.

15. The Ostend Manifesto was
    - A. a treaty among the United States, Britain, and France agreeing to use their joint force to gain independence for Cuba.
    - B. an ultimatum from the United States demanding that Spain give up possession of Cuba.

     * C. a diplomatic dispatch, leaked to the press, suggesting
          that the United States should consider using force to take
          Cuba.
       D. an insult to the United States by Spain which became the
          basis for raids to take over Cuba.

16. Stephen Douglas's proposed compromises in the Kansas-
Nebraska crisis
       A. greatly increased his presidential chances.
    * B. included repealing part of the Missouri Compromise.
       C. inflamed proslavery sentiment against him.
       D. were firmly rejected by Democrats in Congress.

17. The Whig Party was effectively destroyed by strains coming
from
       A. the defeat of Winfield Scott in 1852.
    * B. the passage of the Kansas-Nebraska Act.
       C. the development of the Know-Nothing Party.
       D. John Brown's raid at Harpers Ferry.

18. Passage of the Kansas-Nebraska Act was a victory for
       A. the abolitionists.
    * B. the concept of popular sovereignty.
       C. the immigrant groups in America.
       D. southerners who wanted a transcontinental railroad to run
          west from New Orleans.

19. In the election of 1860, the candidate of the Constitutional
Liberty Party was
       A. Stephen A. Douglas.
       B. John C. Breckinridge.
    * C. John Bell.
       D. Alexander H. Stephens.

20. Charles Sumner was beaten as he sat at his desk in the Senate
       A. because of a slanderous proslavery speech he made.
       B. and sustained injuries that forced him to resign.
    * C. by the nephew of a South Carolina senator he had criti-
          cized.
       D. following debate on the Wilmot Proviso.

21. In the election of 1856
       A. the Republicans nominated Buchanan because of the
          popular stands he had taken on national issues.
       B. only Democrats and Whigs nominated candidates.

* C. only Buchanan appealed to voters in all sections of the country.

   D. the Democratic Party platform called for acceptance of slavery in all parts of the country.

22. In its ruling in *Dred Scott v. Sandford* the United States Supreme Court stated *all but which one* of the following?

* A. Negroes who lived in free states as opposed to free territories could be considered free.

   B. Negroes did not have federal citizenship and therefore could not bring suit in federal courts.

   C. The Missouri Compromise was unconstitutional.

   D. Negroes were so far inferior to whites that they had no rights that a white man was forced to respect.

23. President Buchanan

   A. supported the Lecompton Constitution because he opposed the spread of slavery.

   B. opposed the Lecompton Constitution because he favored the spread of slavery.

   C. opposed the Lecompton Constitution because he was politically dependent on northern congressmen.

* D. supported the Lecompton Constitution because he was dependent on southern congressmen.

24. The Lecompton Constitution

* A. was overwhelmingly rejected by Kansas voters.

   B. was overwhelmingly accepted by Kansas voters.

   C. was unconditionally accepted by the U.S. Congress.

   D. was unconditionally rejected by the U.S. Congress.

25. One important effect of the financial panic of 1857 was that

   A. a new national banking system was adopted the next year to prevent a recurrence of the event.

* B. the South was convinced of the superiority of its economic system.

   C. northern manufacturers were less hurt by the economic reverse than was the agricultural South.

   D. an agreement was made to increase the tariff in 1858 to prevent a further economic decline.

26. Douglas's Freeport Doctrine might be defined as the concept that

   A. slavery could not be prohibited in a territory until that territory became a state.

   B. slavery was immoral and ought to be abolished in all territories of the United States.

* C. even if slavery were permitted in a territory, the people
     could effectively end it by refusing to pass laws to sustain
     it.
  D. if blacks were freed from slavery, they must be given full
     legal and social equality.

27. John Brown's raid at Harpers Ferry resulted in *all but which one
    of the following?*
    A. his execution for treason and inciting insurrection
    B. panic in the slaveholding South
    C. a tendency for southerners to believe that persons who
       wanted to contain slavery were supporters of conspiracy
       and insurrection among the slaves
  * D. some important mending of differences between North and
       South as each section saw the consequences of extremist
       actions

28. At the 1860 Democratic convention in Charleston, South
    Carolina,
    A. northern delegates walked out when a proslavery plank
       was passed.
  * B. southern delegates walked out when a proslavery plank
       was defeated.
    C. delegates nominated Lewis Cass for the presidency.
    D. delegates nominated James Buchanan for reelection to the
       presidency.

29. Buchanan's response to the secession of the southern states was
    A. finally to abandon efforts to compromise.
  * B. to send reinforcements and provisions to Fort Sumter in
       January 1861.
    C. to refuse to take any actions in regard to secession until
       Lincoln took office.
    D. to send diplomatic envoys to the Confederacy to negotiate
       the status of federal forts and other property in the se-
       ceding states.

30. The Crittenden Compromise proposed to
    A. outlaw slavery in the United States after 1865.
  * B. guarantee continuance of slavery in the states where it
       then existed.
    C. guarantee that all new territories would be open to
       slavery.
    D. give slaves full representation rather than allow them to
       count for only three-fifths of a person.

Suggested Essay Questions

1. Explain the issues that led to the Compromise of 1850 and show how the Compromise was fashioned and passed.

2. "The Mexican War may accurately be blamed for causing the Civil War because it opened new wounds between the North and South as it spurred controversy over slavery in the territories acquired from Mexico." Do you agree or disagree? Explain.

3. What various solutions were proposed to deal with the problem of slavery in the territories?

4. At what point (if any) did the war become inevitable? If you could change historical events, what would you do at that point to avoid war?

5. What caused the Civil War? (Your answer should *not* be simply a detailed chronology of events.)

Chapter 16

THE WAR OF THE UNION

This chapter traces the course of the war from Fort Sumter to Appomattox. It covers problems of raising armies, diplomacy, emancipation, financing the war, and political maneuvering in wartime.

Chapter Outline

I. The end of the interim period
   A. Lincoln's inauguration
   B. The conflict begins
   C. Lincoln's initial steps of war
   D. Secession of the upper South
      1. Departure of Virginia, Arkansas, Tennessee, and North Carolina
      2. Creation of West Virginia
   E. Other slave states remain in the Union
      1. Suspension of *habeas corpus* to hold Maryland
      2. Divided Kentucky
      3. The battle for Missouri
   F. Lee's decision to join the Confederacy
   G. First Battle of Bull Run
      1. Basis for confrontation
      2. Military retreat
      3. Impact of battle

II. A modern war
   A. Statistics of war
   B. Nature of the war
   C. Women and the war
   D. The draft
      1. Confederate states
         a. Adoption of conscription
         b. Exemptions
      2. Union states
         a. Terms of conscription
         b. New York City draft riots

III. The war's early course
    A. Strategy
        1. Union
        2. Confederate
    B. Naval action
        1. Ironclad ships
        2. Union seizures along the southern coasts
    C. Actions in the West
        1. General Johnston in western Kentucky
        2. Battle of Shiloh
    D. McClellan's peninsular campaign
        1. McClellan's character
        2. Advance on Richmond
        3. Lee's attack on McClellan
        4. Appointment of Halleck as general-in-chief
    E. Second Battle of Bull Run
    F. Lee's invasion at Antietam
        1. McClellan's mistakes
        2. Lincoln's appointment of Ambrose Burnside
    G. Battle of Fredericksburg
    H. Assessment of war at end of 1862

IV. Emancipation
    A. Lincoln's considerations
    B. The Emancipation Proclamation
    C. Effects of emancipation
    D. Blacks in the military
    E. The abolition of slavery

V. Government during the war
    A. The revolutionary impact of the war
        1. Power shift to the North
        2. Measures passed by the North
    B. Union finances
        1. Increased tariff and excise taxes
        2. Income tax
        3. Issuance of greenbacks
        4. Borrowing
    C. Confederate finances
        1. Tariffs
        2. Direct tax on property
        3. Paper money
    D. Confederate diplomacy
        1. Importance

      2. Emissaries to France and England

      3. Early hopes of recognition

  E. Union politics

      1. Pressure of the Radicals

      2. Actions of the Democrats

      3. Lincoln's suspension of habeas corpus

      4. Democratic campaign of 1864

      5. Election results

  F. Confederate politics

      1. Status of politics in the Confederate system

      2. Problems of states' rights in the Confederacy

VI. Wearing down the Confederacy

  A. Appointment of Joseph E. Hooker to lead the North

  B. Battle of Chancellorsville

  C. Grant's assault on Vicksburg

  D. Lee's invasion at Gettysburg

  E. Union victory at Chattanooga

VII. Defeat of the Confederacy

  A. Grant and Sherman to pursue the war

  B. The wilderness campaign

      1. Grant's strategy

      2. Siege of Petersburg

  C. Sherman's march through the South

      1. Sherman's pursuit of Johnston

      2. Davis replaced Johnston with John B. Hood

      3. Armies move in opposite directions

      4. Sherman's destruction of Georgia

      5. Sherman moves into South Carolina

  D. Lee's effort to escape the Petersburg siege

  E. Surrender at Appomattox

  F. Interpretations of northern victory

  G. Bittersweet victory

Suggestions for Lecture Topics

For this chapter, one of the most useful single books for instructors is Emory M. Thomas's *The American War and Peace, 1860–1877* (1973). Thomas covers, in a more detailed fashion, all the major topics in this chapter.

For a discussion of the life of the common soldiers, see Bell Wiley's *The Life of Johnny Reb* (1943) and *The Life of Billy Yank* (1943).

John Hope Franklin's *The Emancipation Proclamation* (1963) is a good source for a lecture on that topic.

A good way to discuss many of the themes in this chapter is to incorporate them into a lecture on why the North won the war. The best source for such a lecture is *Why the North Won the Civil War*, edited by David Donald (1960). This book discusses five bases for the Union's victory: economic, military, diplomatic, social, and political.

Multiple-Choice Questions

1. In his inaugural address Abraham Lincoln emphasized
    A. the moral wrongness of slavery.
  * B. the "perpetual" nature of the Union.
    C. the loyalty of southerners as demonstrated in the War of 1812.
    D. economic development.

2. The Civil War began when
    A. Union forces at Fort Sumter fired on nearby Confederate positions.
    B. Confederate forces at Fort Sumter fired on nearby Union positions.
    C. Union forces fired on Confederate troops stationed in Fort Sumter.
  * D. Confederate forces fired on Union troops stationed in Fort Sumter.

3. All the following slave states remained in the Union *except*
    A. Missouri.
  * B. Virginia.
    C. Maryland.
    D. Kentucky.

4. In order to keep border states in the Union, Lincoln
    A. canceled elections in those states.
  * B. suspended the writ of habeas corpus.
    C. threatened to "blockade" those states.
    D. did all the above.

5. In the Civil War
    A. over 600,000 men were killed or died of disease.
    B. 50,000 men lost an arm or a leg.
    C. one out of every twelve adult males fought.
  * D. all the above are true.

6. The Anaconda plan
   A. was Gen. P. G. T. Beauregard's strategy for southern victory.
   * B. was Gen. Winfield Scott's strategy for northern victory.
   C. assumed a quick end to the war.
   D. was based on Napoleonic strategy.

7. The first real battle of the war
   * A. was fought near Washington, D.C.
   B. was the Battle of Harpers Ferry.
   C. was a victory for the Union forces.
   D. resulted in tremendous losses for both sides.

8. Which of the following statements about conscription during the Civil War is *not* true?
   A. Only 6 percent of the Union Army was drafted.
   B. In the South, planters with 20 or more slaves were exempted.
   * C. The Union was the first side to use the draft.
   D. Those drafted could find a substitute or pay a fee rather than join the army.

9. Navy actions
   * A. were probably more important than land battles in late 1861 and early 1862.
   B. included a fight between two ironclads, the Confederate *Monitor* and the Union *Merrimack*.
   C. included a fight between two ironclads, the Confederate *Merrimack* and the Union *Virginia*.
   D. were not important in the war until 1863.

10. General Grant's Union victories at Forts Henry and Donelson
    A. captured the South's only north-south railroad.
    * B. forced the Confederates to give up their foothold in Kentucky.
    C. turned into defeats when the Confederates regrouped and forced the Union troops into Indiana.
    D. used infantry exclusively.

11. The Battle of Shiloh
    * A. was at that time the costliest battle in terms of casualties in which Americans had ever fought.
    B. appeared at first to be a Union victory until southern reinforcements arrived.

    C. led to the appointment of Robert E. Lee as General Albert Sidney Johnston's replacement.

    D. allowed the Confederates to regain control of the Tennessee River.

12. General George B. McClellan replaced General Irvin McDowell

    * A. immediately after the Battle of Bull Run.

    B. when McDowell was wounded at Shiloh.

    C. after McDowell was unable to quell the disturbances of the New York City draft riots.

    D. because McDowell moved too slowly.

13. At the Battle of Antietam,

    A. Union forces won an overwhelming victory, thus allowing Lincoln to issue the Emancipation Proclamation.

    B. Union General George McClellan showed rare courage in moving his troops, thereby justifying Lincoln's faith in him.

    * C. a Union soldier recovered important communications from Confederate headquarters.

    D. all the above are correct.

14. Lincoln justified his Emancipation Proclamation on the basis of

    * A. military necessity.

    B. religion.

    C. racial superiority.

    D. congressional power.

15. Robert Smalls

    A. warned Lincoln not to issue the Emancipation Proclamation until after a Union military victory.

    B. was a Union general who freed slaves in South Carolina, Georgia, and Florida, but Lincoln revoked his actions.

    C. was a New York congressman who helped Lincoln write the Emancipation Proclamation.

    * D. was a slave who escaped with his family on a Confederate gunboat.

16. The number of blacks in the Union Army

    A. was small, because a federal law prohibited free Negroes from carrying firearms.

    B. was reduced after Lincoln's Emancipation Proclamation.

    * C. was roughly 200,000, about 10 percent of the Union Army's total manpower.

    D. fell after 1862.

17. With the absence of southern congressmen during the war, Republicans passed all the following *except*
    * A. an act granting citizenship to all blacks.
    B. an act providing for a transcontinental railroad.
    C. the National Banking Act.
    D. the Morrill Land Grant Act.

18. Who commanded the southern troops at Antietam?
    A. Jeb Stuart
    B. James Longstreet
    * C. Robert E. Lee
    D. D. H. Hill

19. Confederate finances
    A. were in better shape than the Union's at the beginning of the war.
    B. were hurt during the war by a marked deflation of the currency.
    C. depended mostly on various income and property taxes.
    * D. depended mostly on new issues of paper money.

20. Jay Cooke
    A. was the Confederate treasury secretary.
    B. was the Confederate secretary of state.
    * C. promoted the sale of bonds for the Union.
    D. sponsored the Contract Labor Act, which aided the importation of immigrant labor.

21. The concept of states' rights
    A. led many southerners to secession in 1860 and 1861.
    B. led many southerners, once in the Confederacy, to challenge the suspension of habeas corpus.
    C. led many southerners, once in the Confederacy, to challenge the legality of conscription and taxes.
    * D. is correctly represented by all the above.

22. Which of the following statements best describes the Civil War at the end of 1862?
    A. Confederates had a definite, though temporary, edge in the East.
    B. Union troops in the West had retreated from their previous gains.
    * C. The war in the East was a virtual deadlock.
    D. After the decisive victories at Antietam and Fredericksburg, Union officers anticipated a quick end to the war.

23. The "Copperheads" were
    A. pro-Confederate Frenchmen who urged their country to support the Confederacy.
    B. Radical Republicans who pushed for a more vigorous prosecution of the war.
  * C. members of the extreme fringe of the peace wing of the Democratic Party.
    D. blacks who served in the Confederate Army.

24. How many southern states seceded?
    A. nine
    B. ten
  * C. eleven
    D. twelve

25. In the election of 1864
    A. Andrew Johnson was the presidential candidate of the Democratic Party.
  * B. Democrats called for an armistice.
    C. Lincoln had the full support of the Republican Party in his campaign for reelection.
    D. Democrats regained control of Congress.

26. In the Confederate election year of 1863,
    A. President Jefferson Davis was almost unanimously re-elected.
    B. President Jefferson Davis was reelected by a small margin.
  * C. many men who opposed Jefferson Davis and secession were elected to the Confederate congress.
    D. Robert E. Lee decided at the last minute not to run against Jefferson Davis.

27. All the following were Union generals *except*
    A. Ambrose E. Burnside.
    B. Joseph E. Hooker.
  * C. Joseph E. Johnston.
    D. George C. Meade.

28. Pickett's Charge, one of the greatest of the Confederacy's military failures, occurred in the Battle of
  * A. Gettysburg.
    B. Chattanooga.
    C. Chancellorsville.
    D. Cold Harbor.

29. Sherman's march through Georgia and the Carolinas
    A. was hampered by the dogged persistence of General Robert E. Lee.
    B. was planned to divert attention from General McClellan's movements to the north.
    C. proved to be the Union's biggest strategic error.
  * D. resulted in the destruction of many southern towns and cities.

30. At Appomattox
    A. Jefferson Davis surrendered.
    B. all the remaining Confederate forces surrendered.
    C. Robert E. Lee, after the bloodiest battle of the war, was captured.
  * D. General Grant allowed the southern soldiers to keep their private horses and sidearms.

Suggested Essay Questions

1. What was the military strategy of each side at the start of the Civil War, and how and why did it change as the war continued?

2. Discuss the aims and success of Confederate diplomacy during the war.

3. Account for the issuance of the Emancipation Proclamation, showing how it was both shrewd military and diplomatic strategy and an effort for humanitarian reform.

4. Describe domestic politics during the war, both North and South. What problems did Abraham Lincoln and Jefferson Davis face? How did they deal with these problems?

5. List and describe briefly the reasons why the North won the Civil War—that is, what were the North's strengths and advantages? Why did the South lose the war? What were her weaknesses and disadvantages?

Chapter 17

RECONSTRUCTION: NORTH AND SOUTH

This chapter covers the effects of the Civil War, Reconstruction under Lincoln, Johnson, and Congress, the impeachment of Johnson, the South during Reconstruction, Grant's administration, and the disputed election of 1876.

Chapter Outline

I. The battle over Reconstruction
   A. The question of Reconstruction
   B. Lincoln and Reconstruction
      1. Lincoln's lenient 10 percent plan
      2. Loyal governments appeared in Tennessee, Arkansas, and Louisiana, but were not recognized by Congress
      3. The stricter Wade-Davis bill
      4. Debates over Reconstruction
      5. Lincoln's assassination
   C. Johnson's plan for Reconstruction
      1. Johnson's philosophy of Reconstruction
      2. Johnson's plan
         a. Exclusion from pardon of those owning property worth over $20,000
         b. States must invalidate secession ordinances, abolish slavery, and repudiate Confederate debt
      3. Most southern states met all of Johnson's requirements
   D. Southern intransigence
      1. Southern states had elected to Congress many ex-Confederate leaders
      2. Southern states had passed repressive Black Codes
      3. Reaction of Radicals
   E. The Radicals
      1. Moderate Republicans drifted toward the Radicals
      2. Radical theories of Reconstruction
         a. Conquered provinces

       b. State suicide

       c. Forfeited rights

  F. Johnson began to lose battle with Congress

    1. Johnson's veto of bill to extend life of Freedmen's Bureau upheld by Senate

    2. Johnson's veto of Civil Rights Acts of 1866 overridden

    3. Johnson's veto of revised Freedmen's Bureau bill overridden

  G. The Fourteenth Amendment

    1. It supported Civil Rights Act of 1866

    2. First section reaffirmed state and federal citizenship and contained important clauses: "privileges and immunities," "due process of law," and "equal protection of the laws"

    3. Southern reaction

  H. Johnson lost support of the American public

    1. Unsuccessful speaking tour of Midwest

    2. In election of 1866, Republicans won over two-thirds majority in each house

II. Reconstructing the South

  A. Congressional Reconstruction

    1. Congress moved to protect its program from President Johnson

       a. Command of the Army Act

       b. Tenure of Office Act

    2. Military Reconstruction Act

       a. Former Confederate states (Tennessee was exempt) placed in five military districts

       b. States must frame new constitutions, grant universal male suffrage, and ratify Fourteenth Amendment

    3. Congress passed law removing Reconstruction cases from the Court's jurisdiction

  B. Impeachment and trial of Johnson

    1. Johnson removed Secretary of War Edwin Stanton in violation of Tenure of Office Act

    2. House of Representatives passed eleven articles of impeachment

    3. In Senate trial, vote to convict was one short

    4. Effects of impeachment on Radicals and Johnson

  C. Republican rule in the South

    1. New governments established in southern states

    2. The work of the Union League

  D. Blacks in politics

        1. Introduced suddenly to politics, many rose to high positions
        2. Black influence in Reconstruction governments has been greatly exaggerated

    E. White Republicans in the South
        1. Carpetbaggers—northern Republicans who allegedly came south for political and economic gain
        2. Scalawags—southern white Republicans

    F. The Republican record
        1. Achievements of Republican governments
        2. Corruption of Republican governments

    G. White terror
        1. Formation of Ku Klux Klan
        2. Prosecution under new federal laws ended most of these activities

    H. Southern conservatives regained power
        1. Klan weakened Negro and Republican morale
        2. North was also concerned with westward expansion, Indians wars, and the economic and political questions of the tariff and currency
        3. Republican control of southern states began to collapse in 1869
        4. By 1876, Radical regimes survived only in Louisiana, Florida, and South Carolina

III. The Grant years
    A. Grant's election
        1. Positions of Democratic and Republican parties and the election of 1868
        2. Grant, an inept political leader, made many unwise appointments

    B. Economic development
        1. Republicans in war years
        2. Acts passed

    C. The problem of the government's debt
        1. Support for monetary expansion
        2. Support for monetary restriction

    D. Scandals in Grant's administration
        1. Jay Gould and Jim Fisk tried to corner the gold market
        2. The Crédit Mobilier scandal
        3. Other scandals disclosed

    E. The Liberal Republicans
    F. Economic distress and the beginning of the Panic of 1873
    G. The Resumption Act of 1875

IV. The election of 1876
  A. Campaigns marked by few real issues and much mud-slinging
  B. Disputed vote count in three southern states
  C. Congress formed special Electoral Commission to resolve problem
  D. The Compromise of 1877
  E. Some promises kept and many broken after Hayes took office
  F. The legacy of Reconstruction

Suggestions for Lecture Topics

A lecture might compare various interpretations of Reconstruction. Two approaches that could be contrasted are William A. Dunning's *Reconstruction, Political and Economic* (1907) and Kenneth M. Stampp's *Reconstruction* (1965).

Fawn Brodie's *Thaddeus Stevens* (1959) could be used as the basis for a lecture assessing the motivations of this leading Radical.

Leon Litwack's *Been in the Storm So Long* (1979) offers a wealth of information for a lecture on the freedmen's experiences.

Compare the interpretation offered in C. Vann Woodward's *Reunion and Reaction* (1951) to the traditional story of the Wormley House agreement.

Multiple-Choice Questions

1. The Thirteenth Amendment
  * A. ended slavery.
    B. said that the nation was "an indestructible Union, composed of indestructible states."
    C. was passed before the war was over.
    D. said that the Confederate debt could not be repaid.

2. During the Civil War, when southern congressmen were absent, the U.S. Congress passed all of the following *except*
    A. the Morrill Tariff of 1861, doubling the average level of duties.
    B. the Homestead Act of 1862, giving 160 acres to settlers who lived on the land for five years.

    C. the National Banking Act of 1863, creating a uniform banking system and currency.

* D. the Carroll Agriculture Act, which set standards governing tenancy on small farms.

3. At the end of the Civil War, the newly freed slaves were given
    A. small plots of land confiscated from southern planters.
    B. forty acres and a mule.
* C. medical and legal assistance from the Bureau of Refugees, Freedmen, and Abandoned Lands.
    D. five dollars for every year they had served in bondage.

4. Under Lincoln's plan for Reconstruction,
    A. loyal governments appeared in five states, but Congress refused to recognize them.
    B. loyal governments were recognized by Congress in three southern states.
    C. 10 percent of elected officials in a state had to be black.
* D. 10 percent of the 1860 voters had to take an oath of allegiance to the Union.

5. The Wade-Davis bill
    A. would have admitted representatives from Tennessee, Arkansas, and Louisiana to Congress in 1864.
* B. was the first congressional plan for Reconstruction.
    C. would have granted congressional authority to Lincoln's Emancipation Proclamation.
    D. included the controversial "ten percent plan."

6. The states that had seceded were simply "out of their proper practical relation with the Union," and the nation's goal following the war was to return them to "their proper practical relation." This statement was made by
    A. Senator Benjamin Wade.
    B. Andrew Johnson.
* C. Abraham Lincoln.
    D. Thaddeus Stevens.

7. In the case of *Texas v. White*, the Supreme Court
    A. decided that Josiah White, a former Confederate soldier, had to stand trial for "atrocities against civilians during the late War of Southern Rebellion."
* B. affirmed the notion of "an indestructible Union."
    C. decided that lands confiscated during the war had to be returned to their original owners.

D. overturned a Texas law barring former Confederates from certain professions.

8. Andrew Johnson's plan for Reconstruction was based on
    A. his strong belief in Negro suffrage.
    B. a strict adherence to the Constitution; hence, since the former Confederate states had left the Union, great changes had to be made in those states before they could reenter the Union.
    * C. a strict adherence to the Constitution; hence, since the Union was indestructible, the former Confederate states had never left it, and Reconstruction was therefore unnecessary.
    D. his "forfeited rights" theory.

9. The Black Codes were designed
    A. by Johnson and his cabinet to ensure the political rights of blacks.
    * B. by southern legislatures to set blacks aside as a caste separate from whites and subject to special restraints.
    C. by Republicans in Congress to ensure the economic rights of blacks.
    D. by the Ku Klux Klan and similar groups as a plan of intimidation of the recently freed slaves.

10. Southern intransigence included all the following *except*
    A. the election of many ex-Confederate leaders to Congress.
    * B. the refusal of every southern state to ratify the Thirteenth Amendment.
    C. the passage of laws that restricted the rights of blacks.
    D. the requirement that blacks enter into strict annual labor contracts.

11. Radical Republicans
    A. included Alexander H. Stephens and George W. Julian.
    B. were, for the most part, motivated by hopes of personal economic gain.
    C. would have supported Lincoln's plan for Reconstruction had Lincoln lived.
    * D. gained strength in 1866.

12. The Civil Rights Act of 1866
    A. had the support of President Johnson, who had urged Congress to pass such a measure.
    B. gave to adult black males the right to vote in local and state—but not national—elections.

* C. was passed over Johnson's veto.

D. was unconstitutional, according to most Radical Republicans.

13. The Fourteenth Amendment forbade any state to do any of the following *except*
    A. abridge the "privileges and immunities" of citizens.
    * B. subject any person to "cruel and unusual punishment."
    C. deprive any person of life, liberty, or property without "due process of law."
    D. deny any person "the equal protection of the laws."

14. In the election of 1866,
    A. Johnson was reelected president by an extremely small margin.
    B. Johnson was reelected president by a large margin.
    * C. Republicans won a majority of seats in each house of Congress, thus assuring that the congressional plan of Reconstruction would pass over Johnson's vetoes.
    D. Democrats still held a slight majority in Congress, but many Democrats were hesitant to support Johnson further.

15. Abraham Lincoln was assassinated
    A. just two months after the war was over.
    B. by a crazed actor who thought Lincoln would be too lenient toward the South.
    * C. by John Wilkes Booth.
    D. All the above are true.

16. The House of Representatives found grounds for impeachment when President Johnson
    A. kept vetoing the legislation of congressional Reconstruction.
    B. refused to appoint military commanders to head the five districts set up by Congress in the Military Reconstruction Act.
    * C. dismissed Secretary of War Edwin Stanton, in violation of the Tenure of Office Act.
    D. pardoned thousands of former Confederates.

17. Which of the following best describes the role of blacks in southern politics during Reconstruction?
    A. Blacks made up a majority in most state legislatures.

    B. Two black governors were elected.

    C. In most areas, black voters overwhelmed white voters for several years.

* D. Sixteen blacks were elected to Congress.

18. During Reconstruction, most of the top positions in the state governments were held by men whom many southern whites called carpetbaggers or scalawags. The difference between the two groups is that

    A. carpetbaggers were southern white Republicans and scalawags were Negro Republicans.

    B. carpetbaggers were northern white Republicans and scalawags were Negro Republicans.

* C. carpetbaggers were northern white Republicans and scalawags were southern white Republicans.

    D. carpetbaggers were southern white Republicans and scalawags were northern white Republicans.

19. Among the accomplishments of Radical Reconstruction were all the following *except*

    A. it set up the beginnings of state school systems.

* B. it relieved the freedmen from continued economic dependence on whites.

    C. it rewrote state constitutions, introducing universal male suffrage and a more equitable apportionment of the legislature.

    D. it repaired some of the physical damage of the Civil War.

20. Which of the following best describes the defeat of the Ku Klux Klan?

* A. President Grant and the Justice Department used the Enforcement Acts of 1870 and 1871 to put an end to Klan activity.

    B. The Klan of 1866 never ended, and is in fact still strong today.

    C. The Justice Department, prosecuting under the Civil Rights Act of 1866, threw most of the Klan leaders in jail, thus breaking the back of the movement.

    D. Militias formed by the Radical regimes in the southern states chased the Klan from the cities and its membership then quickly declined.

21. Radical Reconstruction in the South
    A. ended in some Deep South states as early as 1867, and in all states by 1875.
    B. ended in two states as early as 1869, but continued in some Deep South states until 1890.
    * C. was over by 1877.
    D. was ended by presidential proclamation in 1872.

22. Ulysses S. Grant
    A. was elected president in 1868 despite the heavy black Democratic vote.
    B. brought confidence and honesty to a national government torn by Reconstruction.
    * C. brought little political experience and judgment to the presidency.
    D. pushed for civil service reform throughout his presidency.

23. The plan by Jay Gould and Jim Fisk to corner the gold market
    A. was known as the Crédit-Mobilier scandal.
    B. led to the impeachment of Grant's secretary of war.
    * C. ended on "Black Friday," when President Grant ordered the selling of a large quantity of gold.
    D. led to the Panic of 1873.

24. The Resumption Act, passed by Congress in 1875,
    A. was vetoed by President Grant.
    B. called for the resumption of withdrawing greenbacks.
    * C. allowed for the redemption of greenbacks in gold.
    D. had the support of the National Greenback Party.

25. The so-called "Mulligan Letters"
    A. revealed the extent of corruption of the "Whiskey Ring" in St. Louis.
    * B. linked Republican James G. Blaine to shady railroad deals.
    C. cost Horace Greeley the 1872 Republican presidential nomination.
    D. revealed cases of vote fraud in three states in the election of 1876.

26. In the election of 1876,
    * A. the Democratic and Republican campaigns were based on few real issues.
    B. there were major contested vote counts in three western states.

    C. the main issue dividing the parties was civil service reform.

    D. Democrats for the first time "waved the bloody shirt."

27. The Electoral Commission, set up by Congress in January 1877,
    A. was designed to assure "a free ballot and a fair count" in future presidential elections.
    B. had nine Democratic members and six Republican.
    C. found some instances of fraud in the 1876 election, but decided that the election should stand.
  * D. gave the electoral votes of Florida, Louisiana, and South Carolina to the Republicans.

28. In the Compromise of 1877, Republicans promised all the following *except*
    A. to withdraw federal troops from South Carolina and Louisiana.
    B. to provide funds for southern internal improvements, including a subsidy for a transcontinental railroad along a southern route.
  * C. to pardon all ex-Confederates still disfranchised.
    D. to appoint a southerner to a cabinet post.

29. Charles Sumner
  * A. was a leading Radical Republican during Reconstruction.
    B. was considered the "swing man" on the Electoral Commission.
    C. was implicated in the "Whiskey Ring" scandal.
    D. was implicated in the Crédit Mobilier scandal.

30. Samuel J. Tilden
    A. was a former Confederate from Tennessee who was named postmaster-general under Grant.
    B. was considered the "swing man" on the Electoral Commission.
  * C. was the 1876 Democratic presidential candidate.
    D. called the Compromise of 1877 "the betrayal of the Negro."

Suggested Essay Questions

1. What were the major problems facing the nation in April 1865? What factors stood in the way of a solution to those problems?

2. What were the goals of the reconstruction plans offered by Abraham Lincoln in 1863, by Andrew Johnson in 1865, and by the

Radicals in Congress in 1867? How was each plan going to achieve its goals?

3. What problems did blacks in the South face after Emancipation? What attempts did the government make to solve these problems?

4. What were the major economic issues facing the United States between 1868 and 1877?

5. How was the contested election of 1876 decided? Describe the political, racial, and sectional effects of the decision.

Chapter 18

NEW FRONTIERS: SOUTH AND WEST

This chapter covers the New South, including economic and agricultural developments, the Bourbons, and race relations. It also treats American Indian policy and the western frontier of miners, cowboys, and farmers.

Chapter Outline

I. Prophets and goals of the New South
    A. Henry Grady and his New South speech
    B. The New South creed

II. Economic growth in the New South
    A. Textile mills
    B. The Dukes and Tobacco
    C. Other natural resources
        1. Coal and iron ore
        2. Lumber
    D. Two great forces at the turn of the century
        1. Petroleum
        2. Hydroelectric power

III. Agriculture in the New South
    A. Problems in southern agriculture
        1. Land ownership
            a. Sharecropping
            b. Tenant farming
        2. Credit—the crop-lien system
    B. Result: stagnation

IV. The political leaders of the New South
    A. Definition and evaluation of the term Bourbon
    B. Bourbon ideology
        1. Allied politically with eastern conservatives
        2. Allied economically with eastern capitalists

  C. Effects of Bourbon retrenchment
    1. Education
      a. Greatly reduced spending on education
      b. Need for private philanthropy
    2. Convict leasing
    3. Repudiation of state debts
  D. Achievements of the Bourbons

V. Blacks and the New South
  A. Flexibility in Bourbon race relations
    1. Negro voting
    2. Little strict segregation
  B. Black disfranchisement
    1. Purpose—to allow whites to divide politically
    2. The Mississippi plan
      a. Residence requirement
      b. Disqualification for conviction of certain crimes
      c. Poll tax and other taxes must be paid by February 1
      d. Literacy test (with understanding clause)
    3. Variations of the Mississippi plan (including the "grandfather clause")
    4. Effects of the Mississippi plan
  C. Segregation in the South
    1. The Supreme Court
      a. The *Civil Rights Cases* (1883)
      b. *Plessy v. Ferguson* (1896)
    2. Southern states passes Jim Crow legislation
  D. Lynchings of blacks
  E. Two black leaders
    1. Booker T. Washington and accommodation
    2. W. E. B. Du Bois and protest

VI. Myth and the New South
  A. New South prophets and views of the Old South
  B. The New South itself became a myth
  C. Reconciliation of tradition with innovation

VII. The settlement of the West
  A. The Great Plains slowed settlement
  B. Factors that increased settlement

VIII. The miner in the West
  A. The development of mining communities

B. The great gold, silver, and copper strikes
C. Western states admitted to the Union

IX. Indians in the West
    A. Indians forced to cede lands to the government
        1. Sparadic Indian wars
        2. Chivington's massacre of 450 Indians
    B. *Report on the Condition of the Indian Tribes*
        1. Decision to place Indians on reservations
        2. Agreements at Medicine Creek Lodge and elsewhere
    C. George Custer and the Battle of the Little Big Horn
    D. Continued Indian resistance
        1. Chief Joseph
        2. Capture of Geronimo
        3. The slaughter of the buffalo
    E. Reform of Indian policy
        1. Helen Hunt Jackson
        2. The Dawes Severalty Act
           a. Goal of the Dawes Act
           b. Effect of the Dawes Act

X. Cowboys in the West
    A. Early cattle raising in the West
    B. The great cattle drives
        1. Joseph McCoy and Abilene
        2. The decline of the long drives
    C. Barbed wire and the open-range cattle industry

XI. Farmers in the West
    A. The problem of land
        1. Homestead Act of 1862
        2. The Newlands Reclamation Act of 1901
    B. The problem of water
        1. Effects of the Newlands Act
        2. Other solutions
    C. The farmer's life
    D. Technological advances that aided farmers
    E. Western farms, large and small

XII. The end of the frontier
    A. Frontier line no longer existed after 1890
    B. Frederick Jackson Turner and "The Significance of the Frontier in American History"

Suggestions for Lecture Topics

One lecture could present various interpretations of southern race relations from Reconstruction to the turn of the century. C. Vann Woodward's *The Strange Career of Jim Crow* (3rd ed., 1974) is the key source, but also see Howard Rabinowitz's *Race Relations in the Urban South, 1865–1890* (1978) and Joel Williamson's *The Crucible of Race* (1984).

Ralph K. Andrist's *The Long Death: The Last Days of the Plains Indians* (1964) contains a wealth of information suitable for a lecture on that topic.

A discussion of Frederick Jackson Turner's frontier thesis might be a good way to summarize some of the issues raised in this chapter. See *The Turner Thesis Concerning the Role of the Frontier in American History*, edited by George Taylor (3rd ed., 1972), and Patricia Limerick's recent *The Legacy of Conquest: The Unbroken Past of the American West* (1987).

For a lecture on sharecropping, perhaps the key feature of southern agriculture during this period, see Roger L. Ransom and Richard Sutch's *One Kind of Freedom* (1977) and Robert Higgs's *Competition and Coercion* (1977). These two books, besides containing information on the topic, take opposite sides on a historical debate of current interest: the role of racism in determining tenancy arrangements. Higgs downplays racism as a factor, while Ransom and Sutch see it as significant. Harold Woodman reviews this and other controversies concerning share-cropping in "Sequel to Slavery: The New History Views the Postbellum South" (*Journal of Southern History* 43 [1977]: 523–554).

Multiple-Choice Questions

1. The major prophet of the New South creed was
   * A. Henry W. Grady.
   B. John Taylor.
   C. Edmund Ruffin.
   D. John Ruffin Green.

2. The New South creed emphasized all the following *except*
   A. industrialization in the South.
   B. education in the South.
   * C. women's rights in the South.
   D. racial harmony in the South.

3. The number of cotton mills in the South in the years from 1880 to 1900
   A. is not a good indication of an industrial revolution.
   * B. more than doubled.
   C. decreased when compared to the great expansion of northern mills.
   D. remained about constant.

4. The American Tobacco Company
   A. was started by James Ruffin Green just after the Civil War.
   B. was second only to the Bull Durham Company in cigarette production at the turn of the century.
   * C. was broken up by the Supreme Court in 1911.
   D. was the first such government-owned company in this country.

5. The "Pittsburgh of the South," so named because it was an iron center, was
   * A. Birmingham, Alabama.
   B. Houston, Texas.
   C. Nashville, Tennessee.
   D. Rome, Georgia.

6. In the crop lien system,
   * A. farmers could grow little besides cotton or some other staple crop.
   B. many white farmers were able to buy small plots of land.
   C. farmers could get cheap credit to expand their farms.
   D. farmers found a way to escape the perennial debt into which many of them had fallen.

7. The New South Bourbons
   A. forged a political alliance with eastern liberals.
   * B. forged an economic alliance with eastern capitalists.
   C. generally opposed the Republican laissez-faire policy.
   D. generally opposed the practice of convict leasing.

8. The Bourbons' financial program in general included all the following *except*
   * A. ending tax exemptions for businesses and railroads.
   B. convict leasing.
   C. cutting back on appropriations for education.
   D. repudiating part of the state debts.

9. The term *Bourbons*
   A. celebrated the French origin of most New South leaders.
   * B. was derived from the French Bourbons, whom Napoleon said forgot nothing and learned nothing in the ordeal of the French Revolution.
   C. reflected the fact that several New South leaders in the upper South came from families that had made their fortune as liquor distillers.
   D. was used with pride by New South leaders.

10. Between Reconstruction and 1890, the Bourbons' policy toward race relations
    A. was strict; few blacks were allowed to vote and Jim Crow laws segregated almost all public places.
    B. resulted in the almost-total disfranchisement of blacks by 1880.
    * C. was flexible; many blacks voted, and most of the restrictive Jim Crow laws had not yet been passed.
    D. was based on the idea that blacks, freed from slavery, would develop intellectually to the level of whites.

11. The disfranchisement of blacks in the South
    A. was accomplished soon after the Bourbons came into power.
    B. was often accomplished through the use of the "grandfather clause," which said you could vote only if your grandfather could vote.
    C. was unconstitutional, because the Fourteenth Amendment had explicitly given all citizens the right to vote.
    * D. was designed to allow southern whites to divide politically without giving blacks the balance of power.

12. The Mississippi plan of disfranchisement included all the following *except*
    A. a residency requirement.
    * B. a provision disqualifying anyone who owned less than $300 in personal property.
    C. a provision disqualifying those convicted of certain crimes.
    D. a literacy requirement (with an "understanding" clause, to allow illiterate whites to vote).

13. In the 1883 *Civil Rights Cases*, the Supreme Court ruled that
    * A. a federal Civil Rights Act did not extend to individual action.

    B. segregation on railroad cars was illegal under the Four-
teenth Amendment.

    C. a Louisiana segregation law, under which Homer Plessy, a
New Orleans octaroon, had been convicted, was unconstitutional.

    D. the Fourteenth Amendment's guarantee of "equal protec-
tion of the laws" applied to individual, as well as to
state, action.

14. The lynching of blacks in the South

    A. prompted the passage of a federal antilynching law in
1892.

    B. decreased just before the turn of the century, possibly
because whites could control blacks through the Jim Crow
laws.

*   C. increased at about the same time that Jim Crow laws
spread through the South.

    D. was not much worse at the turn of the century than similar
lynchings in the North.

15. Booker T. Washington

*   A. was born of a slave mother and a white father.

    B. had a Ph.D. in history from Harvard and wrote several
distinguished historical works.

    C. criticized W. E. B. Du Bois's "Atlanta Compromise"
speech.

    D. is correctly represented by all the above statements.

16. The New South prophets

*   A. used the romantic myth of the Old South to bolster self-
esteem and give a sense of identity.

    B. severed all ties to the Old South.

    C. were quick to admit that the romantic myth of the Old
South was largely false, but still praised agrarianism and
the old institution of slavery.

    D. used the Old South as a model for the future.

17. Which of the following statements about the mining frontier is
not true?

    A. The California gold fever ended by 1851.

    B. At many sites, law and order (and stable communities)
followed the prospectors after several years.

*   C. The Comstock Lode was in Nebraska.

    D. Copper was the most important mineral found in Arizona
and Montana.

18. Six states were created from the western territories in the years 1889 and 1890. These territories were not made states before 1889 because
    * A. Democrats in Congress were reluctant to create states out of territories that were heavily Republican.
    B. the lawlessness of many western towns discouraged Congress from admitting the territories as states.
    C. polygamy, as practiced by the Mormons in the West, was unacceptable to Congress.
    D. if large mining firms had been forced to pay state taxes, they would have had to close down.

19. Helen Hunt Jackson's *A Century of Dishonor*
    A. was a best-selling novel about life in the western mining towns.
    B. told the story of four poor families who went west in the 1840s in search of a better life.
    C. exposed prostitution in many western towns and led to reforms.
    * D. focused the nation's attention on the wrongs inflicted on Indians.

20. In the Battle of the Little Big Horn,
    A. Gen. George Custer's troops were massacred by the Cherokee and Seminole Indians.
    * B. some 2,500 Indians annihilated a detachment of 200 soldiers.
    C. Chief Sitting Bull was captured and murdered.
    D. Sioux and Cheyenne Indians won a large chunk of the Montana Territory, which they kept for fourteen years.

21. Following the 1867 "Report on the Condition of the Indian Tribes," Congress decided that the best way to end Indian wars was
    A. to send in the army, under men such as George Custer, to break the morale of the Indians.
    B. systematically to kill most of the buffalo.
    C. to "Americanize" the Indians by offering them an education at the white man's school.
    * D. to force the Indians to live on out-of-the-way reservations.

22. The Dawes Severalty Act of 1887
    A. was designed to "Americanize" the Indians.

    B. gave individual Indians up to 160 acres of land which, for the Indians' protection, the government held in trust for 25 years.

    C. caused the Indians to lose over half their land between 1887 and 1934.

* D. is correctly represented by all the above statements.

23. Chief Joseph

    A. was killed at the Battle of Wounded Knee.

* B. was the peaceful and dignified leader of the Nez Percé Indians.

    C. was forced to sign away his tribe's homeland in the Medicine Creek Lodge agreement.

    D. originated the Ghost Dance to bring on the day of the Indians' deliverance.

24. Joseph G. McCoy created the first great cowtown in

* A. Abilene, Kansas.

    B. St. Louis, Missouri.

    C. Dallas, Texas.

    D. Butte, Montana.

25. Joseph Glidden and John W. Gates

    A. were railroad men who reaped great profits from the early cattle drives.

* B. introduced barbed-wire to cattle ranchers.

    C. made their fame as buffalo hunters, slaughtering thousands of the animals.

    D. led the sheep ranchers against the cattlemen for control of western grazing lands.

26. Which of the following statements about the cowboy's frontier is *not* true?

* A. With two or three notable exceptions, blacks were not allowed to be cowboys.

    B. Texas longhorns were noted more for their speed and endurance than for their value as beef.

    C. Much of the cowboy's equipment had been passed on from Mexico.

    D. Cattle raising had been common since colonial times.

27. The greatest obstacle facing western farmers was

    A. antiquated land laws.

    B. Indian wars.

* C. lack of water.

    D. grasshoppers and other insects.

28. The Newlands Reclamation Act of 1901
    A. sold to settlers the lands created by clearing the timber from the western public lands.
    B. allowed the government to reclaim some of the land once given to railroads.
    C. authorized the government to begin a tremendous tree-planting project to reclaim part of the arid West.
  * D. provided funds for irrigation works.

29. According to the superintendent of the census, the frontier line no longer existed after
    A. 1875.
    B. 1880.
  * C. 1890.
    D. 1900.

30. "The Significance of the Frontier in American History," an essay explaining the American character in terms of the frontier, was written by
  * A. Frederick Jackson Turner.
    B. Henry Adams.
    C. Theodore Roosevelt.
    D. Charles Henry Smith.

Suggested Essay Questions

1. One of the goals of the new South prophets was a diversified agriculture in the South. What factors stood in the way of this goal?

2. In what ways did the Bourbons' emphasis on economy affect the South?

3. Describe the pattern of race relations in the South from the end of Reconstruction to 1900.

4. One might say that the West actually consisted of three frontiers: the miners', the cowboys', and the farmers'. What problems did each of these groups face?

5. Describe the government's policy toward Indians. How did this policy develop over the years, and what were the main factors that influenced its development?

Chapter 19

BIG BUSINESS AND ORGANIZED LABOR

This chapter covers the advances in railroads and manufacturing after the Civil War, the captains of industry, workers in an industrialized America, and the growth of labor unions.

Chapter Outline

I. The growth of the American economy

II. The railroads
   A. The first transcontinental railroad
      1. Increase in railroad building
      2. Pacific Railway bill (1862) authorized transcontinental line on north-central route
         a. Union Pacific Railroad
         b. Central Pacific Railroad and California's Big Four
      3. First transcontinental railroad completed at Promontory Point
   B. Financing the railroads
      1. The Crédit Mobilier Company
      2. Jay Gould
      3. Cornelius Vanderbilt

III. Technological advances
   A. The growth of new industries and the transformation of old ones
   B. Two technological advances that changed people's lives
      1. Alexander Graham Bell and the telephone
      2. Thomas Alva Edison and the electric light

IV. Three great captains of industry
   A. John D. Rockefeller
      1. The Pennsylvania oil rush of 1859
      2. Rockefeller as oil refiner
      3. Growth of Standard Oil
      4. Rockefeller's organization of Standard Oil

B. Andrew Carnegie
   1. Carnegie, railroad and oil
   2. Carnegie and steel
   3. Carnegie and philanthropy
      a. "The Gospel of Wealth"
      b. The worship of success in nineteenth-century America
C. J. Pierpont Morgan
   1. Morgan and investment banking
   2. Morgan and railroads
   3. Morgan and steel

V. Workers in an industrialized America
   A. Rising standard of living
   B. Working conditions
      1. Wages earned and hours worked
      2. Poor safety and health conditions in factories
   C. The change from personal working conditions to impersonal, contractual relationships

VI. Early worker protest
   A. Reasons for the slow growth of unions
   B. The Molly Maguires
   C. The Great Railroad Strike of 1877
      1. Effect of strikes
      2. Reduction of wages was immediate cause
      3. The strikes spread across the country
      4. Failure of the strikes
   D. The rise of unions
      1. Unions in the 1850s and 1860s
      2. The National Labor Union

VII. The Knights of Labor
   A. Founded in 1869 by Uriah S. Stephens
   B. Platform and organization
   C. Under Terence V. Powderly, saw greatest success
      1. Successful strikes against the Union Pacific and Jay Gould's railroads
      2. Growth in membership
   D. Decline of the Knights of Labor
      1. Another strike against Jay Gould failed
      2. The Haymarket Affair
         a. Riot in Haymarket Square
         b. Trial and sentencing of anarchists
         c. Effects on Knights of Labor

    E. Achievements of Knights of Labor

VIII. The American Federation of Labor
    A. Structure of the AFL
    B. Samuel Gompers
        1. Concern for concrete economic gains
        2. Gompers's leadership in the AFL
    C. Membership growth in the AFL

  IX. Two strikes that hurt the union movement
    A. The Homestead Steel Strike of 1892
        1. Reasons for the strike
        2. Battle between strikers and Pinkerton detectives
        3. Strike failed, union dead at Homestead
    B. The Pullman Strike of 1894
        1. Workers forced to live in town of Pullman
        2. Workers turned to Eugene Debs and the American
            Railway Union
        3. Strike tied up most midwestern railroads
        4. Mail cars attached to Pullman cars
        5. Debs jailed and the union called off the strike

   X. Socialism and the unions
    A. Daniel De Leon and the Socialist Labor Party
    B. Eugene Debs and the Social Democrat Party
    C. The Socialist Party of America
        1. Debs in the presidential elections of 1904 and 1912
        2. Successes of the party
        3. Decline of the party

  XI. The Industrial Workers of the World
    A. Origins of the IWW: western mining and lumber camps
    B. Goals of the IWW
        1. To include all workers, skilled and unskilled
        2. To replace the state with one big union
    C. Decline of the IWW
        1. Disputes within the group
        2. William D. "Big Bill" Haywood

Suggestions for Lecture Topics

For a discussion of social mobility in the late nineteenth century, see
Stephen Thernstrom's *Poverty and Progress: Social Mobility in a
Nineteenth-Century City* (1964).

For a lecture on Gilded Age labor, perhaps the best general source is Melvyn Dubofsky's *Industrialism and the American Workers, 1865–1920* (2nd ed., 1985).

A lecture on the so-called robber barons might begin with Matthew Josephson's classic *The Robber Barons* (1934), but also see Hal Bridges's "The Robber Baron Concept in American History" and Edward C. Kirkland's "Divide and Ruin," both in *American History: Recent Interpretations*, edited by Abraham S. Eisenstadt (2nd ed., 1969).

Multiple-Choice Questions

1. The growth of railroads
   - A. was a major cause of the economic expansion at the end of the nineteenth century.
   - B. resulted in an increase in total mileage from about 30,000 in 1860 to almost 200,000 in 1900.
   - C. was greatest in the decade of the 1880s.
   - * D. is correctly represented by all the above statements.

2. A transcontinental railroad was not built before the Civil War because
   - A. the Appalachian Mountains presented great engineering problems.
   - B. Stephen Douglas was able to stop any federal subsidies for the railroads from passage by Congress.
   - * C. the South wanted a southern route for the railroad and the North wanted a northern route.
   - D. many southern states used the states' rights argument to reject federal aid for railroads.

3. The first transcontinental railroad
   - A. was completed in 1885.
   - * B. was built by the Central Pacific and the Union Pacific Railroads.
   - C. followed a southern route through Texas and the Arizona and New Mexico Territories.
   - D. led to the bankruptcy of financial backer and former California governor Leland Stanford.

4. Jay Gould
   - A. was a member of the California "Big Four."
   - B. was known as "the Prince of the Robber Barons" for his devotion to the public good.

  * C. opposed Cornelius Vanderbilt's efforts to take over the Erie Railroad.
  D. controlled 85 percent of the nation's railroad mileage in 1900.

5. Thomas Alva Edison invented all the following *except*
  A. the first successful incandescent lightbulb.
  * B. the air brake for trains.
  C. the phonograph.
  D. the storage battery.

6. The Pennsylvania oil rush of 1859
  * A. far outweighed, in economic importance, the California gold rush of a decade before.
  B. gave George Westinghouse, who was not afraid to speculate by drilling risky oil wells, his start in business.
  C. ended the monopoly that Oklahoma had previously enjoyed in petroleum production.
  D. is correctly described by all the above statements.

7. In 1879, less than ten years after John D. Rockefeller had formed Standard Oil, that company controlled over 90 percent of the nation's oil refining. Which of the following best accounts for Rockefeller's success?
  A. Rockefeller's scientists found new technical processes for refining oil more efficiently.
  B. Rockefeller bought out the Erie Railroad in order to keep transportation charges low.
  * C. Rockefeller proved very adept at corporate organization.
  D. Rockefeller was one of the first industrialists to invest heavily in advertising.

8. Horatio Alger
  * A. wrote rags-to-riches novels.
  B. was Andrew Carnegie's mentor.
  C. was John D. Rockefeller's early business partner.
  D. shot H. C. Frick, president of the Homestead Works.

9. Andrew Carnegie
  A. used much of the fortune he inherited from his father to drill his first oil well.
  B. paid almost $500 million for J. Pierpont Morgan's railroad interests.
  * C. made money in many areas, including oil, railroads, iron and steel, and bridge building.
  D. is correctly described by all the above statements.

10. In "The Gospel of Wealth," Carnegie wrote that a rich man should
    * A. provide means for people to improve themselves.
    B. make provisions in his will for his money to be used for the public good.
    C. give about half of his money to almshouses and similar charities.
    D. return a large share of his wealth to the company that made him rich.

11. Holding companies
    * A. are firms that control the stock of other companies.
    B. were outlawed in New Jersey in 1888.
    C. allowed J. Pierpont Morgan to build a monopoly in the oil-shipping business.
    D. included the Crédit Mobilier and the Credit and Finance Corporation.

12. J. Pierpont Morgan
    A. believed that unrestrained competition was "God's gift to, and the only hope for, American business."
    * B. did not really believe in the free enterprise system.
    C. greatly influenced Carnegie when he was writing "The Gospel of Wealth."
    D. was an inefficient organizer.

13. The first billion-dollar corporation was
    A. Northern Pacific Railroad.
    B. Standard Oil Company.
    * C. United States Steel Corporation.
    D. National Bell Telephone Company.

14. All the following accompanied industrialization between 1865 and 1914 *except*
    A. a rise in real wages and earnings.
    B. a change from personal working relationships to impersonal, contractual relationships.
    * C. shorter workweeks.
    D. poor safety and health conditions in factories.

15. The Molly Maguires
    A. were named for the daughter of George Maguire, the owner of a Pennsylvania coalfield.
    B. accomplished their goals of better wages and working conditions for miners through peaceful arbitration.

* C. aimed to right perceived wrongs against Irish coal workers.
  D. was the first major labor organization for western miners.

16. The Great Railroad Strike of 1877
    A. was led by Eugene V. Debs.
    B. won higher wages for railroad workers.
    C. did not have the support of the public at first, but as the strike (and its violence) spread, so did public sympathy for the strikers.
  * D. ended when the workers, who lacked organized bargaining power, returned to work.

17. The first major national strike occurred in
    A. the 1860s.
  * B. the 1870s.
    C. the mining industry
    D. the textile industry.

18. The National Labor Union
    A. was for its 25 years of existence a major proponent of labor reform.
    B. opposed reforms such as cooperatives and equal rights for women and blacks in favor of simply bargaining with employers to get the best working conditions and wages possible.
    C. was led by Albert Parsons.
  * D. was the first major federation of trade unions.

19. The greatest growth of the Knights of Labor
    A. occurred under the leadership of Uriah S. Stephens.
  * B. occurred in the mid-1880s, when the union had several successful strikes against the railroads.
    C. occurred under the leadership of Terence Powderly, who replaced Stephens in 1879 and personally led every strike by the Knights.
    D. occurred as a result of the Great Railroad Strike of 1877.

20. The Knights of Labor declined for all the following reasons *except*
    A. an unsuccessful strike against Jay Gould in 1886.
  * B. the death of Terence Powderly in 1887.
    C. the Haymarket Affair.
    D. its leadership was devoted more to reform than to the nuts and bolts of organization.

21. The Haymarket Affair
    A. was started by the Knights of Labor.
    B. led to the passage of the Foran Act of 1885.
    C. marked the beginning of the Federation of Organized Trades and Labor Unions.
  * D. was blamed, probably unfairly, on seven anarchist leaders.

22. The American Federation of Labor
  * A. was concerned more with concrete economic gains than with social or political reforms.
    B. was formed in 1869, but experienced most of its growth in the early years of the twentieth century.
    C. was a federation of industrial unions; craft unions could not join until 1948.
    D. could claim as members almost half of all industrial workers in 1920.

23. Which of the following statements about the 1892 Homestead Steel Strike is *not* true?
    A. H. C. Frick, president of Pittsburgh's Homestead Works, wanted to fire many workers.
  * B. Andrew Carnegie privately criticized the management of the Homestead Works.
    C. It turned into a battle between workers and Pinkerton detectives.
    D. When the strike ended, there was no longer an effective union at Homestead.

24. Samuel Gompers
  * A. had been a leader in the Cigarmakers Union.
    B. was a big, gentle man who did not care for the rough-and-tumble world of unionism.
    C. was the first Marxist to head a major American labor organization.
    D. was elected president of the American Federation of Labor in 1878 and served for almost four decades.

25. The Pullman Strike of 1894 ended
    A. when Pullman hired Pinkerton detectives to harass the striking workers.
    B. despite the support of President Grover Cleveland.
  * C. after mail cars were attached to Pullman cars.
    D. when strike leader Richard Olney became ill and could no longer support the strikers' morale.

26. In the case *In re Debs*, the Supreme Court
    A. overturned the conviction of Eugene Debs for destroying private property in Pullman, Illinois.
    B. upheld the conviction of Eugene Debs for destroying private property in Pullman, Illinois.
    C. overturned the conviction of Eugene Debs for inciting a riot.
  * D. upheld the conviction of Eugene Debs for violating a court injunction forbidding the obstruction of interstate commerce or of the transportation of the mails.

27. Daniel De Leon
    A. was the attorney-general of Illinois who obtained an injunction against striking Pullman employees.
    B. was convicted of throwing a bomb at strikers outside the Pullman plant.
    C. published an antisocialist paper in the 1890s.
  * D. was the leading figure in the Socialist Labor Party.

28. Which of the following statements about the Socialist Party of America is *not* true?
  * A. Its support was confined to industrial workers in the Northeast.
    B. In 1912 Eugene Debs, the party's presidential candidate, received almost 900,000 votes.
    C. It was plagued by disagreements over America's participation in World War I.
    D. It elected mayors in 33 American cities.

29. William D. "Big Bill" Haywood
    A. led a private army against the "Wobblies" in Colorado.
    B. was elected mayor of Milwaukee in 1910.
    C. served as editor of *The People*, the organ of the Socialist Labor Party.
  * D. was the leader of the Industrial Workers of the World.

30. The Industrial Workers of the World
  * A. had its origin in the mining and lumber camps of the West.
    B. was less radical than the American Federation of Labor.
    C. ended suddenly when its 1912 textile strike in Lawrence, Massachusetts, failed to win any concessions for the workers.
    D. ended in 1903 when the organization's officers were convicted of embezzling most of its funds.

Suggested Essay Questions

1. Describe the growth of the American economy in the late-nineteenth century and explain how they changed people's lives.

2. "Organization, rather than technological progress or economic growth, was the most important reason for the growth of big business after the Civil War." Is this statement true or false? Explain.

3. How did Andrew Carnegie and Horatio Alger contribute to a philosophical justification for business growth?

4. What factors shaped the growth of labor unions during this period?

5. Compare the aims and achievements of the Knights of Labor, the American Federation of Labor, and the Industrial Workers of the World.

Chapter 20

THE EMERGENCE OF MODERN AMERICA

This chapter covers the growth of cities in late-nineteenth-century America, the new immigration, education, the influence of Darwinian thought in the social sciences and literature, and social reforms.

Chapter Outline

I. The American city in the late-nineteenth century
   A. The growth of cities
      1. Cities in the West
      2. Transportation and industry as factors of growth
      3. Elevators and other engineering advances allowed cities to grow vertically
      4. Streetcars allowed cities to grow horizontally
      5. City planning
   B. Life in the cities
      1. Living conditions
      2. Bosses and city politics
      3. The attraction of the cities

II. Immigration to America
   A. Immigrants a major force in the growth of cities
      1. Numbers of immigrants
      2. Reasons for coming to America
   B. The new immigration
      1. After 1890, most immigrants from southern and eastern Europe
      2. Difference in culture, language, and religion
   C. The nativist response
      1. New immigrants viewed as a threat
      2. The American Protective Association
      3. Immigration restriction
         a. Early laws excluded "undesirables"
         b. Chinese immigrants excluded in 1882

III. Growth of educational opportunities
   A. The spread of public schools

    B. Higher education
       1. Increases in college attendance
       2. Women in higher education
       3. Graduate schools

IV. The rise of professionalism
    A. Education for professionals
    B. Licensing of professionals

V. Theories of social change
    A. Charles Darwin's *Origin of Species* (1859)
    B. Social Darwinism
       1. Herbert Spencer
       2. Tenets of Social Darwinism
       3. William Graham Sumner
    C. Reform Darwinism
       1. A challenge to Social Darwinism
       2. Lester Frank Ward and his *Dynamic Sociology* (1883)

VI. Realism in the social sciences
    A. Law
       1. Oliver Wendell Holmes, Jr., and *The Common Law* (1881)
       2. Law is based on experience, not logic
    B. History
       1. "Scientific" history
       2. Search for origins of institutions

VII. Realism in philosophy
    A. William James and pragmatism
    B. John Dewey and "instrumentalism"

VIII. Realism in literature
    A. Local color
       1. Reasons for its popularity
       2. Early practitioners
       3. Mark Twain
    B. Literary realism
       1. William Dean Howells
       2. Henry James
    C. Literary naturalism
       1. The introduction of scientific determinism into literature
       2. Frank Norris and Stephen Crane
       3. Jack London
       4. Theodore Dreiser

IX. Social criticism in the late-nineteenth century
    A. Henry George's *Progress and Poverty* (1879)
    B. Henry Demarest Lloyd's *Wealth against Commonwealth* (1894)
    C. Thorstein Veblen's *The Theory of the Leisure Class* (1899)

X. The social gospel
    A. The institutional church
    B. Washington Gladden
      1. The social conscience of the middle class
      2. Christian law and industry
    C. The Roman Catholic church and reform
      1. Pope Leo XIII's *Rerum Novarum* (1891) more liberal
      2. American Catholics remained isolated from reform movements

XI. The settlement house movement
    A. Jane Addams's Hull House most famous
    B. Accomplishments of settlement houses

XII. The women's suffrage movement
    A. Women in the workforce
    B. Susan B. Anthony wanted Fourteenth Amendment to include women
    C. Split in the movement
      1. National Woman Suffrage Association promoted many feminist causes
      2. American Woman Suffrage Association promoted only women's suffrage
    D. National American Woman Suffrage Association
      1. Leadership
      2. Accomplishments
        a. Some western states had full suffrage
        b. Fewer and later successes in East
    E. Other women's reform organizations

XIII. The Supreme Court and laissez-faire
    A. Regulation of business by states
    B. Tensions between laissez-faire doctrines and growing sense of reform

Suggestions for Lecture Topics

For a lecture discussing the growth of American cities in the late-nineteenth century, see Sam Bass Warner's *Streetcar Suburbs* (2nd ed., 1978), a case study of Boston.

Oscar Handlin's *The Uprooted* (2nd ed., 1973) would be a good source for a lecture on the new immigration. For a discussion of the nativist response, see John Higham's *Strangers in the Land* (1955).

For a lecture on the influence of Darwinian thought on various aspects of American life, consider Paul F. Boller's *American Thought in Transition: The Impact of Evolutionary Naturalism, 1865–1900* (1969) and Richard Hofstadter's *Social Darwinism in American Thought* (rev. ed., 1955).

John L. Thomas's *Alternative America* (1983) is useful for a discussion of the social critics of the late-nineteenth century.

Finally, for a lecture on the women's suffrage movement, see Eleanor Flexner's *Century of Struggle* (rev. ed., 1975).

Multiple-Choice Questions

1. For the first time, more than half of America's population lived in urban areas after
   A. 1890.
   B. 1900.
   C. 1910.
 * D. 1920.

2. Suburbs grew around many cities in the late-nineteenth century because
   A. a series of fires in downtown Boston made people aware of the dangers of city living.
 * B. the spread of mass transit made commuting to the central city easier.
   C. the cities were running out of room; tall buildings were not yet possible, as the first electric elevator was not invented until 1924.
   D. all the above statements are true.

3. Frederick Law Olmsted
   A. developed the trolley system first used in Richmond, Virginia.
   B. built the first ten-story building, which was located in Chicago.
 * C. planned New York's Central Park.
   D. was an architect whose motto, "Form follows function," indicated his rebellion against Victorian design.

4. Problems in the cities at the turn of the century
   * A. were often handled most efficiently by local political bosses.
   B. were the subjects of Horatio Alger's novels.
   C. were generally solved by the widespread adoption of the "dumbbell" tenement plan.
   D. was the theme of the Columbian Exposition of 1893–1894.

5. After 1890 most immigrants were
   A. from northern and western Europe.
   * B. Jews and Catholics.
   C. of Teutonic and Celtic origin.
   D. from Mexico.

6. The most powerful of the American nativist groups was the
   A. Working Men's Party.
   B. America for Americans Society.
   * C. American Protective Association.
   D. Good Citizens League.

7. The high-water mark of immigration came in which decade?
   A. 1870–1879.
   B. 1880–1889.
   C. 1890–1899.
   * D. 1900–1909.

8. The exclusion of Chinese immigrants
   A. came only after the exclusion of immigrants from eastern Europe.
   * B. was first authorized in 1882, with a ten-year suspension.
   C. was caused mainly by fears of a virulent "Asian flu" that was often fatal to whites.
   D. was opposed by railroad company men.

9. The first university to make graduate work its chief concern was
   * A. Johns Hopkins University.
   B. Duke University.
   C. Yale University.
   D. the University of Georgia.

10. College teachers of the late-nineteenth century
    A. were almost always men.
    B. often taught several diverse subjects.
    C. often did not have advanced training in the subjects they taught.
    * D. are correctly represented by all the above.

11. All the following became more common between the Civil War and 1895 *except*
    A. women's access to higher education.
    B. the licensing of practitioners in certain professional fields.
    * C. core curricula of prescribed courses at major colleges and universities.
    D. public schools.

12. A strict Social Darwinist would object to all the following *except*
    A. the graduated income tax.
    B. sanitation and housing regulations.
    * C. a governmental policy of laissez-faire toward business.
    D. government welfare programs for the handicapped.

13. The man who coined the phrase "survival of the fittest" was
    A. Andrew Carnegie.
    B. Charles Darwin.
    C. William Graham Sumner.
    * D. Herbert Spencer.

14. Lester Frank Ward, chief spokesman for Reform Darwinism,
    A. argued that man, because he was made in the image of God, should not be included among the animals when discussing Darwinism.
    B. challenged religious leaders opposed to Darwin to prove the existence of a human soul or anything else that would set humans apart from animals.
    * C. argued that cooperation, and not competition, would best promote progress.
    D. wrote that man continued to evolve according to Darwin's principles of natural selection.

15. Who was the legal scholar that said, "The life of the law has not been logic, it has been experience"?
    * A. Oliver Wendell Holmes, Jr.
    B. Henry Adams
    C. John Marshall
    D. Leland Stanford

16. One of the major philosophical expressions of the evolutionary idea was *Pragmatism: A New Name for Some Old Ways of Thinking*, written by
    * A. William James.
    B. Henry James.
    C. Henry Adams.
    D. Oliver Wendell Holmes, Jr.

17. John Dewey, proponent of progressive education, believed that
    * A. children should study many subjects as a way of enlarging their personal experience.
    B. children should learn strict habits and standards of behavior early in life.
    C. schools are for academic education; moral and cultural education should come from the family and community.
    D. all the above statements are true.

18. Local colorists
    A. reflected a reunited nation celebrating its cultural diversity.
    B. expressed the nostalgia of an urbanizing and industrializing people.
    C. included George Washington Harris and Joel Chandler Harris.
    * D. are correctly represented by all the above statements.

19. William Dean Howells
    A. was an important literary critic.
    B. wrote several successful novels.
    C. was a proponent of literary realism.
    * D. is correctly represented by all the above statements.

20. In literature, Darwinism showed its greatest influence in a movement that emerged in the 1890s. Authors of this literary school—Frank Norris, Stephen Crane, Jack London, and others—expressed a sort of scientific determinism in their works. This movement is called
    * A. naturalism.
    B. realism.
    C. local color.
    D. socialist fiction.

21. *Sister Carrie* told the story of a woman who achieved great success as an actress, despite her lack of remorse for her somewhat immoral past. The author of *Sister Carrie* was
    A. Carrie Meeber.
    B. Stephen Crane.
    C. Henry James.
    * D. Theodore Dreiser.

22. In *Progress and Poverty*, Henry George argued that
    A. upward mobility in American society was no more than a myth.
    * B. no one should be allowed to make a profit from the land.

    C. the "single-tax" idea was immoral and probably unconstitutional.

    D. all the above statements are true.

23. Thorstein Veblen
* A. wrote about "conspicuous consumption" and "conspicuous leisure."
    B. wrote a book exposing the practices of Standard Oil.
    C. argued that too many industrial experts were becoming business managers.
    D. defended the productive efficiency of big business against its critics.

24. One of the earliest leaders of the social gospel movement in America was
* A. Washington Gladden.
    B. De Witt Talmage.
    C. Russell Conwell.
    D. Henry Ward Beecher.

25. Settlement houses were established to assist
    A. abused wives.
    B. alcoholics and drug addicts.
* C. slum dwellers.
    D. unwed mothers.

26. All the following statements about settlement houses are true *except*
    A. Jane Addams's Hull House was one of the most famous.
    B. they often organized political support for laws to help the poor.
    C. they brought cultural and educational opportunities to the slums.
* D. their Jewish orientation offended many non-Jews.

27. In 1869 the women's movement split on the issue of
    A. whether to grant suffrage to black as well as white women.
    B. the role of women in the religious professions.
    C. the political involvement of settlement houses in women's rights.
* D. whether or not the movement should concentrate on female suffrage to the exclusion of other feminist causes.

28. Which of the following statements best describes the status of women's suffrage in 1912?
      A. Women could vote in a few northeastern cities, but no state had adopted women's suffrage.
    * B. Nine states, all in the West, had adopted women's suffrage.
      C. Over a dozen states in the West and North allowed women to vote.
      D. Women's suffrage was confined to the Northeast.

29. Pope Leo XIII's *Rerum Novarum*
      A. declared erroneous such ideas as liberalism and rationalism.
    * B. expressed a new Catholic social doctrine condemning the poverty and degradation caused by capitalism.
      C. forbade workers to join labor unions.
      D. condemned women's suffrage.

30. The New York Consumers League
      A. organized boycotts to lower food prices.
      B. was formed by men who opposed female merchants in the marketplace.
    * C. sought to make the public aware of degrading labor conditions.
      D. promoted laissez-faire in business.

Suggested Essay Questions

1. Describe the growth of women's rights in this period. What accomplishments were made? What obstacles held the movement back?

2. How did immigration to America change in the latter half of the nineteenth century, and what was the response to that change?

3. Compare Social Darwinism and Reform Darwinism. What were the basic assumptions of each movement?

4. How did late-nineteenth-century American literature reflect the impact of Darwinian thought?

5. Among the responses to urbanization was the rise of the social gospel movement and settlement houses. Describe each of these, showing what problems each tried to correct and how they went about their tasks.

Chapter 21

GILDED AGE POLITICS AND AGRARIAN REVOLT

This chapter covers Gilded Age politics; the issues of the currency, tariffs, and civil service reform; the discontent of farmers; the rise of agrarian political movements; and the triumph of metropolitan and industrial values.

Chapter Outline

I. Gilded Age politics
   A. The traditional view of Gilded Age politics
      1. Few real differences between political parties
      2. Factors shaping Gilded Age politics
         a. Parties evenly divided
         b. No "strong" chief executive in Gilded Age
      3. Alliance between politics and business
      4. Voter turnout extremely high
   B. A newer view of Gilded Age politics
      1. Cultural conflicts between ethnic and religious groups shaped political parties
      2. The Republican Party—political insiders and active reformers
      3. The Democratic Party—political outsiders
      4. Immigration and politics
      5. Prohibition and politics

II. The administration of Rutherford B. Hayes
   A. Civil service reform
      1. Republican Party split between Stalwarts and Half-Breeds
      2. Hayes's policy toward civil service reform
      3. The removal of Chester A. Arthur and Alonzo Cornell
   B. Limiting the role of government

III. The administrations of James A. Garfield and Chester A. Arthur
   A. Garfield as president
      1. Election of 1880
      2. Garfield's assassination

    B. Arthur as president
        1. Arthur and reform
           a. Independence from the Stalwarts
           b. Pendleton Civil Service Act (1883)
        2. Attempts to lower tariff

IV. The first administration of Grover Cleveland
    A. Election of 1884
        1. Republicans
           a. James G. Blaine and the "Mulligan letters"
           b. Rise of the Mugwumps
        2. Democrats
           a. Grover Cleveland and early career of reform
           b. Cleveland and the potential scandal of an illegitimate child
        3. Last-minute blunders by Blaine
    B. Cleveland as a president
        1. Civil service reform
           a. Promised support for Pendleton Act
           b. But he removed many Republican officeholders
        2. Opposition to pension raids on Treasury
        3. Railroad regulation: the Interstate Commerce Commission
        4. The tariff
           a. Annual message of 1887 devoted entirely to tariff
           b. Bill for modest tariff reduction died in Congress

V. The administration of Benjamin Harrison
    A. Election of 1888
        1. Tariff was main issue
        2. Corruption and the phony "Murchison letter"
        3. Cleveland won popular vote, but lost election in electoral college
    B. Harrison as president
        1. Many federal officeholders removed on partisan grounds
        2. Pensions for Union veterans doubled
        3. Sherman Antitrust Act, 1890
        4. Sherman Silver Purchase Act, 1890
        5. McKinley Tariff of 1890
    C. Midterm elections of 1890
        1. Great Republican losses
        2. Reasons for Republican losses

VI. The problems of farmers
    A. Decline in commodity prices
        1. Domestic overproduction
        2. International competition
    B. Railroads and middlemen
        1. High railroad rates
        2. Little bargaining power
    C. High tariffs
    D. Debt
        1. Crop liens and land mortgages
        2. Forced to grow cash crops
    E. Inadequate currency
        1. Per-capita currency in circulation decreased 10 percent from 1865 to 1890
        2. The "Crime of 73"—Congress halted coinage of silver

VII. The Grange
    A. Oliver H. Kelley founded the Grange in 1867
        1. Membership in the Grange
        2. Goals of the Grange
    B. "Granger Laws"
        1. Regulation of railroad and warehouse rates
        2. Supreme Court upheld warehouse regulation in *Munn v. Illinois* (1877)
    C. Decline of the Grange
        1. Failure of economic ventures
        2. The Greenback Party

VIII. The Farmers' Alliance
    A. The growth of the Alliance
        1. Reasons for growth
        2. The Alliance and women
    B. The economic program of the Alliance
        1. Cooperatives and exchanges
        2. The subtreasury plan
    C. The Alliance and politics
        1. Western successes
            a. Record
            b. Mary Elizabeth Lease
            c. "Sockless Jerry" Simpson
        2. Southern successes
            a. Influenced Democratic Party
            b. Tom Watson

IX. The Populist Party
    A. Formed in Cincinnati in May 1891
    B. Omaha Platform (July 4, 1892)
        1. Finance
        2. Transportation
        3. Land
    C. Election of 1892
        1. James B. Weaver as Populist presidential candidate
        2. Weaver received over a million popular votes, carried four states

X. The Depression of 1893
    A. Cleveland's second administration
    B. Worker unrest
        1. In 1894, 750,000 workers on strike
        2. Millions unemployed
        3. Coxey's Army marched on Washington
    C. Midterm elections of 1894
        1. Republican victories
        2. Populists elected 13 congressman
    D. Depression focused attention on currency issue
        1. Repeal of the Sherman Silver Purchase Act
        2. Populists and the silver question

XI. The election of 1896
    A. Candidates and positions
        1. Republicans nominated William McKinley on gold-standard platform
        2. Democrats nominated pro-silver William Jennings Bryan after his "cross of gold" speech
        3. Rather than split silver vote, Populists also nominated Bryan
    B. Victory for McKinley
        1. Bryan carried most of the West and South
        2. Bryan unable to attract votes of midwestern farmers and eastern workers

XII. The new era
    A. The triumph of metropolitan and industrial America over rural and agrarian America
    B. New gold discoveries ended the depression
    C. The coming of the Spanish-American War ended much controversy over tariffs and the currency

Suggestions for Lecture Topics

For a discussion of the ethnocultural basis of Gilded Age politics, see Paul Klepper's *The Third Electoral System, 1853–1892* (1979).

A lecture on the Populists could take several approaches. John D. Hicks's *The Populist Revolt* (1931) includes a useful discussion of the farmers' grievances. Compare this with Lawrence Goodwin's *The Populist Moment* (1978). Another lecture—one that students will find unforgettable—could interpret Frank L. Baum's *The Wizard of Oz* as an allegory of the Populist revolt; see Henry M. Littlefield's "The Wizard of Oz: Parable on Populism" (*American Quarterly* 16 [1964]: 47–58). Finally, for a lecture on the important election of 1896, see Robert F. Durden's *The Climax of Populism* (1965).

Multiple-Choice Questions

1. One issue on which Democrats and Republicans differed in the Gilded Age was
   A. immigration.
   B. civil service reform.
   C. the regulation of big business.
   * D. the tariff.

2. Which of the following was *not* a factor in shaping Gilded Age politics?
   A. Politics was seen more as a way to get office than a way to press certain issues.
   * B. Business remained separate from politics.
   C. In national politics, neither party could keep both a majority in Congress and a president in the White House.
   D. None of the presidents in this period could be described as a strong leader.

3. Voters in the Gilded Age
   A. were not concerned with the issues of civil service reform, currency, the tariff, immigration, and monopolies.
   B. were deeply concerned with corruption in national politics.
   * C. turned out in large numbers—70 percent to 80 percent voter turnout was not rare.
   D. were usually unaware of the candidates' stands on issues.

4. Which of the following would probably *not* have been a Republican in the Gilded Age?
    A. a New England Protestant
    * B. a German immigrant
    C. a nativist
    D. a black man

5. Which of the following would probably *not* have been a Democrat in the Gilded Age?
    A. a southern white
    B. a Jewish immigrant
    * C. a prohibitionist
    D. an atheist

6. The Stalwarts
    A. were a faction in the Democratic Party.
    B. generally favored a lenient southern policy.
    * C. were led by Roscoe Conkling.
    D. generally favored civil service reform.

7. Which of the following best describes Rutherford B. Hayes's policy of civil service reform?
    A. Hayes was able to get several civil service reform bills through Congress, but the new laws were not enforced..
    B. Hayes was against civil service reform, but Congress passed several bills over his vetoes.
    C. Hayes was personally against civil service reform, but he signed several bills into law for political expediency.
    * D. Hayes was unable to get civil service reform legislation through Congress, but in an executive order set up his own rules for merit appointments.

8. Chester A. Arthur
    A. was elected to the presidency with less than half of the popular vote.
    B. died in office of Bright's disease.
    C. was elected to the presidency despite untrue rumors concerning gambling debts circulated by the Democrats just before the election.
    * D. was connected with the New York Customs House corruption before he became president.

9. The Pendleton Civil Service Act
   * A. provided for appointments to a number of government jobs on the basis of competitive exams.
   B. was signed into law by James Garfield in 1883.
   C. was the leading issue in the election of 1884.
   D. set up the first racial quotas for government service jobs.

10. During the campaign for the presidential election of 1884, many prominent Republican leaders and supporters left the party because
   A. the Mugwumps, a reform faction, had gained power within the party.
   B. Grover Cleveland was named as the father of an illegitimate child.
   * C. the discovery of more "Mulligan letters" further linked candidate James G. Blaine to the railroads.
   D. the party refused to take a firm stand on the tariff.

11. Grover Cleveland
   A. was the first Democrat elected to the White House since 1856.
   B. thought that "just as the people support the government, so should the government support the people."
   C. refused to fire federal workers on partisan grounds.
   * D. is correctly described by all the above statements.

12. The Interstate Commerce Act was created
   * A. initially to regulate the railroads.
   B. despite President Cleveland's veto.
   C. because the railroads refused to turn over to the government 30 million acres of land subject to forfeiture.
   D. all the above are true.

13. In 1887, President Cleveland devoted his entire annual message to the tariff. Congress reacted by
   A. significantly reducing the tariff.
   B. significantly increasing the tariff.
   * C. refusing to reduce the tariff significantly, despite Cleveland's call for such a reduction.
   D. refusing to increase the tariff significantly, despite Cleveland's call for such an increase.

14. Benjamin Harrison was elected president
   A. in a campaign waged mainly on the issue of currency reform.

    * B. although he received fewer popular votes than the loser, Grover Cleveland.

    C. despite publication of the phony "Murchison letter," linking him to British free-traders.

    D. in the only Gilded Age campaign not marred by dirty tricks and personal attacks on the candidates.

15. During the first two years of President Benjamin Harrison's term,

    A. Congress passed the Sherman Antitrust Act.

    B. the pension rolls of Union veterans almost doubled.

    C. Republicans controlled both the White House and Congress for the only time between 1875 and 1895.

    * D. all the above statements are true.

16. The Sherman Silver Purchase Act of 1890

    A. decreased by about one-third the amount of silver purchased by the federal government.

    * B. had the support of senators from the new western states.

    C. did not have the support of debt-ridden farmers, who were afraid of the inflation it might cause.

    D. limited the amount of silver an individual could buy in one year, but not the overall amount he could own.

17. In 1890,

    * A. Democratic candidates for Congress were the big winners.

    B. Republican candidates for Congress were the big winners.

    C. Benjamin Harrison lost in his bid for reelection.

    D. Benjamin Harrison won in his bid for reelection.

18. The so-called "Crime of '73" referred to

    * A. the congressional decision to drop the provision for the coinage of silver.

    B. the revised tariff issued in 1873 that raised duties nearly 50 percent.

    C. the arrest of eight farmers who were protesting unfair railroad rates.

    D. President Cleveland's veto of a bill to aid victims (mainly farmers) of a severe Texas drought.

19. "Sockless Jerry" Simpson

    A. was secretary of agriculture under Harrison.

    B. was the economist whose books influenced passage of the Sherman Silver Purchase Act.

    C. was a leading Union veteran and, for a time, pension commissioner.

    * D. was a Kansas Populist leader.

20. Between 1865 and 1890, the per-capita amount of currency in circulation
    A. stayed fairly constant.
    B. increased by about 10 percent.
    C. increased by about 30 percent.
  * D. decreased by about 10 percent.

21. Mary Elizabeth Lease
    A. founded the Patrons of Husbandry (the Grange).
  * B. advised farmers to "raise less corn and more hell."
    C. was the presidential candidate of the Greenback Party in 1892.
    D. wrote the 1892 Omaha Platform for the People's Party.

22. The Supreme Court case of *Munn v. Illinois* (1877)
  * A. upheld a law involving warehouse regulation.
    B. overturned "Granger Laws" in that state.
    C. upheld the constitutionality of the Bland-Allison Act.
    D. allowed the Farmers' Alliance to have separate organizations for Negro members.

23. Which of the following statements about the subtreasury plan is *not* true?
    A. The plan allowed farmers to store their crops in government warehouses and secure a loan at low interest for up to 80 percent of their crop's value.
  * B. The plan would have helped large farmers at the expense of small farmers.
    C. The plan allowed farmers to hold their crops for a good price.
    D. Through the issue of new legal-tender notes, the plan promoted inflation.

24. All of the following were included in the 1892 Omaha platform of the People's Party *except*
  * A. halting the free and unlimited coinage of silver.
    B. increasing the amount of currency in circulation to $50 per capita.
    C. nationalizing the railroads.
    D. restricting immigration.

25. Coxey's Army
    A. put down a rebellion of farmers in eastern Kansas.
  * B. demanded that the federal government provide unemployed people with meaningful work.

    C. marched down several of New York's main streets to protest Cleveland's failure to end the Depression of 1893.

    D. was led by future president Theodore Roosevelt.

26. The party that benefited most from the Depression of 1893 elections of 1894 was the

    A. Populist.

*   B. Republican.

    C. Democrat.

    D. Greenbackers.

27. "You shall not crucify mankind upon a cross of gold!" This statement was made by

*   A. William Jennings Bryan, at the 1896 Democratic convention.

    B. William McKinley, at the 1896 Republican convention.

    C. Grover Cleveland, in a speech before Congress.

    D. Thomas E. Watson, in the Georgia state legislature.

28. In the presidential election of 1896, William Jennings Bryan

    A. was the candidate of both the Democratic and Populist parties.

    B. carried most of the states in the West and South.

    C. could not win the votes of urban workers in the Northeast.

*   D. is correctly described by all the above statements.

29. One factor that helped end the Depression of 1893 was

    A. the Dingley Tariff of 1893, which lowered the average duty by over one-third.

*   B. new discoveries of gold which led to inflation.

    C. the increased production needs of World War I.

    D. a series of price supports for distressed farmers.

30. One theme of Gilded Age politics was

*   A. the triumph of business and industry.

    B. the triumph of agricultural interests.

    C. the rise of the common man.

    D. the extension of government into the private sphere.

Suggested Essay Questions

1. Describe Gilded Age politics. What were the main issues? What factors influenced voters to be either Republican or Democrat?

2. Describe the controversy over civil service reform in the Gilded Age. Which groups favored such reforms? What types of reforms did they achieve?

3. What problems did American farmers face in 1890?

4. What were the main planks of the 1892 Omaha platform of the Populist Party? How would these provisions have helped solve the problems farmers faced?

5. "By the end of the Gilded Age, the values of a metropolitan and industrial America had triumphed over those of a rural and agrarian America." What evidence supports this statement?

Chapter 22

THE COURSE OF EMPIRE

This chapter covers American diplomacy after the Civil War, the reasons for American expansion, and American foreign policy through the administration of Theodore Roosevelt.

Chapter Outline

I. Diplomacy after the Civil War
    A. Little concern for foreign affairs
        1. Domestic affairs seemed important
        2. "Free security" for America
    B. Purchase of Alaska

II. Expansion in Pacific
    A. Americans had been interested in Pacific islands for many years
    B. Samoa
    C. Hawaii
        1. Boom in sugar growing as result of trade agreement with United States
        2. In 1887 Americans in Hawaii forced king to grant constitutional government
        3. When Liliuokalani ascended to throne and tried to restore power, Americans staged revolution
        4. Rebels refused to disband, proclaimed Republic of Hawaii

III. Reasons for American expansion
    A. Markets
    B. Naval power
        1. Alfred Thayer Mahan argued that national greatness and prosperity depended on sea power
        2. The expansion of the navy
    C. Racial thought
        1. Social Darwinism seemed to justify imperialism
        2. Alleged Anglo-Saxon superiority
        3. Josiah Strong and the sanction of religion

IV. The Spanish–American War
  A. "Cuba libre"
    1. Rebellion broke out in Cuba
    2. American views of the Cuban revolt
      a. "Butcher" Weyler
      b. Yellow journalism
    3. President Cleveland refused to interfere
  B. America headed for war
    1. McKinley elected on platform endorsing Cuban independence
    2. Spain offered Cuba autonomy in return for peace
    3. de Lôme letter
    4. Explosion of the *Maine*
    5. Spain gave McKinley power to secure peace through negotiations
    6. The United States declares war on Spain
      a. Congress declared Cuba independent
      b. Teller Amendment said America did not want Cuba
    7. Reasons America went to war
      a. Popular pressure
      b. Business community demanded quick settlement
      c. Political expediency
  C. Campaigns
    1. Manila
    2. Cuba
  D. The end of the war
    1. Armistice and peace protocol signed
    2. War casualty figures

V. The annexation debate
  A. The demand for annexation of the Philippines
    1. Little demand before the war
    2. McKinley's reasons for annexation
      a. National honor
      b. Commerce
      c. Racial superiority
      d. Altruism
    3. Other areas annexed at this time
      a. Hawaii (1898)
      b. Wake Island (1898)
  B. The Treaty of Paris in the Senate
    1. Opposition
    2. William Jennings Bryan influenced vote to approve

C. Attempts to subdue Filipino insurrectionists
D. Anti-imperialist groups strong in America

VI. Organizing America's new acquisitions
    A. Philippines
        1. Philippine Government Act (1902) made Philippines an unorganized territory
        2. Tydings-McDuffie Act (1934) offered independence in ten years
    B. Puerto Rico
        1. Foraker Act (1900) established civil government
        2. U.S. citizenship in 1917
    C. Cuba
        1. Trouble between military government and Cuban rebels
        2. Platt Amendment

VII. The Far East
    A. The Open Door
        1. Following the Sino-Japanese War, China attracted the great powers in a scramble for control
        2. Open-Door Policy, outlined by Secretary of State John Hay urged major powers to keep China trade open to all countries on an equal basis
    B. The Boxer Rebellion
        1. When Chinese nationalists laid siege to foreign embassies in Peking, multinational force went in to relieve embassies
        2. Hay urged other countries to "preserve Chinese territorial and administrative integrity"

VIII. The rise of Theodore Roosevelt
    A. The election of 1900
        1. Democrats chose William Jennings Bryan as presidential candidate on anti-imperialist platform
        2. Republicans chose William McKinley again, with Theodore Roosevelt as vice-presidential candidate, on pro-imperialist platform
        3. Victory for Republicans
    B. Assassination of McKinley made Roosevelt president
    C. Roosevelt's character

IX. America's relations with Japan
    A. Fear of Japan in Philippines
        1. Taft-Katsura Agreement
        2. Root-Takahira Agreement

B. Mutual distrust
    1. Fear of "yellow Peril"
    2. "Gentlemen's Agreement"

X. Roosevelt's foreign policy
  A. The Panama Canal
    1. American moves for a canal
      a. Hay-Pauncefote Treaty (1901) ratified
      b. Hay-Herrán Treaty (1903) ratified, but Colombian senate held out for $25 million
      c. Colombian province of Panama, with American aid, claimed independence and got canal contract from United States
    2. America built the canal
      a. Colombia resented America's actions concerning Panama
      b. Canal opened (1914)
  B. The Roosevelt Corollary
    1. An economic crisis in the Dominican Republic seemed to invite foreign intervention
    2. Roosevelt announced his Corollary to the Monroe Doctrine—the United States could intervene in its neighbors' affairs to forestall foreign intervention
    3. In the Dominican Republic, the United States installed a customs collector who applied part of the revenues to debt payments

XI. America and Europe
  A. At Roosevelt's insistence, countries met in conference to settle question of French domination in Morocco
  B. Roosevelt won the 1906 Nobel Peace Prize
  C. In show of goodwill and force, Roosevelt sent American navy on tour around the world

Suggestions for Lecture Topics

Emily S. Rosenberg's *Spreading the American Dream* (1982) describes the reasons and justifications for American expansionism. This would be a good source for an introductory lecture for the chapter.

A lecture on the anti-imperialists would be useful. See Robert L. Beisner's *Twelve against Empire* (1968).

Instructors who wish to lecture on military aspects of the Spanish-American War will find G. J. A. O'Toole's *The Spanish War* (1984) to be a good source of information. David F. Trask's *The War with Spain in 1898* (1981) is more comprehensive.

For a lecture on the Panama Canal, see David McCullough's *The Path between the Seas* (1977). This is a big book, but it is full of interesting details.

Multiple-Choice Questions

1. The United States wanted to acquire some control over the Pacific island groups of Samoa and Hawaii
   A. because of oil deposits found there.
   B. despite Secretary of State William Seward's urgings for Americans to resist the expansionist impulse.
   * C. because the islands offered strategic locations for naval bases.
   D. despite the Treaty of Washington (1871), which ceded the islands to the Russians.

2. Queen Liliuokalani
   A. was forced by Americans living in Hawaii to grant a constitutional government for the islands in 1899.
   B. welcomed American sugar planters to Hawaii.
   C. was an American pretender to the Hawaiian throne.
   * D. opposed the Americanization of Hawaii.

3. John Hay
   A. was Grover Cleveland's secretary of state.
   B. was James Garfield and Chester Arthur's secretary of state.
   * C. established the "Open Door" policy to preserve Chinese territorial and administrative integrity.
   D. was appointed by President Cleveland to a special commission to investigate the Hawaiian situation.

4. *The Influence of Sea Power upon History, 1660–1783*, a book arguing that national greatness arose from sea power, was written by
   A. Albert J. Beveridge.
   B. John Fiske.
   * C. Alfred Thayer Mahan.
   D. John W. Burgess.

5. Josiah Strong
    A. argued in his book *American Political Ideas* that Anglo-Saxons were destined to dominate the globe.
  * B. wrote *Our Country: Its Possible Future and Its Present Crisis*, which added the sanction of religion to the expansionists' argument.
    C. was one of the earliest government officials to speak out against imperialism.
    D. used Darwinian concepts to show how American expansionism hurt the people of the areas America annexed.

6. Which of the following occurred first?
  * A. America's purchase of Alaska
    B. America's annexation of Hawaii
    C. America's treaty with Samoa for a naval base at Pago Pago
    D. passage of the Teller Amendment

7. Americans felt secure after the Civil War because
    A. militarily strong neighbors in the Western Hemisphere could help protect America.
  * B. wide oceans acted as buffers on each side.
    C. by 1870 the United States had the strongest navy in the world.
    D. all the above statements are true.

8. The term "yellow journalism" arose from
    A. the use of native reporters in the press coverage of the battles in the Philippines.
    B. the press coverage of the trials of three Cuban officials who were accused of accepting bribes in the form of gold shipments from insurrectionists.
  * C. the circulation war between William Randolph Hearst's New York *Journal* and Joseph Pulitzer's New York *World* during the Cuban crisis.
    D. the use of propaganda in underground newspapers published by the Cuban insurrectionists.

9. America went to war against Spain because of all of the following *except*
    A. the buildup of public pressure for war.
  * B. Spain's refusal to discuss terms for peace and Cuba's independence.

   C. Spanish General Valeriano Weyler's alleged mistreat-
      ment of Cuban civilians.
   D. Americans compared the Cuban insurrection to their own
      American Revolution.

10. The Battleship *Maine*
    A. exploded as it left Miami for Cuba.
  * B. became a battle cry in the Spanish-American War, al-
       though blame for the explosion could never be fixed.
    C. was carrying arms to the Cuban insurrectionists.
    D. disappeared at sea with no trace, but William R. Hearst's
       newspapers claimed that Spain had ordered it sunk.

11. The first major victory for American forces in the Spanish-
    American War was at
    A. San Juan Hill.
    B. Santiago.
  * C. Manila Bay.
    D. Havana.

12. In the Spanish-American War,
    A. America's victory could in large part be attributed to
       expert preparation.
  * B. more American soldiers died from disease than in battle.
    C. the American victory in the decisive battle at Santiago
       depended on assistance from German forces.
    D. America finally settled the question of freedom of the
       seas.

13. Which of the following territories did America *not* gain from
    the Treaty of Paris following the end of the Spanish-American
    War?
    A. Guam
    B. Puerto Rico
  * C. Cuba
    D. The Philippines

14. The Treaty of Paris
  * A. was opposed by most Democrats and Populists.
    B. was ratified in the Senate over the protests of William
       Jennings Bryan.
    C. provided for Spain to pay to the United States $10,000 for
       each American soldier killed in the war.
    D. provided for Hawaiian autonomy.

15. The de Lôme letter
    A. revealed the location of Spanish troops in Cuba.
    B. was the first of the Cuban insurrectionists' overtures for peace.
    C. blamed the destruction of the battleship *Maine* on Spanish agents.
  * D. referred to President McKinley as a weak and cowardly leader, thus further straining relations between the United States and Cuba.

16. In the election of 1900,
    A. Democratic candidate William Jennings Bryan disagreed with Republican candidate William McKinley on imperialism, but not on tariff reduction or monetary policy.
    B. there were few differences in the platforms of the two parties.
  * C. the nation's return to prosperity was probably the Republicans' biggest asset.
    D. Republicans promised to end America's policy of annexation.

17. The Tydings-McDuffie Act of 1934
  * A. offered independence to the Philippines in ten years.
    B. provided American troops to put down a revolt in the Philippines.
    C. granted Puerto Rico its commonwealth status.
    D. made inhabitants of Puerto Rico citizens of the United States.

18. All of the following opposed America's annexation of the Philippines *except*
    A. Andrew Carnegie.
    B. Samuel Gompers.
  * C. Albert J. Beveridge.
    D. William James.

19. The Platt Amendment to the Army Appropriation Bill of 1901
    A. removed General Leonard Wood, who opposed American annexation of Cuba, from his post as Cuba's military governor.
    B. arranged for a Cuban election to decide the issue of annexation.
  * C. sharply restricted the independence of Cuba's new government.
    D. set up the Army Yellow Fever Commission under Dr. Walter Reed.

20. Which president sent the "Great White Fleet" around the world in a show of America's naval might?
    A. Grover Cleveland
    B. Benjamin Harrison
    C. William McKinley
  * D. Theodore Roosevelt

21. The Hay-Herrán Treaty
    A. ended the Spanish-American War.
    B. ended the insurrection in the Philippines.
  * C. concerned America's right to build a canal in Panama.
    D. failed to pass in the Senate.

22. The most important reason for American expansionism in the 1890s was
  * A. economic (to gain markets and raw materials).
    B. military (to obtain naval bases and coaling stations).
    C. racial (to spread the superior characteristics of Anglo-Saxon institutions and peoples).
    D. religious (to spread Christianity).

23. In the so-called Gentlemen's Agreement of 1907, President Roosevelt
  * A. stopped the flow of Japanese immigrants to America.
    B. acknowledged Japan's dominance of Korea.
    C. agreed not to bring American armed forces into the Russo-Japanese War.
    D. agreed to help finance the Russian effort to seize Korea from the Japanese.

24. As a result of Japan's show of strength in the Russo-Japanese War,
    A. the United States Congress voted financial and military aid to Korea to help prevent a Japanese invasion of the Korean peninsula.
    B. America was quick to send money and support troops to aid Russia.
    C. Congress lifted the limitations it had previously set on Japanese immigration.
  * D. Americans began to doubt the security of the Philippines.

25. The "Boxer Rebellion" took place in
    A. 1891.
  * B. 1900.
    C. the Philippines.
    D. Puerto Rico.

26. When the United States and Colombia could not agree on a price for the Canal Zone,
    - A. the matter was submitted to an international board for arbitration.
    - B. Roosevelt sent the army to Colombia to force Colombian leaders to accept the U.S. offer.
    - * C. the Colombian province of Panama rebelled against Colombia.
    - D. Colombian leaders offered the deal to the British.

27. The Roosevelt Corollary
    - A. encouraged American bankers to help finance the shaky Latin American governments.
    - * B. stated that the United States could intervene in the affairs of Western Hemisphere countries to forestall the intervention of other powers.
    - C. rescinded most of the provisions of the Monroe Doctrine.
    - D. justified American intervention in the Far East.

28. Emilio Aguinaldo
    - * A. was the Filipino rebel leader.
    - B. led the Spanish forces against Teddy Roosevelt's Rough Riders.
    - C. was installed as Cuba's governor in 1898.
    - D. was the martyred leader of the Cuban rebellion.

29. Which of the following statements about Teddy Roosevelt is *not* true?
    - A. He had been sick as a child.
    - B. He was known as an outdoorsman.
    - C. He was a historian.
    - * D. He became president when Harrison was assassinated.

30. Roosevelt's intervention in the Russo-Japanese War and the Moroccan dispute
    - A. strained America's relations with Russia.
    - * B. won for Roosevelt the Nobel Peace Prize of 1906.
    - C. involved the use of armed forces without the consent of Congress.
    - D. weakened his image around the world.

Suggested Essay Questions

1. What were the reasons for American expansionism at the turn of the century? What justifications did Americans offer for expansionism?

2. How did Hawaii become part of the United States?

3. Describe the steps leading to America's war with Spain in 1898. Was war justified?

4. What effect did American ownership of the Philippines have on U.S. foreign policy?

5. What was the Open Door Policy, and how did it come about?

Chapter 23

PROGRESSIVISM: ROOSEVELT, TAFT, AND WILSON

This chapter covers the antecedents and main features of progressivism and the domestic policies of the administrations of Roosevelt, Taft, and Wilson.

Chapter Outline

I. Elements of progressive reform
    A. Paradoxes in progressivism
        1. Progressivism as a "more respectable" populism
        2. Elements of conservatism in progressivism
    B. Antecedents to progressivism
        1. Populism
        2. The Mugwumps
        3. Socialism
    C. The muckrakers

II. Features of progressivism
    A. Greater democracy
        1. Direct primaries
        2. The initiative, referendum, and recall
        3. Popular election of senators
    B. "The gospel of efficiency"
        1. Frederick W. Taylor and efficiency
        2. New ideas for municipal government—commission system and the city-manager plan
        3. Robert La Follette and the "Wisconsin Idea"
    C. Corporate regulation
        1. The trend toward regulation
        2. Who should do regulating
    D. Social justice
        1. Labor laws
            a. Child labor
            b. The Supreme Court and state labor laws
        2. Prohibition

III. Roosevelt's progressivism—first term
   A. Trusts
      1. Roosevelt thought effective regulation better than attempts to restore competition
      2. Decision in *United States v. E. C. Knight* (1895) held manufacturing to be intrastate activity
      3. Supreme Court ordered the Northern Securities Company dissolved
   B. Anthracite coal strike of 1902
      1. Workers struck for more pay and fewer hours
      2. Mine owners closed mines
      3. Roosevelt threatened to take over the mines, forcing the owners to submit to arbitration panel
   C. More regulation
      1. An act created the Department of Commerce and Labor, including the Bureau of Corporations
      2. The Elkins Act made it illegal to take as well as give railroad rebates
      3. Break up of Standard Oil and American Tobacco
   D. The election of 1904

IV. Roosevelt's progressivism—second term
   A. The Hepburn Act of 1906
      1. Gave the Interstate Commerce Commission power to set maximum rates
      2. Other provisions of act
   B. Movement to regulate food processors and makers of drug and patent medicines
      1. Upton Sinclair's *The Jungle* and meat-packers
      2. The Meat Inspection Act (1906)
      3. The Pure Food and Drug Act (1906)
   C. Conservation
   D. The election of 1908
      1. Roosevelt handpicked William Howard Taft as his successor
      2. Taft won over Democratic candidate William Jennings Bryan

V. Taft's progressivism
   A. Taft's early career
   B. Tariff reform
      1. Taft wanted lower tariff
      2. New tariff raised many rates
      3. Fearful of party split, Taft backed new tariff

      C. Ballinger-Pinchot controversy
        1. When Chief of Forestry Gifford Pinchot discovered possible corrupt dealings by Secretary of the Interior Richard Ballinger, he went public with his accusations
        2. Fired by Taft for insubordination
        3. Tarnished Taft's image as progressive
      D. The Taft-Roosevelt break
        1. Review of accomplishments of Taft's administration
        2. Although Roosevelt won most Republican state primaries, Taft controlled party machinery and won nomination
        3. Roosevelt became the nominee of the Progressive Party

VI. The election of 1912
      A. The rise of Woodrow Wilson
      B. Taft had little chance in the election
      C. Roosevelt's "New Nationalism"
        1. Influence of Herbert Croly
        2. Hamiltonian means to achieve Jeffersonian ends
      D. Wilson's "New Freedom"
        1. Influence of Louis Brandeis
        2. Restoration of an economy of small-scale competitive units
      E. Election figures—victory for Wilson
      F. Significance of the election of 1912
        1. A high-water mark for progressivism
        2. Brought Democrats back into effective national power
        3. Brought southerners back into national and international affairs

VII. Wilson's progressivism
      A. Relied more on party politics than popular support to pass reforms
      B. Underwood-Simmons Tariff (1913)
        1. Lowered average duty by about one-fifth
        2. To replace lost revenue, began income tax
      C. The Glass-Owen Federal Reserve Act (1913)
      D. Wilson and trusts
        1. The Clayton Antitrust Act of 1914
          a. Outlawed price discrimination, "tying" agreements, interlocking directorates in large corpo-

rations, and the practice whereby a corporation buys up the stock of its competitors to gain control of the market
- b. Farm labor organizations exempted
2. Wilson's administration showed friendly attitude toward business
E. Little social-justice legislation before 1916
F. A resurgence of progressivism
1. Wilson added to his progressive record to form a broad base of support for 1916 election
2. Farm reforms—Federal Farm Loan Act (1916) and Smith-Hughes Act (1917) funded farm demonstration agents and agricultural and mechanical education in high schools
3. Labor reform
- a. Keating-Owen Act (1916) excluded from interstate commerce goods manufactured by children under fourteen
- b. Adamson Act (1916) provided for eight-hour day for railroad workers
G. Under Wilson, progressivism became a movement for positive government

VIII. Paradoxes of progressivism
A. Disfranchisement of blacks
B. Decisions made more by faceless policy-makers
C. Decline in voter participation

Suggestions for Lecture Topics

Arthur S. Link and Richard L. McCormick's *Progressivism* (1983) is a good recent overview of the subject that would be a useful start for several lectures. See also the relevant portions of Otis L. Graham, Jr.'s *The Great Campaigns: Reform and War in America, 1900–1928* (1971).

A discussion of the various historical interpretations of progressivism would be both interesting and instructive. See *The Progressive Era*, edited by Lewis L. Gould (1974), and *Progressivism: The Critical Issues*, edited by David M. Kennedy (1971).

For a lecture comparing Woodrow Wilson and Theodore Roosevelt, use John M. Cooper's *The Warrior and the Priest* (1983) or John Blum's *The Progressive Presidents* (1980).

Robert M. Crunden's *Ministers of Reform* (1982) answers the question "What is Progressivism?" by discussing the spectrum of reform leaders and their achievements. Louis Filler's older *Crusaders for American Liberalism* (1939, published in 1968 as *The Muckrakers*) would also be good for a lecture that approaches progressivism by looking at the leaders involved.

Multiple-Choice Questions

1. Which of the following would *not* be considered an antecedent to progressivism?
     A. populism
     B. the Mugwumps
   * C. the Stalwarts
     D. the Socialist Party

2. The author of *Wealth against Commonwealth* was
   * A. Henry Demarest Lloyd.
     B. Lincoln Steffens.
     C. Ida M. Tarbell.
     D. Ray Stannard Baker.

3. The Sixteenth Amendment
     A. authorized the popular election of senators.
     B. gave women the right to vote.
     C. called for direct primaries.
   * D. authorized the federal income tax.

4. Frederick W. Taylor
     A. was an Oregon reformer responsible for many progressive measures enacted there.
   * B. was the original "efficiency expert."
     C. wrote *How the Other Half Lives*.
     D. was the progressive governor of Wisconsin.

5. The most influential proponent of efficiency in government was
     A. Joseph W. Folk.
     B. Charles Evans Hughes.
   * C. Robert M. La Follette.
     D. Hoke Smith.

6. The commission plan of city government was first adopted in
   * A. Galveston, Texas.
     B. Staunton, Virginia.
     C. Richmond, Virginia.
     D. Durham, North Carolina.

7. Progressives concerned with social justice called for
    A. child labor laws.
    B. regulations on the hours of work for women.
    C. prohibition.
  * D. all the above.

8. During the anthracite coal strike of 1902,
  * A. President Theodore Roosevelt won more support for his use of the "big stick" against big business.
    B. thousands of striking miners marched on Washington, starting a riot that lasted three days.
    C. President Theodore Roosevelt threatened to use the army to force strikers back to work.
    D. arbitrators awarded the miners all their demands.

9. In the case of *Lochner v. New York* (1905), the Supreme Court
    A. ruled that immigrants could vote in state, but not national, elections.
  * B. struck down a ten-hour workday law because it violated the workers' "liberty of contract."
    C. upheld an Alabama prohibition law.
    D. broke up the American Tobacco Company.

10. The Hepburn Act of 1906
    A. was the first federal law regulating railroads.
  * B. authorized the Interstate Commerce Commission to set maximum rates for railroads.
    C. in effect outlawed the Northern Securities Company.
    D. is correctly described by all the above statements.

11. The title of the Upton Sinclair novel that showed the need for the Meat Inspection Act of 1906 was
    A. *Chicago.*
    B. *Jaws.*
  * C. *The Jungle.*
    D. *Maggie.*

12. In the area of conservation, Theodore Roosevelt
    A. believed strongly that natural resources should be preserved, but felt that this was a matter for state, not federal, action.
    B. angered many conservationists by his appointment of Gifford Pinchot, a businessman with no experience in conservation, as head of the Division of Forestry.
  * C. used the Forest Reserve Act to withdraw some 125 million acres of timberland from use.

    D. vetoed a bill authorizing a National Conservation Commission.

13. William Howard Taft, the Republican candidate for president in 1908,
 * A. was Roosevelt's choice as his successor.
   B. was described by many journalists as "the ultimate politician."
   C. found solid support from voters only in the South and Southwest.
   D. was, in the Republican tradition, opposed to a lower tariff.

14. The Ballinger-Pinchot controversy
   A. resulted in the immediate dismissal of Secretary of the Interior Richard A. Ballinger for his involvement in corrupt land dealings.
   B. proved to the public that Taft supported the conservation of America's resources.
 * C. contributed to the growing rift between Taft and Roosevelt.
   D. is correctly represented by all the above statements.

15. As president, Taft
   A. was able to unite a faction-ridden Republican Party with his towering personality.
   B. opposed the Sixteenth and Seventeenth Amendments.
   C. brought less than one-third the number of antitrust suits then were prosecuted under Roosevelt.
 * D. in four years withdrew more public lands than Roosevelt had in nearly eight.

16. Taft won the nomination of the Republican Party for president in 1912
   A. because of his good showing in the presidential primaries.
   B. despite a bargain for delegate votes between Roosevelt and Robert M. La Follette.
 * C. because his forces controlled the convention machinery.
   D. although he had indicated in 1910 that he would not seek a second term.

17. Woodrow Wilson is correctly represented by all the following *except*
   A. he was a college professor and president.
 * B. he was the leading Roman Catholic politician at the turn of the century.

     C. he was the progressive governor of New York.

     D. he was influenced by Louis D. Brandeis.

18. Theodore Roosevelt's "New Nationalism"
  * A. meant that government intervention, once identified with business interests, should be used to achieve democratic goals.
  B. was a conservative philosophy of a limited role of government.
  C. favored the growth of big business.
  D. meant that the federal government should concern itself with problems of social justice, and let big business take care of itself.

19. Federal money for farm demonstration agents was provided by
  * A. the Smith-Lever Act.
  B. the La Follette Farm Education Act.
  C. the Keating-Owen Act.
  D. the Glass-Owen Act.

20. The election of Wilson in 1912
  A. brought the Democrats into effective national power for the first time in over half a century.
  B. signaled the return of southerners to national and international affairs for the first time since the Civil War.
  C. altered the character of the Republican schism.
  * D. is correctly described by all the above statements.

21. To get support for his progressive reforms, Wilson
  A. did not trust Congress, so he usually took his case directly to the people.
  B. acted through a bipartisan coalition of Progressives.
  * C. relied on the party loyalty of Democrats.
  D. found he could not trust most Democratic congressmen to stick with him.

22. The Underwood-Simmons Tariff
  A. raised the average tariff, and hence was supported by Wilson.
  B. raised the average tariff, and hence was opposed by Wilson.
  C. lowered the average tariff, and hence was opposed by Wilson.
  * D. lowered the average tariff, and hence was supported by Wilson.

23. Herbert Croly
    * A. wrote *The Promise of American Life* (1909).
    B. was the direct source of much of Taft's political philosophy.
    C. argued that the federal government should restore competition rather than regulate monopolies.
    D. is correctly represented by all the above statements.

24. The Clayton Antitrust Act, passed in 1914,
    A. was more lenient toward big business than were previous acts.
    * B. outlawed price discrimination and "tying" agreements.
    C. contained a clause explicitly including farm labor organizations in the application of the act.
    D. was considered by Wilson to be the crowning achievement of his administration.

25. Despite the progressiveness of most of Wilson's administration,
    A. he declined to endorse an amendment for women's suffrage in his first term.
    B. he allowed the spread of Jim Crow practices in the federal government.
    C. he withheld support from federal child-labor legislation.
    * D. all the above statements are true.

26. Few major pieces of social-justice legislation were passed under Wilson until 1916. More were passed beginning in 1916 because
    A. by 1916 the rift in the Republican Party (which opposed such legislation) had grown so wide that the Democrats controlled Congress.
    B. Wilson could not persuade Congress to pass such legislation until 1916.
    * C. Wilson saw the need to build a coalition of progressives for the 1916 election.
    D. most of the necessary social-justice legislation had been passed under President Taft.

27. Wilson's program of reform for farmers
    A. was based on the subtreasury plan, which finally passed in Congress some two decades after the Populists first proposed it.
    B. included the Keating-Owen Act.

    * C. included the Warehouse Act of 1916 and the Federal Farm Loan Act.

    D. was based on the idea that farmers should help themselves rather than look to the government for assistance.

28. The Adamson Act
    A. provided workmen's compensation for federal employees.
    B. excluded from interstate commerce goods manufactured by children under the age of fourteen.
    C. provided dollar-matching grants to states for highways.
    * D. provided an eight-hour day for railroad workers.

29. The greatest contribution of progressive politics was the establishment and acceptance of which of the following progressive features?
    A. a greater democratization of government
    B. the "gospel of efficiency"
    C. the regulation of big business
    * D. the public-service concept of government

30. In the progressive period,
    A. reform movements were comprised, for the most part, of the upper class and social elites.
    B. voter turnout remained high.
    * C. many groups—blacks, the poor, the unorganized—had little influence.
    D. all the above statements are true.

Suggested Essay Questions

1. What were the main features of progressivism? Describe each.

2. Which of the progressive presidents was most progressive? Explain.

3. What were the major reforms of the progressive era?

4. How did Wilson's victory in the 1912 election change the role of Democrats and southern statesmen in national affairs?

5. "From its beginning to its end, the progressive movement was, more than anything else, paradoxical." What evidence could be used to support this statement?

Chapter 24

WILSON AND THE GREAT WAR

This chapter covers foreign affairs in Wilson's administration, the war in Europe, American neutrality and preparedness, America's entry into the war, domestic affairs during World War I, Wilson's Fourteen Points and his fight for the Versailles Treaty, and the transition from war to peace in America.

Chapter Outline

I. Wilson's foreign policy
  A. Idealistic diplomacy
    1. Secretary of State William Jennings Bryan
    2. America called to advance democracy and moral progress
  B. Mexico
    1. General Victoriano Huerta established military dictatorship
    2. Incident at Tampico allowed Wilson to intervene
    3. The downfall of Huerta
    4. Pancho Villa
    5. Carranza's more liberal Mexican government
  C. In Caribbean, American marines helped put down disorders

II. The United States and the European war
  A. The beginning of the war
    1. Assassination of Austrian Archduke Franz Ferdinand
    2. The European system of alliances
      a. Central Powers (Germany, Austria-Hungary, Italy)
      b. Triple Entente (France, Great Britain, Russia)
  B. America's initial reaction
    1. Wilson urged Americans to be neutral
    2. Many immigrants for the Central Powers
    3. Old-line Americans for the Allies
    4. Role of propaganda

C. American neutrality strained
 1. Financial assistance to Allies
 2. Freedom of the seas
  a. Importance of sea power in European war
  b. British ordered ships carrying German goods via neutral ports to be stopped
 3. German submarine warfare
  a. Germans declared a war zone around the British Isles and threatened to sink any ships there
  b. German sinking of two ships divided the administration on a course of action
  c. *Lusitania* sunk; among 1,198 dead were 128 Americans
  d. America protested through a series of notes
  e. Unwilling to risk war, Secretary of State William Jennings Bryan resigned (June 1913)
 4. *Arabic* pledge
D. The debate over preparedness
 1. Sinking of the *Lusitania* contributed to demands for a stronger army and navy
  a. National Security League organized
  b. Wilson's war preparation plans announced (November 1915)
  c. Some were against preparedness
 2. Increases in the military
  a. National Defense Act doubled the regular army and authorized a National Guard
  b. Naval Construction Act authorized up to $600 million for three-year program of enlargement
 3. Revenue Act of 1916
E. Election of 1916
 1. Republicans nominated Charles Evans Hughes
 2. Democrats nominated Wilson again
 3. Wilson campaigned on peace and a progressive platform
 4. Wilson won in close race
F. Wilson's last efforts for peace
 1. Wilson asked each side to state its war aims
 2. Wilson said that America should share in laying the foundations for lasting peace
 3. Germany announced its new policy of unrestricted submarine warfare
 4. Wilson broke diplomatic relations with Germany
 5. The Zimmerman telegram

III. America's entry into the war
    A. Declaration of war
    B. Reasons for war
    C. America's early role in the war
        1. American contributions to Allied naval strategy
            a. Convoy system
            b. Minefield across North Sea
        2. Liberty Loan Act helped finance British and French war efforts
        3. Token army of under 14,500 men under John J. Pershing sent to France
        4. Selective Service Act

IV. The home front
    A. Regulation of industry and the economy
        1. Food and Fuel Administrations
            a. Herbert Hoover used propaganda campaigns and voluntary methods to conserve food
            b. Harry Garfield introduced Daylight Saving Time and "Heatless Mondays" to conserve fuel
        2. War Industries Board
        3. United States Employment Service placed four million workers in war-related jobs
    B. Mobilizing public opinion—the Committee on Public Information
        1. Headed by George Creel
        2. "Expression, not repression"
    C. Civil liberties
        1. Public opinion, aroused to promote war, turned to "Americanism" and witch-hunting
        2. Espionage and Sedition Acts
            a. Over 1,500 prosecutions with more than 1,000 convictions
            b. In *Schenck v. United States*, Supreme Court upheld acts

V. America in the war
    A. Until 1918, American troops played only a token role
    B. The "race for France"
        1. Second Battle of the Marne (July 15)
        2. By November Germany was retreating all along the front
    C. Wilson's plan for peace
        1. The Fourteen Points

        a. Open diplomacy
        b. Freedom of the seas
        c. Removal of trade barriers
        d. Reduction of armaments
        e. Impartial adjustment of colonial claims
        f. Evacuation of occupied lands
        g. National self-determination
        h. A League of Nations
   2. Allies accepted Fourteen Points as basis for peace, with two exceptions
        a. Reserved right to discuss freedom of the seas
        b. Demanded reparations for war damages
   3. Armistice signed on November 11, 1918
   4. Intervention in Russia

VI. Wilson's fight for the peace
   A. Wilson's domestic strength was declining
      1. The unraveling of his progressive coalition
      2. Democrats lose in the elections of 1918
      3. Wilson failed to invite any prominent Republicans to assist in the negotiations
   B. The negotiations in Paris
   C. The League of Nations
      1. For Wilson, the most important point
      2. Article X pledged members to consult on military and economic sanctions against aggressors
      3. Organization of the League
      4. Republican opposition
      5. Amendments adopted to Wilson's plan
   D. Other negotiations
      1. France pushed for several harsh measures against Germany
        a. Territorial concessions
        b. Reparations
      2. Problems with Wilson's principle of national self-determinism
      3. The issue of reparations
        a. France wanted to use demands for reparations to cripple Germany
        b. Wilson agreed to clause where Germany accepted responsibility for war and thus for its costs
        c. Reparations Committee ultimately decided that Germany owed $33 billion

VII. Wilson's fight for the treaty
    A. Opposition in Senate
        1. The irreconcilables
        2. The reservationists
    B. Henry Cabot Lodge began his attack on the treaty
    C. Wilson took his case to the American people
        1. Delivered 32 addresses in 22 days
        2. Suffered stroke on October 2
        3. Now he refused to compromise on treaty
    D. The Senate vote on the Versailles Treaty
        1. On the treaty with reservations, Wilsonians and irreconcilables combined to defeat ratification
        2. On the treaty without reservations, reservationists and irreconcilables combined to defeat ratification
    E. The official end of the war by joint resolution of Congress

VIII. From war to peace
    A. Economic transition
        1. Postwar boom
        2. Labor unrest
    B. Racial friction
    C. The Red Scare
        1. Fear of a social revolution (like Russia's)
        2. Most violence was the work of the lunatic fringe, but many Americans saw it all as "Bolshevism"
        3. Role of A. Mitchell Palmer, attorney-general, in promoting the Red Scare
        4. The Red Scare began to evaporate by the summer of 1920

Suggestions for Lecture Topics

For a lecture on Wilsonian diplomacy, see Arthur S. Link's *Wilson the Diplomatist* (1957) and the relevant portions of Otis L. Graham, Jr.'s *The Great Campaigns* (1971).

Instructors who wish to lecture on the military aspects of World War I will find Edward M. Coffman's *The War to End All Wars* (1968) useful.

David M. Kennedy's *Over Here* (1980) describes the effect of the war on American society and is a good source for a lecture on that topic. Maurine Weiner Greenwald's *Women, War, and Work* (1980) covers that more specialized topic.

Multiple-Choice Questions

1. Which of the following statements best describes the diplomatic stance of Woodrow Wilson and William Jennings Bryan?
   - A. America must, above all else, protect American interests around the world.
   - B. America must not interfere in the affairs of other nations.
   - * C. America has been called to spread democracy and moral progress throughout the world.
   - D. America should prove its might wherever and whenever possible.

2. Faced with the situation of a military dictator ruling neighboring Mexico, President Wilson said that
   - A. America must recognize de facto power to maintain world credibility.
   - * B. America should not recognize governments that do not rest on the consent of the governed.
   - C. America should follow the principles of Social Darwinism and recognize the dictator.
   - D. America must recognize the dictator as long as he "salutes the flag," or shows respect for America.

3. Pancho Villa
   - A. was captured and executed by General John J. Pershing in 1914.
   - B. led the Mexican forces against an unsuccessful invasion by American marines and sailors at Vera Cruz.
   - C. led the rebellion against Mexican President Porfirio Díaz.
   - * D. killed a number of Americans in an attempt to provoke American intervention in Mexico.

4. Which of the following was *not* a member of the Central Powers?
   - A. Austria-Hungary
   - B. Germany
   - * C. Russia
   - D. Turkey

5. Before the United States entered the war, American investors had loaned
   - A. no significant amounts of money to the Allies or the Central Powers, to maintain neutrality.
   - B. approximately equal amounts of money to the Allies and the Central Powers, to maintain neutrality.

C. great amounts of money to the Central Powers and very little to the Allies.

* D. almost eight times more money to the Allies than to the Central Powers.

6. Early in 1915 in response to the British blockade the German government announced that

A. Germany would submit to the blockade rather than create a threat to peace with the United States.

* B. enemy merchant ships and neutral ships found in the waters around the British Isles were liable to be sunk.

C. only ships carrying the British flag need feel threatened by the German navy.

D. Germany's diplomatic ties with England were severed.

7. President Wilson's response to the sinking of the *Lusitania*

A. led to the resignation of Edward M. House, his secretary of state.

B. included a speech where he said that if Germany were responsible for the killing of any more Americans, then a state of war would exist between the United States and Germany.

C. was conciliatory.

* D. was a series of notes demanding that Germany stop such actions and pay reparations.

8. The war preparation plans that Wilson announced in November 1915

A. had the approval of almost all Americans.

B. provided more money for the new air force than for the army and navy combined.

* C. were financed in part from the income tax increases of the Revenue Act of 1916.

D. had the support of Robert La Follette and other progressives.

9. In the presidential election of 1916, the Republicans

A. nominated Theodore Roosevelt.

* B. lost by a small margin.

C. nominated Woodrow Wilson for reelection, and won by a large margin.

D. ran on a platform of social legislation, neutrality, and women's suffrage.

10. Late in 1916 Wilson asked each of the belligerent powers to state its war aims. The Allies responded that they intended to do all the following *except*
    A. break up the Austro-Hungarian Empire.
    B. exact reparations.
    C. destroy Germany's military strength.
    * D. annex several German island possessions in the South Pacific.

11. The Zimmerman telegram
    * A. asked for help from Mexico in the case of war between Germany and the United States.
    B. announced Germany's decision to wage unrestricted submarine warfare.
    C. announced the addition of three countries to the Central Powers.
    D. caused the United States to break diplomatic relations with Germany.

12. In the cases of *Schenck v. United States*, the supreme Court
    A. struck down as unconstitutional the Lever Food and Fuel Act, which had created the Food and Fuel Administrations.
    * B. upheld the convictions of men who had circulated pamphlets against the draft.
    C. ruled that labor organizations as such did not fall under the jurisdiction of the War Industries Board.
    D. overturned the Espionage and Sedition Acts.

13. George Creel
    A. was the energetic leader of the War Labor Policies Board.
    * B. said that the best way to influence public opinion on the war was "expression, not repression."
    C. was the first and most celebrated conviction under the Espionage Act of 1917.
    D. was convicted under the "clear and present danger" doctrine.

14. Of all the mobilization agencies, the most important was the
    A. Food Administration.
    B. Emergency Fleet Corporation.
    * C. War Industries Board.
    D. War Labor Board.

15. The Fuel Administration
    * A. introduced the nation to Daylight Saving Time and "heatless Mondays."
    B. was headed by Herbert Hoover.
    C. operated the nation's railroads during the war.
    D. was the most important agency under the War Industries Board.

16. Under the Espionage and Sedition Acts of Wilson's administration,
    A. there were 25 prosecutions and 10 convictions.
    B. speaking or writing against Germany or Italy became a crime.
    * C. criticism of government leaders or war policies was outlawed.
    D. was aimed more at "middle America" rather than at socialists or other radicals.

17. The congressional resolution for war
    * A. passed overwhelmingly.
    B. was based, more than anything else, on the discovery of the Zimmerman telegram.
    C. came in April 1916.
    D. was divided strictly along party lines.

18. The largest American action of the war was
    * A. the Meuse-Argonne offensive.
    B. the Second Battle of the Marne.
    C. at Château-Thierry.
    D. just inside the German lines, near Metz.

19. Wilson's Fourteen Points called for all the following *except*
    A. self-determination for Europe's various nationalities.
    * B. more discreet diplomacy.
    C. freedom of the seas.
    D. reduction of armaments.

20. The armistice ending the war
    A. was signed in April 1917.
    * B. assured the Germans that the Fourteen Points would be the basis for the peace conference.
    C. ended the fighting for Bulgaria, Turkey, Austria-Hungary, and Germany.
    D. allowed the Germans to keep their submarines, ships, and railroads.

21. In the midterm elections of 1918,
    * A. the Democrats lost both houses of Congress.
    B. labor, eastern businessmen, and western farmers expressed support for Democratic policies.
    C. Republican victories in the South were offset by heavy losses in the Northeast.
    D. Wilson asked voters to elect progressive candidates of either party.

22. To what did Wilson refer when he spoke of "the heart of the League"?
    A. The League of Nations army, which would enforce peace.
    B. The Permanent Court of Justice, which would rule on international disputes.
    * C. Article X, which would pledge members to consult on military and economic sanctions against aggressors.
    D. The Assembly, which would allow each League member an equal voice.

23. On the question of reparations,
    A. Wilson agreed with French and English officials that Germany should have to pay only for civilian damages.
    B. Wilson argued that the German people should not be further humiliated by having to pay.
    C. Germany finally agreed to pay just over $3 million.
    * D. French and British officials took a much harder stance toward Germany than Wilson wished to.

24. The leader of the reservationists—those who insisted on limiting the participation of the United States in the League of Nations—was
    A. Herbert Hoover.
    * B. Henry Cabot Lodge.
    C. Henry White.
    D. Thomas R. Hardwick.

25. To win support for the Versailles Treaty, Wilson
    A. agreed to weaken Article X, which provided for collective action against aggressors.
    * B. decided to take his case to the people and appeal to public opinion.
    C. refused to accept any changes by the reservationists.
    D. insisted that the League of Nations would never be more than a "paper organization."

26. When the Versailles Treaty came before the Senate,
    A. the Senate refused to ratify the treaty; it was not ratified until the reservationists' amendments had been added, in 1920.
    * B. Wilsonians refused to vote for an amended treaty.
    C. the Senate ratified it almost immediately, although several senators had wanted changes.
    D. the Senate refused to ratify it, and the United States remained technically at war with Germany until the end of World War II.

27. The postwar economic boom was fueled by all the following *except*
    A. pent-up demand and wartime savings.
    B. American supremacy in overseas trade.
    C. a valuable cotton crop in 1919.
    * D. an upswing in business growth after 1921.

28. A race riot in which 38 people were killed and 537 injured took place in July 1919 in
    A. Albany, New York.
    B. Birmingham, Alabama.
    * C. Chicago, Illinois.
    D. Detroit, Michigan.

29. The Red Scare of 1919–1920 was most influenced by
    A. the massive steel strikes around Chicago and western Pennsylvania.
    B. the tremendous growth of the Socialist Party during World War I.
    * C. the shock of the Bolshevik revolution in Russia and actions of a "lunatic fringe."
    D. the demobilization of the American army.

30. The attorney-general who played a large role in the government's involvement in the Red Scare was
    A. J. Edgar Hoover.
    B. Harry Daugherty.
    C. Louis L. Post.
    * D. A. Mitchell Palmer.

Suggested Essay Questions

1. Why did America enter the war in Europe when it did? Why did it not enter before?

2. Describe Wilson's Fourteen Points, discussing not only the details but also the overall philosophy behind them.

3. Describe the economic mobilization for war on the American home front.

4. Why did the reservationists and the irreconcilables oppose the Treaty of Versailles? How effective was their opposition?

5. How and why were civil liberties curtailed during World War I? What was the effect of these curtailments?

Chapter 25

SOCIETY AND CULTURE BETWEEN THE WARS

This chapter covers the defensive mood of the 1920s (nativism, the Klan, fundamentalism, and Prohibition), the new morality, the women's movement, the "New Negro," the influence of science on social thought, the influence of modernism in literature and art, and the southern literary renaissance.

Chapter Outline

I. The defensive mood of the 1920s
   A. America seemed to be changing, and these changes posed a threat to the older orthodoxies
   B. Nativism
      1. Sacco and Vanzetti
         a. Arrested for robbery and murder
         b. Executed more for their political beliefs
      2. Immigration restriction
         a. New immigration quota law in 1924 favored old immigration from northern and western Europe
         b. New law allowed unrestricted immigration from Western Hemisphere countries
      3. The new Ku Klux Klan
         a. Unlike predecessor, devoted to "100% Americanism"
         b. Decline of the Klan
   C. Fundamentalism
      1. William Jennings Bryan and other leaders against the teaching of evolution
      2. The Scopes trial in Dayton, Tennessee
         a. The Tennessee anti-evolution law and the civic boosters of Dayton
         b. Bryan, Clarence Darrow, and the trial
      3. Death of Bryan and the decline of fundamentalism
   D. Prohibition
      1. Early prohibition movements
      2. Eighteenth Amendment ratified in 1919

   3. Problems of enforcement
   4. Organized crime
      a. Prohibition gave new source of income
      b. Al Capone
   5. Decision to continue enforcement of Prohibition
E. Defensive temper of the 1920s partly a reaction to social and intellectual revolution

II. The new morality
   A. A revolution in manners and morals
   B. F. Scott Fitzgerald chronicled the revolution
   C. Growing awareness of Sigmund Freud's theories prompted discussion of sex
   D. Sex in books, magazines, and movies
   E. By 1930, the revolution was fading

III. The women's movement
   A. Suffrage
      1. Alice Paul and the militant movement
      2. Carrie Chapman Catt and the National Suffrage Association
      3. Woodrow Wilson finally endorsed the "Anthony Amendment"
      4. Nineteenth Amendment ratified in 1920
   B. The Equal Rights Amendment
      1. Introduced in Congress in 1923
      2. Congress did not adopt amendment until 1972; it then failed ratification
   C. Working women
      1. Increases in number of voting women
      2. Most still traditional occupations

IV. The "New Negro"
   A. In the Great Migration, almost 15 percent of blacks born in the South moved north
   B. Harlem Renaissance
      1. Literary and artistic movement
      2. Writers of the Harlem Renaissance
   C. Negro nationalism
      1. Promoted black cultural expression and black exclusiveness
      2. Marcus Garvey the leading spokesman
   D. The NAACP
      1. Organized in 1910
      2. Main strategy of NAACP was legal action

       3. NAACP's attack on lynching

V. Science and social thought
   A. Isaac Newton's universe had been an ordered one with absolute standards; an infinite progress in knowledge seemed possible
   B. The work of Albert Einstein showed that everything is relative
   C. Werner Heisenberg's Uncertainty Principle indicated that human knowledge of the universe is limited
   D. Relativity and anthropology
      1. "Culture" has no absolutes; therefore one cannot judge another culture
      2. Ruth Benedict and Margaret Mead showed the diversity of cultures around the world

VI. The modernist movement in literature and art
   A. Features of modernism
   B. Modernism in art
   C. Modernism in literature
      1. Varieties of expression
      2. Major figures
         a. Ezra Pound
         b. T. S. Eliot
         c. Gertrude Stein
         d. F. Scott Fitzgerald
         e. Ernest Hemingway
   D. Writers and social significance
      1. John Steinbeck
      2. Richard Wright

VII. The southern renaissance
   A. H. L. Mencken announced "The Sahara of the Bozart"
   B. Writers in the southern renaissance
      1. Thomas Wolfe
      2. William Faulkner

VIII. The rediscovery of America

Suggestions for Lecture Topics

Two books that cover the period between World War I and the Depression are William E. Leuchtenburg's *The Perils of Prosperity, 1914–1932* (1958) and Frederick Lewis Allen's *Only Yesterday* (1931).

These books contain a wealth of information for lectures on a variety of topics concerning those years.

Several books discuss aspects of the defensive temper of the 1920s in greater detail than the two books above and would be useful for lectures on those topics. For nativism, see John Higham's *Strangers in the Land* (1955); for the Ku Klux Klan, see David M. Chalmers's *Hooded Americanism* (1965); for the Scopes trial, see Ray Ginger's *Six Days or Forever?* (1958); and for Prohibition, see Norman H. Clark's *Deliver Us from Evil* (1976).

For the other side of the twenties, see relevant sections of the Leuchtenburg and Allen books. The following sources would be useful for lectures on specific topics: for women's suffrage, see Eleanor Flexner's *Century of Struggle* (rev. ed., 1975); for the cultural side of the black movement, see Jervis Anderson's *This Was Harlem* (1982); and for the literature of the decade, see Frederick J. Hoffman's *The Twenties* (rev. ed., 1962).

Multiple-Choice Questions

1. Nicola Sacco and Bartolomeo Vanzetti
   A. were convicted of bombing eight army supply trucks.
   * B. were two Italian-born anarchists sentenced to death and executed in the 1920s even though there was doubt as to their guilt.
   C. were finally exonerated of the charges of payroll robbery and murder.
   D. would not have been convicted had it not been for the Ku Klux Klan.

2. The immigration quota law passed in 1924
   A. favored immigrants from southern and eastern Europe.
   * B. completely excluded people from East Asia.
   C. set strict limits on immigration from Mexico.
   D. rescinded the "Gentlemen's Agreement" accepted during Theodore Roosevelt's administration.

3. William J. Simmons was
   A. the defense attorney at the Sacco and Vanzetti trial.
   B. the prosecuting attorney at the Sacco and Vanzetti trial.
   * C. founder of the Ku Klux Klan.
   D. the newspaper reporter who exposed Ku Klux Klan activities in an effort to discredit the organization, but only brought more publicity to it.

4. The 1925 Scopes trial
   A. pitted William Jennings Bryan, former presidential candidate and self-confessed agnostic, for the prosecution against fundamentalist Clarence Darrow for the defense.
   * B. concerned a bill that had outlawed the teachings of evolution in Tennessee public schools.
   C. marked the beginning of a large fundamentalist movement in America.
   D. is correctly described by all the above statements.

5. The militant feminist who worked for the Equal Rights Amendment was
   * A. Alice Paul.
   B. Mrs. Frank Leslie.
   C. Clara Bow.
   D. Margaret Bourke-White.

6. The author of *This Side of Paradise,* a novel of student life at Princeton, was
   A. H. L. Mencken.
   B. Thomas Wolfe.
   * C. F. Scott Fitzgerald.
   D. Samuel Hopkins Adams.

7. The Amendment banning the manufacture or sale of intoxicating liquors was ratified in
   A. 1929.
   B. 1915.
   * C. 1919.
   D. 1926.

8. Which Amendment to the Constitution gave women the right to vote?
   A. Seventeenth
   B. Eighteenth
   * C. Nineteenth
   D. Twentieth

9. The movement of southern blacks to the North beginning about 1915
   A. is called the "Great Migration."
   B. created a steady growth in black political influence.
   C. involved over 13 percent of the South's native black population by 1930.
   * D. is correctly described by all the above statements.

10. The author of *Cane*, considered by many to be the greatest single work of the Harlem Renaissance, was
    A. Claude McKay.
    * B. Jean Toomer.
    C. Du Bose Heyward.
    D. Langston Hughes.

11. The United Negro Improvement Association
    A. sponsored black artists and writers.
    * B. was led by Marcus Garvey.
    C. promoted Booker T. Washington's idea of racial peace through accommodation.
    D. was the forerunner of the National Association for the Advancement of Colored People (NAACP).

12. In the case of *Norris v. Alabama* (1935), the Supreme Court
    A. struck down Oklahoma's grandfather clause.
    B. invalidated a residential segregation law in Louisville.
    C. upheld the Texas Democrats' white primary.
    * D. ruled that the systematic exclusion of blacks from Alabama juries had denied black defendants equal protection of the law.

13. Which of the following statements about fundamentalists is *not* true?
    A. Governor Miriam "Ma" Ferguson of Texas supported them, and H. L. Mencken did not.
    * B. They stressed that the Bible should be studied in light of modern scholarship.
    C. They argued that the Bible could no be reconciled with evolution.
    D. Their belief was grounded in a literal interpretation of the Bible.

14. The "new physics" of Albert Einstein, Werner Heisenberg, and others helped to undermine the concept of absolute standards. In anthropology this was reflected in
    A. a movement to study the physical evidence of man's origins.
    B. attempts to show that other societies had not developed in several important areas to the extent that ours had.
    * C. attempts to understand other cultures without imposing American or European values on them.
    D. a number of comparative studies of human and ape communities.

15. The modernist movement is correctly represented by all of the following *except*
    * A. it replaced views of conflict with Victorian ideals of peace and bliss.
    B. it explored the irrational as an essential part of human nature.
    C. it viewed the universe as turbulent and unpredictable.
    D. it embraced uncertainty as a desirable condition.

16. Harriet Monroe
    * A. started *Poetry: A Magazine of Verse* and brought to light many modernist writers, including Conrad Aiken, Edna St. Vincent Millay, and Carl Sandburg.
    B. was a modernist painter whose experimental art shocked many people in 1919.
    C. founded and was the first editor of *New Republic*.
    D. wrote stories based on Afro-American folktales.

17. "The Waste Land," a difficult poem that became the favorite of many modernist readers because of its sense of disillusionment and its suggestion of a burned-out civilization, was written by
    A. Ezra Pound.
    * B. T. S. Eliot.
    C. Gertrude Stein.
    D. Vachel Lindsay.

18. The novels of Ernest Hemingway
    * A. pictured a desperate search for the meaning of life and the cult of masculinity.
    B. portrayed utopian communities in a socialist society.
    C. attacked the corruption of machine politics in the large cities.
    D. traced the philosophical connections between twentieth-century America and eighteenth-century England.

19. The Ku Klux Klan of the 1920s was based mainly on
    * A. "100 percent Americanism."
    B. prohibition.
    C. white supremacy.
    D. fundamentalist religious beliefs.

20. One of the chief originators and propagators of the modernist style and the author of the phrase "the lost generation" was
    * A. Gertrude Stein.
    B. John Steinbeck.

    C. Dorothy Parker.

    D. Vachel Lindsay.

21. Richard Wright

    A. was the foremost black historian of the 1920s and 1930s.

    B. wrote *Dubious Battles*, a novel about a fruit-pickers' strike in California.

*   C. wrote *Native Son,* a story of racial injustice.

    D. won fame with his *Novels of the Commonwealth,* a realistic social history of Virginia.

22. "The Sahara of the Bozart," an essay describing the (supposed) lack of culture in the South, was written by

    A. Ellen Glasgow.

    B. Donald Davidson.

    C. Bigger Thomas.

*   D. H. L. Mencken.

23. Three of the following four novels were written by the same author. Which was not?

    A. *The Sun Also Rises*

    B. *A Farewell to Arms*

    C. *The Old Man and the Sea*

*   D. *Black Boy*

24. Three of the following four novels were written by the same author. Which was not?

    A. *Light in August*

    B. *The Sound and the Fury*

*   C. *The Grapes of Wrath*

    D. *As I Lay Dying*

25. The decade of the 1920s

    A. was one of prosperity and optimism for some Americans.

    B. was one of despair and doubt for some Americans.

    C. was one of frivolity and loosening morals for some Americans.

*   D. is correctly described by all the above statements.

26. One of the most skillful creators of modernist literature described southerners in the mythical Yoknapatawpha County in such novels as *Absalom! Absalom!* and *Sartoris.* This writer was

    A. Ellen Glasgow.

*   B. William Faulkner.

      C. Thomas Wolfe.

      D. Quentin Compson.

27. *For Whom the Bell Tolls*
      A. was an epic poem by Carl Sandburg portraying the patriotism of the American people through history.
      B. was John Dos Passos's vision of an America divided into two nations.
      C. was written by F. Scott Fitzgerald.
   * D. was written by Ernest Hemingway.

28. Al Capone
   * A. was the most celebrated criminal of the 1920s.
      B. was imprisoned for bootlegging, but officials were never able to convict him of murder.
      C. was so successful at bootlegging that President Hoover agreed with a 1931 commission report that recommended the end of Prohibition.
      D. is correctly represented by all the above statements.

29. All the following were reactions against modernism *except*
      A. the Ku Klux Klan.
      B. fundamentalism.
   * C. the new poetry.
      D. Prohibition.

30. The modernist temper and the defensive temper of the 1920s met in an atmosphere of
      A. unity.
   * B. conflict.
      C. stagnation.
      D. tolerance.

Suggested Essay Questions

1. Describe the defensive temper of the 1920s. What factors contributed to it?

2. What were the political and cultural manifestations of a new sense of identity among black in the 1920s?

3. How did the scientific work of Albert Einstein and Werner Heisenberg influence American thought?

4. "The major theme in American society in the 1920s was the theme of newness." Is this statement true or false? Explain.

5. Describe the influence of modernism in literature and art.

Chapter 26

REPUBLICAN RESURGENCE AND DECLINE, 1920–1932

This chapter covers the transformation of progressivism; domestic affairs in the administrations of Harding, Coolidge, and Hoover; the Republican prosperity of the 1920s; and the first three years of the Depression.

Chapter Outline

I. The transformation of progressivism
   A. Wilson's progressive coalition had dissolved by 1920
   B. Progressivist impulse transformed to move for good government and public services

II. Harding's administration
   A. The election of 1920
      1. Warren Harding won the Republican nomination
      2. James Cox won the Democratic nomination
      3. Victory for Harding
   B. Harding as president
      1. Appointments included good and bad choices
      2. Harding lacked self-confidence as president
      3. Policies of Andrew Mellon
         a. Tax reductions for the rich
         b. A higher tariff
      4. Harding named conservative advocates of big business to head major regulatory agencies
   C. Corruption in Harding's administration
      1. Scandals of the Ohio Gang
      2. The Teapot Dome scandal
         a. Albert Fall of the Interior Department allowed private companies to exploit government-owned oil deposits
         b. Harding troubled by the scandals
      3. Harding's death spared him from public disgrace

III. The rise of Calvin Coolidge
   A. Became president at Harding's death

     B. Coolidge's quiet character

     C. Election of 1924

        1. Coolidge, who controlled the party machinery, won the Republican nomination

        2. John W. Davis named candidate of divided Democratic party

        3. Progressive, Farmer-Labor, and Socialist parties named Robert La Follette

        4. Landslide victory for Coolidge

IV. Republican prosperity in the 1920s

     A. Much of prosperity fueled by growth of consumer-goods industries

        1. Growing consumer culture

        2. Motion pictures

        3. Radio broadcasting

     B. Advances in transportation

        1. Airplanes

           a. Acts providing government subsidies for manufacturers

           b. Charles Lindbergh's flight

        2. Automobiles

           a. Provided market for steel, glass, rubber, textiles, oil, and so forth

           b. The good-roads movement

V. Coolidge's administration

     A. Economic stabilization

        1. Herbert Hoover (secretary of commerce) and "associationalism"

           a. Hoover's *American Individualism* (1922)

           b. Standardization in industry and business

           c. Promoted trade associations

        2. Supreme Court upheld trade associations

     B. Agricultural policies

        1. Agriculture still weak in the 1920s

        2. Commodity-marketing associations

        3. The Farm Bloc

           a. A coalition of western Republican and southern Democratic congressmen

           b. Legislation to aid farmers

        4. The McNary-Haugen bill

           a. Plan to dump surplus crops on world market to raise prices on home market

           b. Vetoed by Coolidge

C. Labor policies
  1. Employers used various devices to keep out unions
      a. Open shop allowed employers not to hire unionists
      b. "Yellow-dog" contracts forced workers to agree not to join union
      c. "Industrial democracy" and "welfare capitalism" offered workers alternatives to unions
  2. Union membership declined in 1920s

VI. Hoover's administration
  A. Election of 1928
      1. Republicans nominated Herbert Hoover
      2. Democrats nominated Alfred Smith
      3. The images of the candidates
      4. Victory for Hoover
  B. Hoover as progressive and humanitarian
  C. For farmers, Hoover endorsed the Agricultural Marketing Act, which supported farm cooperatives
  D. The Hawley-Smoot Tariff raised duties to all-time high
  E. The economy out of control
      1. The Florida real-estate boom
      2. Increased speculation in the stock market
      3. The stock market peaked on September 3, 1929

VII. Hoover in the Depression
  A. The stock market had its worst day on October 29
  B. Hoover's first action was to express hope, though wages fell and unemployment rose
  C. Reasons for the crash
      1. Economic factors
      2. Governmental policies
  D. Hoover's attempts at recovery
      1. Asked businessmen to let profits suffer before purchasing power
      2. Increased opportunities for employment and credit
      3. The "Hooverization" of America
  E. In elections of 1930 Republicans lost control of both houses of Congress
  F. More attempts at recovery
      1. The Reconstruction Finance Corporation, to keep financial institutions open
      2. Glass-Steagall Act increased loan opportunities
      3. Federal Home Loan Act provided financing for home mortgages

4. The Emergency Relief and Construction Act provided funds for public works programs

VIII. Protests against Hoover's policies
    A. Farmers protested with strikes and violence
    B. Veterans
       1. The Bonus Expeditionary Force marched on Washington demanding immediate payment of bonus
       2. Congress rejected their demands, but many veterans stayed in Washington
       4. Army was used to evict veterans

Suggestions for Lecture Topics

For a lecture on Herbert Hoover, Joan Hoff-Wilson's sympathetic *Herbert Hoover: Forgotten Progressive* (1975) would be a good source.

For a discussion of the setbacks for labor, see Irving Bernstein's *The Lean Years* (1960).

John Kenneth Galbraith's *The Great Crash, 1929* (1955) would be a good source for a lecture on the causes and effects of the stock market crash.

Multiple-Choice Questions

1. The progressive coalition that had elected Woodrow Wilson president dissolved by 1920 for all the following reasons *except*
  * A. farmers favored a continuation of the wartime price controls.
    B. intellectuals became disillusioned because of popular support for Prohibition and the antievolution movement.
    C. organized labor viewed the Democrats as unsympathetic.
    D. a number of the progressives' main goals had been achieved.

2. Harding's secretary of the treasury, Andrew W. Mellon,
    A. favored retaining the high wartime level of taxation in order to build up the public treasury.
  * B. favored a reduction of the high wartime level of taxation, but mainly for the rich.
    C. favored a reduction of the high wartime level of taxation, but mainly for the poor and middle class.

    D. favored only a slight reduction of the high wartime level of taxation, but compensated for that by supporting a general reduction of the tariff.

3. On the issue of regulating big business, President Harding
   A. showed his support for regulation by pressuring Congress to pass stricter laws.
   * B. named conservative advocates of big business to head the Interstate Commerce Commission and the Federal Trade Commission.
   C. and his administration brought a record number of suits against corporations.
   D. named Robert La Follette, a former leading progressive, to head a government commission to investigate unfair business practices.

4. The biggest scandal of the Harding administration
   A. led to an attempt to impeach Harding that fell just four votes short of success in the House of Representatives.
   B. concerned a corrupt U.S. Customs official who had regularly allowed Chinese imports into this country duty-free.
   C. was the indictment, while in office, of Attorney-General Harry Daugherty for fraudulent handling of German assets seized after World War I.
   * D. involved the leasing of government-owned oil deposits to private companies.

5. Which of the following characteristics best describes Warren G. Harding as president?
   A. corrupt
   * B. lacking self-confidence
   C. cocky
   D. conniving

6. In the 1924 election,
   A. Calvin Coolidge barely won the nomination of a faction-ridden Republican Party.
   B. John W. Davis, the Democratic candidate who had the solid support of his party, almost upset Calvin Coolidge.
   * C. Robert La Follette, running as a third-party candidate, received a large number of votes.
   D. all the above statements are true.

7. Harding's accomplishments as president included all the following *except*
    A. creating a remarkable economic boom.
    B. playing a forceful role in pushing legislation through Congress.
    C. playing a forceful role in shaping foreign policies.
  * D. integrating previously racially segregated government departments.

8. Coolidge's attorney general was
  * A. Harry Daugherty.
    B. Henry A. Wallace.
    C. indicted for looting veterans' hospitals.
    D. found dead in his Washington apartment, one of several suicides in Coolidge's administration.

9. The first radio commercial aired in the same year that the 500th radio station began broadcasting. The year was
  * A. 1922.
    B. 1929.
    C. 1931.
    D. 1933.

10. After World War I the aircraft industry in America foundered. Which of the following was *not* a factor in the revival of the aircraft industry?
    A. the psychological boost provided by Charles Lindbergh's solo flight across the Atlantic
    B. an act which subsidized the industry through airmail contracts
    C. an act which, among other things, began federal aid to establish airports
  * D. the Grayson Act of 1929, which mandated the use of radar-tracking equipment at major passenger airports and authorized federal funds to assist in its installation

11. The rise of the automobile
    A. was aided by Henry Ford's business innovations.
    B. meant an increased market for steel, rubber, glass, and textiles.
    C. quickened the good roads movement.
  * D. all the above are true.

12. Herbert Hoover's *American Individualism* was published in 1922. As secretary of commerce, Hoover applied the philosophy

of that book to the relationship between government and business by

    A. endorsing laissez-faire policies to allow businesses to govern themselves.

*   B. supporting the trade-association movement.

    C. pushing for stricter regulation of big business in order to protect individual Americans.

    D. supporting trust-busting legislation and Justice Department lawsuits.

13. The "Ohio gang"

    A. rivaled Charlie Chaplin in box office receipts in the 1920s.

*   B. was a gang of Harding's old friends who were named to political office.

    C. was the name of Sinclair Lewis's short story about the consumer culture.

    D. was the first coast-to-coast radio broadcast.

14. In the 1920s, farm prices

    A. kept at their high wartime levels.

    B. kept at their low wartime levels.

*   C. fell sharply.

    D. rose sharply.

15. The Farm Bloc

*   A. was a coalition of western Republicans and southern Democrats.

    B. pushed the McNary-Haugen Act into law.

    C. failed in its efforts to extend credit to cooperative associations and to exempt farm organizations from antitrust laws.

    D. is correctly represented by all the above.

16. In "yellow-dog" contracts, employers

    A. agreed to submit all grievances to an arbitration panel whose decision was binding.

*   B. forced workers to agree to stay out of unions.

    C. agreed to hire only union workers.

    D. maintained the right to cut wages at any time and for any reason.

17. In the 1920s, labor unions

    A. won a number of important victories in the Supreme Court.

    B. had the active support of Attorney-General Harry Daugherty.

* C. lost about 1.5 million members.
  D. were helped by the prosperity of the decade.

18. In the election of 1928,
    A. the biggest issue on which the Republican and Democratic parties differed was support of labor unions.
    * B. the Republicans and the Democrats ran on almost identical platforms.
    C. the Democratic platform endorsed the enforcement of the Volstead Prohibition Act while the Republican platform pledged repeal of Prohibition.
    D. Republicans promised to reduce the protective tariff.

19. Alfred E. Smith, the Democratic candidate for president in 1928, lost the election because
    A. voters did not want a former Methodist minister from Nebraska who had written two books on the evils of drinking.
    * B. Americans were pleased with the Republican prosperity of the 1920s.
    C. he offended Catholic and immigrant voters.
    D. all the above statements are true.

20. President Herbert Hoover's progressive and humanitarian reforms included all the following *except*
    A. supporting the Agricultural Marketing Act, which gave financial assistance to farm cooperatives.
    B. rejecting "red hunts" or interference with the peaceful picketing of the White House.
    C. seeking financial assistance for all-black Howard University.
    * D. supporting a bill to provide federal assistance to lower-income families.

21. The Hawley-Smoot Tariff of 1930
    A. pleased farmers because it raised the protective tariff on agricultural imports but lowered it on manufactured imports.
    B. displeased farmers because it lowered the protective tariff on agricultural imports but raised it on manufactured imports.
    * C. raised the average duty on manufactured and agricultural imports to an all-time high.
    D. moderately reduced the average duty on manufactured and agricultural imports.

22. Part of the reason for the stock market crash was
    A. the high rate of inflation in the 1920s.
    B. Andrew Mellon's tax policies, which had especially hurt the wealthy who might otherwise have bought more stocks.
    * C. the buying of great amounts of stock "on margin."
    D. the low tariff, which allowed imports to corner several important American markets.

23. In 1929 America's wealth was unevenly distributed—one-third of the personal income went to only 5 percent of the population. This helped to cause the crash because
    * A. as production increased, demand declined.
    B. corporations no longer had sufficient capital to expand their productive capacities.
    C. many people no longer had extra money to invest in stocks.
    D. Americans with less spending power began buying cheaper imported goods rather than American-made goods.

24. All the following were governmental policies that contributed to the crash *except*
    * A. increased taxes on upper levels of income.
    B. hostility toward labor unions (which worsened income balances).
    C. high tariffs.
    D. lax enforcement of antimonopoly laws.

25. Hoover's early efforts to end the Depression included
    A. cutbacks in public works, to shore up the public treasury.
    B. a stricter credit policy by the Federal Reserve, to stop the flow of "easy money" available for speculation.
    C. an increase in aid to farmers, to allow them to produce more.
    * D. asking businessmen to maintain wages and avoid layoffs, in order to keep purchasing power strong.

26. In the elections of 1930
    A. Herbert Hoover was soundly defeated by Franklin D. Roosevelt.
    B. Herbert Hoover won a second term as president, but by a very small margin.
    C. the stock market crash was not a major factor in the way people voted.
    * D. Republicans lost control of both houses of Congress.

27. In 1931, just as economic indicators were beginning to rise,
    A. New York's Chase Manhattan Bank closed, increasing the investors' panic and setting off runs on other banks.
    * B. Austria's largest bank closed, triggering a panic that swept through Europe and caused European investors to withdraw their American gold and dump their American securities.
    C. a drought in the Midwest caused crop failures that raised food prices and thus increased panic.
    D. Andrew Mellon's tax increase of 1928 took effect, suddenly lessening the purchasing power of the average consumer.

28. The Reconstruction Finance Corporation
    A. was the old War Finance Corporation brought back to life for a new purpose.
    B. offered emergency loans to banks, farm mortgage associations, building and loan societies, and other such businesses in order to prevent bankruptcies.
    C. was criticized for its alleged favoritism to business.
    * D. is correctly represented by all the above statements.

29. In the early years of the Depression, farmers
    A. were hurt by passage of the Garner Farm Assistance Act, which actually cut farm assistance by nearly 70 percent.
    B. were aided by the Grain and Cotton Stabilization Corporations, which bought surplus crops and thus kept prices high.
    C. supported Hoover's Emergency Relief and Construction Act, which provided loans to prevent bankruptcy or to expand operations.
    * D. often lost their farms as their incomes continued to fall.

30. The Bonus Expeditionary Force
    A. consisted of angry farmers who sometimes acted outside the law to prevent the foreclosure of mortgages on their farms.
    B. toured the country to create support for the Communist Party.
    * C. marched on Washington in an attempt to get immediate payment of a veterans' bonus that Congress had voted in 1924.
    D. was a special division within the army created to help local authorities deal with disturbances.

Suggested Essay Questions

1. How had the progressivism of the prewar period been transformed by the 1920s? What factors led to the transformation?

2. How might the 1920s be called "the decade of prosperity"?

3. What did Warren G. Harding mean by "normalcy"?

4. Discuss the various causes of the stock market crash, paying particular attention to government policies that helped bring on the crash.

5. Describe Herbert Hoover's attempts at recovery in the first three years of the Depression. Which of his policies were effective? What more might he have done?

Chapter 27

FRANKLIN D. ROOSEVELT AND THE NEW DEAL

This chapter covers FDR's election, the first Hundred Days, opposition to the New Deal from the left and the Supreme Court, the second Hundred Days, labor and the New Deal, the slump of 1937, economic policy and the New Deal, and the legacy of the New Deal.

Chapter Outline

I. From Hoover to FDR
- A. The parties in 1932
  - 1. Republicans
    - a. Renominated Herbert Hoover
    - b. Atmosphere of defeat
  - 2. Democrats
    - a. Battle between John Nance Garner and FDR
    - b. Accepting nomination, FDR promised "a new deal for the American people"
- B. FDR's rise
  - 1. Early political career
  - 2. Platform
  - 3. Voters had confidence in FDR
- C. The election of 1932
- D. FDR takes office
  - 1. The long wait
    - a. Four months until inauguration
    - b. Depression's panic spread
  - 2. FDR's inauguration
    - a. Speech stressed hope and promised change

II. The first Hundred Days
- A. Strengthening America's finances
  - 1. The banking crisis
    - a. FDR declared four-day banking holiday
    - b. Emergency Banking Relief Act
    - c. FDR's "fireside chats" assured banks' safety

          d. By March 15, banking crisis over
     2. The end of Prohibition
     3. The problem of debt
          a. Farm Credit Administration
          b. Home Owners' Loan Corporation
     4. Banking and investment reforms
          a. Federal Deposit Insurance Corporation
          b. Federal Securities Act
     5. Devaluing the currency
  B. Relief Measures
     1. Civilian Conservation Corps
     2. Federal Emergency Relief Administration
     3. Civil Works Administration
     4. Works Progress Administration
  C. Agricultural recovery
     1. The Agricultural Adjustment Act
     2. Commodity Credit Corporation
     3. Supreme Court, in *United States v. Butler*, ended AAA
     4. Soil Conservation and Domestic Allotment Act
     5. Second Agricultural Adjustment Act
  D. Industrial recovery—the National Industrial Recovery Act
     1. Public Works Administration
     2. National Recovery Administration
          a. Codes of fair practice
          b. Criticism of the NRA
          c. Legacy of the NRA
  E. The Tennessee Valley Authority
     1. Started as power and nitrate plants at Muscle Shoals, Alabama
     2. New objectives: overall regional planning
     3. Rural Electrification Administration helped spread electricity through rural areas

III. Opposition to the New Deal
  A. Early support for Roosevelt's programs
  B. Criticism from the right
  C. Thunder on the left
     1. Huey Long
     2. Francis Townsend
     3. Charles Coughlin
     4. Pushed Roosevelt to "steal the thunder" of the left
  D. The Supreme Court and the New Deal
     1. Struck down part of NIRA
     2. Entire New Deal seemed in danger

IV. The second Hundred Days
   A. National Labor Relations Act
   B. Social Security Act
   C. Revenue Act of 1935 (Wealth Tax Act)

V. The election of 1936
   A. FDR's popularity
   B. Republicans
      1. Alfred M. Landon nominated
      2. Began campaign on a moderate note, but soon turned to attacks on the New Deal
      3. Hope that voters on the left would pull votes from FDR
   C. Democrats create a new electoral coalition
   D. Landslide victory for FDR

VI. FDR and the Supreme Court
   A. The Court's decisions seemed to endanger the New Deal
   B. FDR decided to enlarge the Court, to enable him to appoint pro–New Deal justices
   C. Court-packing scheme met with much opposition
   D. Court-packing became unnecessary

VII. Labor in the New Deal
   A. Growth of unions
   B. Industrial unions
      1. Movement to organize workers in mass-production industries
      2. Craft unions in AFL opposed to industrial unions
      3. Formation of CIO
   C. The CIO
      1. Success in automobile industry
      2. Success in steel industry
      3. CIO had soon unionized much of industrial America

VIII. The slump of 1937
   A. Reasons for slump
   B. Economic theories
      1. Less government spending and a balanced budget
      2. Renewed spending and opposition to monopolies
   C. Roosevelt endorsed ideas of second group

IX. Later reforms
   A. Wagner-Steagall Housing Act
   B. Bankhead-Jones Farm Tenant Act

C. Fair Labor Standards Act

X. The legacy of the New Deal
   A. FDR and the Democratic Party
     1. Southern Democrats drifted toward a coalition with conservative Republicans
     2. The conservative opposition
     3. FDR's efforts to cleanse Democratic Party
     4. Factions in Democratic Party
   B. The emergence of the broker state
     1. Through the 1930s the power of the national government was vastly enlarged
     2. FDR had taken the road between the extremes of laissez-faire and socialism
     3. Rise of a government whose role was a broker, mediating among interest groups

Suggestions for Lecture Topics

One useful lecture would emphasize the differences between the first and second New Deals. Consult William E. Leuchtenburg's *Franklin D. Roosevelt and the New Deal, 1932–1940* (1963) for information.

Alan Brinkley's *Voices of Protest* (1982) would be a good source for a discussion of the "thunder on the left."

For a lecture that examines the legacy of the New Deal, see *Fifty Years Later: The New Deal Evaluated*, edited by Harvard Sitkoff (1985). William E. Leuchtenburg's "The Achievements of the New Deal," the closing essay in the book, is especially useful for a lecture on that topic.

Multiple-Choice Questions

1. In the presidential election of 1932,
   * A. radical Socialist and Communist Party candidates won nearly one million votes.
   B. Franklin D. Roosevelt's training as vice-president under Herbert Hoover helped him win the Democratic nomination.
   C. Republican John Nance Garner won the electoral votes of only six states.
   D. Franklin D. Roosevelt promised to continue the economic policies of Herbert Hoover.

2. Between the election in November 1932 and Roosevelt's inauguration in March 1933,
    A. leading economic indicators showed an upswing in the nation's economy.
    B. many banks that had been closed since 1929 reopened.
    C. President Hoover asked Roosevelt to consult with congressional leaders on "this most serious matter of national concern."
    * D. the panic of the Depression spread.

3. To increase the public's confidence in American banks, Roosevelt did all the following in March 1933 *except*
    A. declare a four-day banking holiday.
    * B. double the percentage of total deposits that banks were required to keep on hand, available for withdrawal.
    C. persuade Congress to pass the Emergency Banking Relief Act.
    D. assure the public of the safety of banking institutions in his first radio fireside chat.

4. Roosevelt abandoned the gold standard in order to
    * A. raise prices.
    B. create deflation.
    C. increase the value of the dollar.
    D. reduce the nation's abundance of gold.

5. The main purpose of the Civilian Conservation Corps was
    A. to train young men for the Army Corps of Engineers.
    * B. to provide work relief for young men.
    C. to give young women an opportunity to earn money for higher education.
    D. to promote conservation practices by the general public.

6. The Federal Emergency Relief Administration
    A. was headed by Harry L. Hopkins.
    B. gave financial assistance to the needy through direct cash payments as well through work.
    C. was actually administered through the states.
    * D. is correctly represented by all the above.

7. The Civil Works Administration
    A. was the only relief agency that lasted to the end of the Depression.
    * B. gave financial assistance to the needy through work relief, although many of its projects were "make-work" jobs.

C. allowed the federal government little control over how the relief money was used.

D. is correctly represented by all the above.

8. The goal of the Agricultural Adjustment Act of 1933 was to raise farm income through
    * A. cutbacks in production.
    B. intensive farming.
    C. marketing quotas.
    D. state and federal subsidies.

9. The Agricultural Adjustment Act was ruled unconstitutional
    A. in the case of *Bankhead v. United States.*
    B. because benefit payments for farmers came from general funds rather than from some special tax.
    * C. after it had helped increase farm income by nearly 60 percent from 1932 to 1935.
    D. because the Supreme Court held that farm production was an interstate activity and thus beyond the reach of state action.

10. The Public Works Administration
    A. was created by an amendment to the second Agricultural Adjustment Act.
    B. provided make-work jobs such as raking leaves and digging ditches to provide relief for the hard-core unemployed.
    * C. attempted to "prime the pump" of business with new expenditures.
    D. was ruled unconstitutional by the Supreme Court in the Hoosac Mills case (1936).

11. The labor standards in the National Recovery Administration's codes of fair practice
    A. set a 40-hour workweek.
    B. set a minimum weekly wage.
    C. forbade child labor under the age of sixteen.
    * D. did all the above.

12. Among the objectives of the Tennessee Valley Authority were all the following *except*
    A. the production of cheap electric power.
    * B. the development of air transportation.
    C. general industrial development.
    D. soil conservation.

13. The author of the Share Our Wealth program, which would have liquidated personal fortunes and guaranteed a minimum income for almost all Americans, was
    A. Charles E. Coughlin.
    B. Francis E. Townsend.
    C. John W. Davis.
    * D. Huey P. Long.

14. In the case of *Schechter Poultry Corporation v. United States*, the Supreme Court
    A. overturned the Farm Credit Act.
    * B. overturned the National Industrial Recovery Act.
    C. decided that Schechter was involved in interstate, not local, trade.
    D. upheld the constitutionality of the second Agricultural Adjustment Act.

15. The act passed by Congress in July 1935 that gave workers the right to bargain through unions and prohibited employers from interfering with union activities was
    * A. the Wagner Act.
    B. the Guffey-Snyder Employment Act.
    C. the Adamson Act.
    D. the Wheeler Act.

16. Which of the following statements about the Social Security Act of 1935 is *not* true?
    A. It was, according to Roosevelt, the "supreme achievement" of the New Deal.
    B. It committed the national government to a broad range of welfare activities.
    C. It provided old-age pensions.
    * D. It was based on a progressive tax that took a larger percentage of higher incomes.

17. The Revenue Act of 1935 (sometimes called the Wealth Tax Act)
    A. provided for a regressive tax.
    B. increased federal revenue significantly, and thus helped finance the New Deal.
    * C. raised taxes on incomes above $50,000.
    D. created a more equal distribution of wealth in America.

18. In the presidential election of 1936,
    A. Roosevelt easily defeated Republican William Lemke.
    B. Republicans won most of the western farm vote and northern ethnic vote and almost upset Roosevelt.

* C. Republicans hoped that third-party action might throw the election to them.
  D. Roosevelt's opponents were afraid to make the New Deal a campaign issue, and hence campaigned on the tariff and foreign affairs.

19. Which of the following groups would have been least likely to support Roosevelt in the election of 1936?
    A. intellectuals
    B. labor unions
* C. wealthy businessmen
    D. blacks

20. The Wagner Act
    A. was upheld by the Supreme Court in the case of *United States v. Butler*.
    B. gave jobs to several thousand unemployed miners.
* C. reinstated rights that workers first gained through a section of the National Industrial Recovery Act.
    D. was struck down by the Supreme Court in 1936.

21. Shortly after his second inauguration, Roosevelt sent to Congress his "court-packing" scheme. This became unnecessary, however, when
    A. the Supreme Court ruled that the president, and not Congress, has authority to adjust the number of justices.
    B. the Supreme Court agreed to an extension of the number of justices.
    C. Congress took from the Supreme Court's jurisdiction cases involving the New Deal.
* D. the Supreme Court began reversing previous decisions and upholding the New Deal.

22. The Committee for Industrial Organization
    A. began as a rival to the American Federation of Labor.
    B. was mainly interested in craft unions.
* C. experienced extremely rapid growth in the few years following 1936.
    D. was led by Samuel Gompers.

23. Labor's "new direction" in the late 1930s was toward
    A. decentralization of union organization.
* B. industrial unions.
    C. women in unions.
    D. the Republican Party.

24. The 1937 economic slump was caused in part by
    * A. a sharp decrease in government spending.
      B. a sharp rise in private spending.
      C. the huge government deficit.
      D. the repeal of the Revenue Act of 1935.

25. The Farm Security Administration
      A. administered the Agricultural Adjustment Act of 1938.
    * B. offered loans to marginal farmers to keep them from sinking into tenancy.
      C. provided federal subsidies for the expansion of large farms.
      D. established educational programs to teach farmers new agricultural methods.

26. The conservative Democratic opposition to the New Deal
    * A. was heaviest in the South.
      B. succeeded in removing three of Roosevelt's cabinet members.
      C. emerged in 1939.
      D. supported plans to replace FDR with Charles Coughlin as the Democratic presidential candidate in 1936.

27. The Wagner-Steagall National Housing Act
      A. was one of the last New Deal measures Roosevelt was able to pass.
      B. assisted in slum clearance and public housing.
      C. set up the United States Housing Authority in the Department of the Interior.
    * D. is correctly represented by all the above.

28. The Fair Labor Standards Act did all the following *except*
      A. set a minimum wage of 40 cents an hour.
      B. set a minimum work week of 40 hours.
      C. prohibit child labor under the age of sixteen.
    * D. forbid racial discrimination in hiring for certain jobs.

29. In the elections of 1938,
      A. Roosevelt was defeated for reelection.
    * B. Roosevelt's attempts to "purge" the Democratic Party were largely unsuccessful.
      C. Republicans won control of the House and the Democrats kept a majority of only two in the Senate.
      D. Republicans won control of the Senate and Democrats kept a majority of only two in the House.

30. The most significant legacy of the New Deal was
   A. minimum standards for labor.
   B. financial reforms.
   C. agricultural reforms.
 * D. the rise of the "broker state."

Suggested Essay Questions

1. Describe the gains made by labor during the New Deal.

2. How did the "thunder on the left" shape New Deal policies?

3. Why did Roosevelt attempt to "pack" the Supreme Court? Did Roosevelt achieve his goals?

4. How did New Deal reforms attempt to raise farm prices and stabilize industry?

5. How did the nation's perceptions of the role of government—its powers and responsibilities—change in the 1930s?

Chapter 28

FROM ISOLATION TO GLOBAL WAR

This chapter covers American foreign policy between the wars, the portents of war in Europe and Asia, American neutrality, the war in Europe, American aid to Britain, and Japanese aggression leading to Pearl Harbor.

Chapter Outline

I. Postwar isolation
   A. America and the League of Nations
   B. War debts and reparations
      1. German reparations
      2. Johnson Debt Default Act of 1934
   C. Disarmament
      1. Concern for growth of Japanese power
      2. Strains in Japanese-American relations
      3. Washington Armaments Conference (1921)
         a. Five-Power Naval Treaty: tonnage limits, moratorium on capital shipbuilding, no further fortification of Pacific possessions
         b. Four-Power Treaty: each would respect others' Pacific possessions
         c. Nine-Power Treaty: agreed to support the Open-Door Policy and the territorial integrity of China
         d. Effect of treaties
   D. Attempts to outlaw war
      1. Growth of peace societies and programs
      2. Kellogg-Briand Pact (Pact of Paris)
         a. Signers agreed never to go to war with each other
         b. Effect of the pact

II. The "Good Neighbor" Policy
   A. Policy of peace and noninvolvement in Latin America
   B. Examples

      1. American forces pulled out of the Dominican Republic and Nicaragua

      2. Peacefully solved problem with Mexico of expropriation of American oil properties

      3. Platt Amendment, with its provisions allowing intervention in Cuba, abrogated

III. War clouds
    A. In the Far East
      1. Rise of Kuomintang (National Party) in China
      2. Japanese seizure of Manchuria
    B. In Europe
      1. Italy
        a. Mussolini had wide appeal
        b. By 1925 Mussolini was dictator
      2. Germany
        a. Hitler and National Socialist (Nazi) Party
        b. Reichsführer in 1934
    C. America's reaction
      1. Isolationism
      2. Diplomatic recognition of Soviet Russia
    D. The war clouds spread
      1. Japan, Spain, and Italy
      2. Germany
        a. Hitler's early attacks and conquests
        b. When Hitler invaded Poland, Britain, and France declared war on Germany

IV. American neutrality
    A. Nye Committee suggested that "merchants of death" might have pushed America into World War I
    B. Neutrality Act of 1935
      1. Forbade sale of arms or munitions to belligerents
      2. Weakness of act soon became apparent
    C. America and the Spanish Civil War
      1. Roosevelt refused to intervene
      2. Neutrality laws extended to cover civil wars
    D. Neutrality Act of 1937
      1. Provisions
      2. In Chinese-Japanese confrontation, Roosevelt did not invoke act—a step away from isolationism
    E. Roosevelt's "quarantine" speech—another step from isolationism
    F. United States ended commercial treaty with Japan
    G. Neutrality against Germany weakened

       1. After the German occupation of Czechoslovakia, Roosevelt no longer pretended to be impartial
       2. Neutrality Act of 1939
       3. American attitudes continued to vacillate

V. The storm in Europe
   A. *Blitzkrieg* (Spring 1940)
      1. Denmark, Belgium, Norway, and the Netherlands
      2. Mussolini entered the war
      3. The fall of France
   B. American defense
      1. Increased defense budget
      2. National Defense Research Committee set up to coordinate military research
   C. Aid for Britain
      1. Battle of Britain ended threat of German invasion
      2. United States gave 50 "overage" destroyers to Britain in return for leases on naval and air bases
   D. First peacetime conscription in American history
   E. Continued debate in America

VI. The election of 1940
   A. The candidates
      1. Republicans chose Wendell Willkie
      2. Democrats chose Roosevelt again
   B. The campaigns
      1. Roosevelt too busy to campaign
      2. Willkie attacked FDR's foreign policy
   C. Roosevelt won an unprecedented third term

VII. The Lend-Lease Act
   A. Provisions
   B. Isolationists opposed to bill

VIII. War continued to spread in Europe
   A. German victories and defeats
   B. The Atlantic Charter
   C. German attacks on American vessels
   D. American reaction
      1. Convoying ships
      2. End of neutrality

IX. The storm in the Pacific
   A. Japanese aggressions
      1. Movement into French Indochina
      2. Tripartite Pact with Germany

  3. Nonaggression pact with Russia
B. America's reaction
  1. Restricted oil exports to Japan
  2. Organized the armed forces of the Philippines into the U.S. Army
C. Japanese-American negotiations
D. Japanese attack on Pearl Harbor
E. The same day, Japan attacked the Philippines, Guam, Midway, Hong Kong, and the Malay Peninsula
F. America entered the war

Suggestions for Lecture Topics

For a lecture on American foreign policy during this period, see Selig Adler's *The Uncertain Giant* (1965). Joan Hoff-Wilson's *American Business & Foreign Policy, 1921–1933* (1971), stressing the role of business, would also be useful.

The first section of *Franklin D. Roosevelt and the World Crisis, 1937–1945* (1973), edited by Warren F. Kimball, contains useful information for a lecture on isolationism and the question of neutrality.

For an interesting lecture on the attack on Pearl Harbor, see Gordon W. Prange's *At Dawn We Slept* (1981) or John Toland's *Infamy* (1982).

Multiple-Choice Questions

1. The spirit of isolationism in the United States in the 1920s was seen in all the following *except*
    A. the Red Scare.
    B. the tight immigration laws.
  * C. the low tariff walls.
    D. the popular theme of "100 percent Americanism."

2. The Lansing-Ishii Agreement
    A. allowed the Japanese special tariff concessions in the Philippines.
    B. almost doubled the number of Japanese immigrants allowed into the United States.
  * C. admitted that Japan had "special interests" in China.
    D. limited the number of submarines Japan and the United States could have.

3. Which of the following statements about war debts from World
War I is *not* true?
    A. The debts caused anti-American feelings in Europe.
    B. France and England could not repay the debts until they
    collected reparations from Germany.
    C. Most European nations defaulted on their debts during the
    Great Depression.
  * D. The Johnson Debt Default Act issued loans to the Allies in
    the 1920s so they could keep up payments.

4. America's "Good Neighbor" policy
    A. allayed Canadian fears of American intervention there.
    B. included economic and military aid to the Allies.
    C. was demonstrated in 1926 when marines were sent to
    Nicaragua to help put down disorders.
  * D. included nonintervention in Latin America.

5. The Washington Armaments Conference of 1921
    A. was called in part because of America's fear of a British
    invasion in the Philippines.
  * B. resulted in an agreement limiting the military-ship ton-
    nage of participants.
    C. in effect gave the United States supreme naval power in
    the western Pacific.
    D. is correctly described by all the above statements.

6. In the Five-Power Naval Treaty, the signatories agreed to all
the following provisions *except*
    A. to refrain from further fortification of their Pacific
    possessions.
    B. to build no capital ships for ten years.
    C. to limit naval tonnage.
  * D. to respect the Monroe Doctrine.

7. The Pact of Paris (the Kellogg-Briand Pact)
  * A. outlawed war among signatories as an instrument of
    national policy.
    B. reduced the Allied war debt.
    C. limited the size of America's standing army.
    D. was defeated in the Senate.

8. Despite the general spirit of isolationism in the 1920s, America
was involved in world affairs. This could be seen in all the
following *except*
    A. the worldwide connections of American business.
    B. American overseas loans and investments.

* C. America's membership in the League of Nations.
  D. America's overseas possessions.

9. American foreign policy in Latin America in this period included all the following *except*
    A. withdrawing American marines from Nicaragua and Haiti.
    B. the Clark Memorandum.
  * C. rejection of the Pan-American Conference.
    D. a treaty with Cuba abrogating the Platt Amendment.

10. Benito Mussolini's rise to power in Italy
    A. followed the death of President Hindenburg. King Victor Emmanuel
    B. followed Hitler's rise in Germany.
    C. followed his successful invasion of Ethiopia.
  * D. came about largely because he promised to restore order to a country torn by dissension.

11. A renewal of diplomatic relations with the Soviet Union came about
    A. mainly because of the threat of Nazi Germany.
    B. under President Harding.
  * C. in 1933, thanks to FDR
    D. despite FDR's objections.

12. In the 1938 agreement signed at Munich,
    A. Mussolini agreed not to invade Albania.
  * B. Britain and France agreed to let Hitler have the Sudetenland.
    C. Japan joined Germany and Italy in the "Anti-Comintern Pact."
    D. Hitler achieved the union of Austria and Germany.

13. Britain and France went to war with Germany
    A. to keep Germany from seizing Czechoslovakia.
    B. when Mussolini conquered Ethiopia.
  * C. when Hitler invaded Poland.
    D. after Japan joined Italy and Germany in the "Anti-Comintern Pact."

14. The Nye Committee
  * A. investigated the role of bankers and munitions makers in America's entry into World War I.
    B. recommended that Europeans appease Hitler by allowing him to annex Czechoslovakia.

    C. compiled an official list of America's international obligations under existing treaties.

    D. condemned the actions of the "merchants of death," those foreign mercenaries who had committed atrocities against European civilians during World War I.

15. The Neutrality Act of 1935
    A. was directed against Japanese action in China.
    B. allowed the American navy to stop and search Italian ships on the high seas.
  * C. forbade the sale of arms and munitions to belligerent nations.
    D. stopped German and Italian military aid to Francisco Franco.

16. Why was Roosevelt hesitant to intervene in the Spanish Civil War?
  * A. He wanted to keep the fight localized.
    B. The Neutrality Act of 1938 forbade intervention.
    C. Catholics favored the Spanish Republic.
    D. Germany and Italy were supporting the Spanish Republic, but their aid was slight.

17. The so-called "moral embargo"
  * A. was on oil and similar products.
    B. restricted shipments of arms to China in 1936.
    C. restricted shipments of arms to Spain in 1937.
    D. was passed by Congress over Roosevelt's veto.

18. Which of the following events happened first?
    A. Congressional approval of the Neutrality Act of 1937
  * B. Hitler's reoccupation of the Rhineland
    C. the German invasion of France
    D. the fall of the Spanish Republic

19. The Neutrality Act of 1939
  * A. allowed the United States to sell arms on a cash-and-carry basis to England and France.
    B. failed to pass Congress by only four votes.
    C. renewed America's isolationist stance toward the war in Europe.
    D. was passed over Roosevelt's veto.

20. Which of the following was *not* an isolationist in 1940–1941?
    A. Charles A. Lindbergh

   * B. Henry L. Stimson
     C. Herbert Hoover
     D. Charles A. Beard

21. On September 2, 1940, Roosevelt agreed to send 50 "overaged" destroyers to Britain in return for
     A. Republican promises not to ask for a peacetime draft.
   * B. 99-year leases on a series of naval and air bases.
     C. a renegotiated payment schedule of the Allies' war debt from World War I.
     D. congressional approval of a draft registration act.

22. The America First Committee
     A. pushed for more aid to England and France in order to defend America.
   * B. argued that a Nazi victory in Europe would pose no threat to American national security.
     C. urged an immediate declaration of war on Germany.
     D. drew most of its support from the East and West Coasts and the South.

23. Wendell L. Willkie
     A. was Roosevelt's vice-presidential candidate in 1940.
     B. wrote *The Road to War: America, 1914–1917*, which argued that the United States should have kept out of World War I.
     C. was the leading congressional opponent of the Lend-Lease Act.
   * D. was the Republican presidential candidate in 1940.

24. With the Lend-Lease Act,
   * A. Roosevelt moved further away from isolationism.
     B. Roosevelt was able to please both isolationists and internationalists.
     C. American aid to England was reduced by about one-half.
     D. England became the "arsenal of democracy."

25. The Atlantic Charter included all the following principles *except*
     A. freedom of the seas.
     B. economic cooperation.
   * C. division of German and Italian colonies.
     D. self-determination of all peoples.

26. When the Germans began attacking American ships,
    A. Roosevelt asked Congress to declare war on Germany.
    * B. Congress in effect repealed the neutrality acts through new legislation lifting those bans.
    C. Roosevelt ordered ships to avoid combat zones.
    D. Roosevelt broke diplomatic relations with Germany.

27. In response to Japanese encroachments in Indochina in 1940 and 1941, Roosevelt
    A. froze all Japanese assets in the United States and sent 200,000 troops to the Philippines.
    B. sent 200,000 troops to China.
    * C. sent financial aid to China and restricted oil exports to Japan.
    D. declared a naval blockade of Japan.

28. Before any negotiations could proceed with the Japanese, the United States demanded that Japan
    A. give up its recently acquired territory in New Zealand.
    B. sign an agreement not to attack Russia.
    * C. withdraw completely from China.
    D. pay England and Holland for the oil and other resources it had taken from their colonies.

29. One way in which the Japanese attack at Pearl Harbor was not a total success was that the Japanese
    A. failed to disable the American planes lined up on airfields.
    * B. ignored shore installations and oil tanks.
    C. did not immediately follow up with assaults on other American and British positions in the Pacific.
    D. withdrew their attack before significantly damaging any of the battleships in the harbor.

30. The congressional resolution for war
    A. came just four days after the Japanese attack on Pearl Harbor.
    B. passed unanimously.
    C. came just after Italy and Germany showed their support for Japan by declaring war on America.
    * D. reflected the mood of America, which had suddenly decided against neutrality.

Suggested Essay Questions

1. Describe the Atlantic Charter and explain its significance.

2. How were attempts at disarmament and outlawing war in the 1920s ineffective?

3. What was the "Good Neighbor" Policy ? How did it reflect the general foreign-policy mood of the nation?

4. Describe the major steps in America's move away from neutrality between 1935 and 1941.

5. Discuss the negotiations between the United States and Japan in 1940 and 1941. How did the actions of each contribute to war?

Chapter 29

THE WORLD AT WAR

This chapter covers World War II, its effects on American society, and the Yalta agreements.

Chapter Outline

I. America's early battles
   A. Setbacks in the Pacific
      1. Collapse along the Pacific
      2. Surrender of the Philippines
      3. Japanese strategy
      4. Battle of the Coral Sea
   B. Battle of Midway
      1. American cryptanalysts had broken Japanese code
      2. Heavy Japanese losses
      3. A turning point in the Pacific war
   C. Setbacks in the Atlantic
      1. Devastation from German submarines
      2. American response

II. Mobilization at home
   A. Mobilization of the armed forces
   B. Economic mobilization: Gross National Product doubled
   C. Financing the war
      1. Taxation
      2. Borrowing from the public
   D. Impact of the war on the economy
      1. Rise in wages and spending
      2. Office of Price Administration
      3. Wage and farm price controls
      4. Overall, economic controls a success

III. Social effects of the war
   A. On women
      1. 200,000 women joined the armed forces
      2. 6,000,000 women entered the civilian workforce
      3. Changed attitudes toward sex roles

B. On blacks
  1. Blacks in armed forces—usually in segregated units
  2. Blacks in war industries
      a. A. Philip Randolph's March on Washington
      b. Discrimination in defense work forbidden
      c. Revived migration from the South
  3. Challenges to other forms of discrimination
  4. Conservative white reaction
C. On Japanese-Americans
  1. Over 100,000 sent to War Relocation Camps
  2. Federal compensation to survivors in 1983
D. Wartime domestic conservatism
  1. Elections of 1942 showed gains for Republicans
  2. Many New Deal agencies cut or abolished
  3. Actions against labor
      a. Smith-Connally War Labor Dispute Act
      b. State legislation

V. The war in Europe
  A. Decision to move against Germany first
    1. Nazis posed greater threat to western hemisphere
    2. Still, more Americans went to Pacific in 1942
  B. Aspects of joint conduct of war
    1. Agreement on war aims
    2. Disagreement on strategy
        a. Americans wanted to strike directly across the English Channel
        b. British wanted to wait and build up forces
  C. The North Africa campaign
    1. Eisenhower's landing
    2. German surrender
  D. Agreements at Casablanca
    1. Cross-channel invasion further postponed
    2. Atlantic antisubmarine campaign planned
    3. Agreement to end war only with "unconditional surrender" of all enemies
  E. Sicily and Italy
    1. Invasion of Sicily
    2. Italian surrender
    3. German control of northern Italy
    4. The battle for Rome
  F. Strategic bombing of Europe
    1. Anglo-American cooperation
    2. Impact
  G. The Teheran Conference

        1. Included Roosevelt, Churchill, and Stalin
        2. Decisions
          a. Planning for the D-Day invasion and the Russian offensive
          b. Russia promised to enter war against Japan
    H. D-Day
        1. Eisenhower in command of Operation "Overlord"
        2. The invasion
        3. Slowing momentum of the drive on Germany

V. The war in the Pacific
    A. Guadalcanal offensive
    B. MacArthur in New Guinea
    C. Nimitz in the Central Pacific
        1. The Gilberts
        2. The Marshalls
        3. Battle of the Philippine Sea
        4. Battle of Leyte Gulf
          a. Decision to use the Philippines for staging area
          b. The largest naval battle in history and loss of most of Japan's remaining sea power

VI. The election of 1944
    A. Republicans nominate Thomas E. Dewey
    B. Democrats named Truman for vice-president
    C. Victory for Roosevelt

VII. Closing on Germany
    A. German counteroffensive
    B. Allied moves against Germany

VIII. The Yalta Conference
    A. Roosevelt's ideas
        1. Ensure that Russia joined the war against Japan
        2. Form a world organization—the United Nations
    B. The division of Germany and Berlin
    C. Russia "given" eastern Europe
        1. Question of Poland
        2. Other eastern European areas
        3. Russia wanted a buffer zone between it and Germany
    D. Yalta's legacy
        1. Soviet violations
        2. Secret agreements concerning the Far East

IX. Collapse of the Third Reich
    A. Roosevelt's death

B. Collapse of Germany
  1. Mussolini and Hitler dead
  2. Unconditional surrender
C. Discovery of the Nazi Holocaust

X. Collapse of Japan
  A. Allied moves toward an invasion of Japan
    1. The Philippines
    2. Iwo Jima
    3. Okinawa
  B. The atomic bomb
    1. Development of the bomb
    2. Decision to use the bomb
      a. Target chosen
      b. Potsdam Declaration threatened bombing if Japan did not surrender immediately
    3. Devastation of the bomb
      a. At Hiroshima
      b. At Nagasaki
    4. Japanese surrender
      a. Emperor allowed to keep his throne under the authority of the Allied supreme commander
      b. Formal surrender signed

XI. The final ledger on the war
  A. Estimates of death and destruction
  B. Impact on America and Russia

Suggestions for Lecture Topics

A lecture on the war's effects on American society could use John Morton Blum's *V Was for Victory* (1976) and Richard Polenberg's *War and Society* (1972) as sources.

The relevant chapters in Russell F. Weigley's *The American Way of War* (1973) would be a useful basis for a discussion of how military strategists pursued the war in both theaters.

For a lecture on the decision to drop the atomic bomb and historians' interpretations of that decision, see the chapter in *After the Fact*, edited by James West Davidson and Mark Hamilton Lytle (2nd ed., 1986). Another good lecture could use Paul S. Boyer's *By the Bomb's Early Light* (1985); Boyer shows how the bomb quickly came to influence all aspects of American culture.

Multiple-Choice Questions

1. A. Philip Randolph
    A. headed the Office of Economic Stabilization.
    * B. headed the Brotherhood of Sleeping Car Porters.
    C. led American forces in the Philippines from 1941 to 1942.
    D. was Franklin D. Roosevelt's attorney-general.

2. The Battle of Midway
    * A. was the turning point of the war in the Pacific.
    B. was fought in the Coral Sea.
    C. was fought to a draw.
    D. cost the United States almost one-third of its naval force.

3. The purpose of the War Production Board was to
    * A. direct industrial conversion to war production.
    B. finance the building of war plants.
    C. oversee military-scientific research and development.
    D. publish and distribute American propaganda.

4. Which of the following statements on financing the war is true?
    * A. FDR supported, and Congress opposed, increases in income taxes.
    B. Congress supported, and FDR opposed, increases in income taxes.
    C. Unlike the case in World War I, war bonds played an insignificant role in World War II.
    D. Because of high wartime taxes, the national debt grew only slightly.

5. The Office of Price Administration
    A. froze wages and farm prices.
    B. was designed to raise consumer prices.
    * C. rationed tires, sugar, coffee, gasoline, and other items.
    D. is correctly represented by all the above.

6. The Fair Employment Practices Committee
    A. offered women job opportunities in defense industries.
    B. had authority to bring suit against employers who refused to comply with its "equal pay for equal work" directive.
    * C. persuaded many employers to hire blacks, even though it had no power of enforcement.
    D. was established under the Civil Rights Act of 1941.

7. By the end of World War II, how many women had entered the workforce?
   - A. 250,000
   - B. 600,000
   - C. 2,000,000
   - * D. 6,000,000

8. Nisei were
   - A. low-cost but efficient bombs developed for mass use in Germany.
   - * B. Americans of Japanese descent.
   - C. female naval personnel.
   - D. small-bore automatic rifles developed in 1942 and mass-produced in a converted bicycle factory.

9. During the war, domestic politics was marked by
   - * A. a growing conservatism.
   - B. continued concern for New Deal programs.
   - C. the "liberalization" of southern Democrats.
   - D. the unrestrained growth of labor unions.

10. All the following were significant reasons for the Allies' decision to fight Hitler first *except*
    - A. Nazi forces posed more of a threat to the western hemisphere.
    - * B. Japan was no longer a threat after 1941.
    - C. German war potential was greater.
    - D. Germany was more advanced in science than Japan, and was therefore more likely to come up with a devastating new weapon.

11. In 1941, FDR and Churchill
    - A. revoked the Atlantic Charter.
    - B. agreed on an early cross-Channel invasion of Germany.
    - C. named General H. H. "Hap" Arnold to head the Allied naval force.
    - * D. agreed on general war aims but not on specific strategies.

12. Erwin Rommel
    - A. was England's chief delegate at the Allies' war talk in Washington in 1942.
    - * B. headed Germany's forces in North Africa.
    - C. was a French Nazi collaborator.
    - D. wrote *The Way to Win*, a book highly critical of FDR's war policies.

13. All the following statements about labor during the war are true
    except
    A. the Smith-Connally War Labor Dispute Act was intended
       to keep labor problems from hurting the war effort.
    B. about a dozen states passed laws restricting union
       activities.
    C. unions benefited from the growth of the civilian
       workforce.
  * D. union membership decreased 35 percent during the war.

14. Following the Allied victory in Sicily,
    A. Mussolini's forces held off the Allied force advancing on
       Italy for 15 months.
    B. Mussolini committed suicide.
  * C. Italy joined the Allies.
    D. the Allies turned their attention to Egypt.

15. The strategic bombing of Germany in 1943
  * A. employed pilots and planes from the air forces of England
       and the United States.
    B. cut significantly into German war production.
    C. was effective in breaking German civilian morale.
    D. was aimed only at high-tech war industries.

16. The meeting of the Big Three leaders (Roosevelt, Churchill, and
    Stalin) to plan an invasion of France and a simultaneous Russian
    offensive took place in
  * A. Teheran.
    B. Paris.
    C. Geneva.
    D. Casablanca.

17. The head of Operation "Overlord" was
    A. Omar Bradley.
  * B. Dwight D. Eisenhower.
    C. George Patton.
    D. Douglas MacArthur.

18. The new strategy used in the Pacific in 1943 was
    A. attacking only the smallest Japanese naval vessels.
    B. attacking the northern islands first, then moving south-
       ward.
  * C. isolating the Japanese strongholds, leaving them to "die
       on the vine."
    D. firebombing the islands to destroy all the foliage where
       Japanese could hide.

19. All the following statements about the Battle of Leyte Gulf are true *except*
    A. it was the largest naval engagement in history.
    B. the Japanese lost almost all of their remaining sea power.
    C. it followed naturally the Allied invasion of the Philippines.
    * D. German submarines were almost able to repel the advancing Allied naval forces.

20. In the election of 1944,
    A. Roosevelt won an unprecedented third term.
    B. the Democratic candidate for vice-president was Thomas E. Dewey.
    C. the vote in the southern states was, for the first time in history, overwhelmingly Republican.
    * D. the Republicans argued that America needed younger leaders.

21. Following their quick sweep across France, the Allies
    * A. lost momentum in the fall of 1944.
    B. just as quickly captured most of Germany.
    C. were forced to retreat to their pre-1944 lines.
    D. were surrounded and nearly defeated in the Ruhr Valley.

22. To ensure that Russia joined the war against Japan, Roosevelt agreed to all the following *except*
    A. continued Russian control of Outer Mongolia.
    B. Russia's acquisition of the Kurile Islands from Japan.
    * C. recognition of Russian sovereignty over Manchuria.
    D. Russia's recovery of rights and territory lost after the Russo-Japanese War in 1905.

23. The Yalta Conference
    A. met early in 1944.
    B. discussed mainly wartime strategy.
    C. planned an invasion of France to coincide with a Russian offensive.
    * D. gave Russia control of eastern Germany.

24. When the advancing Russian front reached Poland in 1944,
    A. Russia promised not to try to influence the Polish government.
    B. Poles welcomed a Communist government.
    * C. the Russians installed a puppet government.
    D. the Polish government-in-exile left London to govern its country again.

25. President Roosevelt died
    A. just one week after the surrender of Germany.
  * B. in Warm Springs, Georgia.
    C. on the Atlantic Ocean while returning from the Yalta Conference.
    D. of leukemia.

26. V-E Day
  * A. celebrated the defeat of Germany.
    B. celebrated the defeat of Japan.
    C. was in 1944.
    D. followed the Allied win at Okinawa.

27. The Battle of Okinawa
    A. was most significant for serving as a staging area for later attacks on Japan.
  * B. was most significant for wearing down the remaining Japanese defenses.
    C. was relatively bloodless.
    D. came just before the reconquest of the Philippines.

28. The development of the atomic bomb that was dropped on Hiroshima
    A. was opposed by most Americans.
  * B. was the responsibility of the Manhattan Project.
    C. was the responsibility of a group of scientists headed by Albert Einstein.
    D. cost just over $20 million.

29. The Japanese surrender
  * A. allowed the emperor to keep his throne under the authority of an Allied supreme commander.
    B. came just hours after an atomic bomb virtually destroyed the city of Hiroshima.
    C. saved thousands of lives, because Americans had a second atomic bomb they had threatened to use.
    D. left only Russia for the Allies to defeat to end World War II.

30. The cost of World War II
    A. included military expenditures and property losses for all involved nations of perhaps $70 million.
  * B. included over 40 million military and civilian dead.

    C. was more costly for the United States (in proportion to population) than for any other major power.

    D. is correctly described by all the above statements.

Suggested Essay Questions

1. Discuss the major steps in America's industrial and economic mobilization for World War II.

2. Describe the effects of World War II on women, blacks, Japanese-Americans, and labor.

3. What military and economic factors influenced the Allied victory in the Pacific?

4. Describe the agreements made during the war that shaped the postwar world. In your view, did Roosevelt "sell out" to the Russians at Yalta? Explain.

5. Why did America drop the atomic bomb on Japan? Was the action justified?

Chapter 30

THE FAIR DEAL AND CONTAINMENT

This chapter covers domestic and foreign affairs in the Truman administration, including demobilization, the Cold War, the Korean War, and the second Red Scare.

Chapter Outline

I. Demobilization under Truman
  A. Harry Truman
    1. Background and character
    2. Domestic proposals of 1945
  B. Demobilization
    1. Rapid reduction of armed forces
      a. By 1950, armed forces down to 600,000
      b. The baby-boom generation
    2. Demobilization did not bring depression
      a. Unemployment pay and other Social Security benefits
      b. Servicemen's Readjustment Act of 1944
      c. Pent-up demand for consumer goods
  C. The problem of inflation
    1. Demands for wage increases
    2. Strikes
    3. Truman's response to economic problems
      a. The gradual death of the Office of Price Administration
      b. Price controls ended after 1946

II. Truman's early domestic policies
  A. Congressional elections of 1946
    1. Discontent with Democrats
    2. Republicans won majorities in both houses of Congress
  B. Record of the Republican Congress
    1. Taft-Hartley Act
      a. Restrictions on labor

        b. Passed over Truman's veto

        c. Effect of act

    2. Tax reduction

        a. Truman felt that the government debt should be reduced

        b. Congress overrode Truman's veto of a $5-billion tax cut

    3. National Security Act

        a. Response to the congressional investigation of Pearl Harbor

        b. Created the National Military Establishment, the National Security Council, and the Central Intelligence Agency

    4. Presidential Succession Act—Speaker of the House and president pro tempore of the Senate to follow the vice-president

    5. Twenty-second Amendment—limited presidents to two full terms

III. Development of the Cold War

   A. The United Nations

     1. Background

     2. Outline of the United Nations

     3. Ratification of the United Nations charter

   B. Differences with the Soviets

     1. Problems in eastern Europe

        a. Russian violations of the Yalta agreements

        b. Communist takeovers

     2. Postwar settlement treaties confirmed Soviet control of eastern Europe

     3. Proposals to control atomic energy

   C. The policy of containment

     1. Formulated by George F. Kennan

     2. The Truman Doctrine

        a. Communist influence in Turkey and Greece

        b. Financial aid "to support free peoples who are resisting attempted subjugation"

     3. The Marshall Plan

        a. War damage and dislocation in Europe invited Communist influence

        b. Economic aid to all European countries offered in the European recovery program

        c. European response

     4. Dividing Germany

        a. Merger of Allied zones
        b. Berlin blockade and airlift
        c. Creation of East and West Germany
    5. North Atlantic Treaty Organization (NATO)
        a. Members
        b. Pledged signers to treat an attack against one as an attack against all
        c. Counterpart in eastern Europe
    6. Establishment of Israel

IV. Domestic politics
    A. Division of the Democratic Party
        1. Southern conservatives upset over Truman's civil rights stand
        2. Democratic left upset at Truman's firing of Henry Wallace
    B. Truman's strategy for 1948
        1. To shore up New Deal coalition
        2. New departure—emphasis on civil rights
    C. The 1948 election
        1. Republicans nominated Thomas E. Dewey
        2. Democrats nominated Truman and included a strong civil rights plank
            a. Southern conservatives formed the States' Rights Democratic Party ("Dixiecrats") and nominated J. Strom Thurmond
            b. The Democratic left formed the Progressive Party and nominated Henry Wallace
        3. Election results
            a. Truman won in major upset
            b. Split in Democratic Party helped Truman
            c. Democratic majorities in Congress
            d. A vindication of the New Deal
        4. Fair Deal proposals
            a. Truman won on higher minimum wage and extension of Social Security, rent controls, farm price supports, housing, and rural electrification
            b. Truman lost on civil rights bills, national health insurance, federal aid to education, and repeal of the Taft-Hartley Act

V. The Cold War heats up
    A. Truman's foreign policy
    B. China

      1. History of the Communist movement in China
        a. Rise of Mao Tse-tung
        b. U.S. support for Chiang Kai-shek
      2. Nationalists forced to Formosa (Taiwan)
      3. United States sought to shore up friendly Asian regimes
    C. Problems of the Atomic Age
      1. Russia detonated its first atom bomb
      2. Truman ordered construction of the hydrogen bomb
      3. Call for buildup of conventional forces to provide options to nuclear war

VI. The Korean War
    A. America's entry
      1. Korea from World War II to 1950
      2. North Korean forces invaded South Korea
      3. United Nations sanctioned aid to South Korea
      4. Truman ordered American military forces to Korea under U.N. auspices
    B. America in the Korean War
      1. General Douglas MacArthur commanded U.N. forces
      2. Chiefly an American affair
      3. Congress never voted a declaration of war
    C. Military developments
      1. Decision to invade the North
      2. Chinese Communists entered the war
    D. Dismissal of MacArthur
      1. Different views of the Korean War
      2. MacArthur openly criticized Truman
      3. MacArthur dismissed
      4. Public reaction
        a. Initially in favor of MacArthur
        b. Senate investigation justified Truman
    E. End of the war
      1. Snags in negotiations
      2. Truce signed
      3. Cost of the war

VII. Another Red Scare
    A. Evidences of espionage
    B. Truman's loyalty program
    C. The Hiss case
      1. Whittaker Chambers, former Soviet agent, accused Hiss of passing secret documents
      2. Hiss convicted of perjury

    D. The Rosenbergs executed
    E. Joseph McCarthy's witch-hunt
       1. Rise of McCarthy
       2. His anti-Communist tactics
    F. McCarran Internal Security Act
       1. Passed over Truman's veto
       2. Attempt to control Communist activities

VIII. Assessment of the Cold War

Suggestions for Lecture Topics

For a lecture showing how Truman tried to carry out the promises of the New Deal, see Alonzo L. Hamby's *Beyond the New Deal: Harry S. Truman and American Liberalism* (1973).

Michael Mandelbaum's *The Nuclear Question* (1979) goes beyond the chronology of this chapter, but could be used now (or later) for a lecture on America's nuclear policy.

Multiple-Choice Questions

1. The domestic program that Harry Truman sent to Congress in September 1945
    A. was a setback for laborers.
  * B. continued and enlarged the New Deal.
    C. addressed only the problem of demobilization.
    D. reversed most of his predecessor's policies.

2. During the 1950s
    A. international tensions decreased.
    B. the birth rate dropped.
  * C. the army had less than 10 percent of the number of men it had at its peak in World War II.
    D. all the above were true.

3. Among the factors that cushioned the economic impact of demobilization after World War II were all the following *except*
    A. unemployment pay and other Social Security benefits.
    B. the "G.I. Bill of Rights."
  * C. reductions in business investments.
    D. the pent-up demand for consumer goods.

4. The main economic problem faced by Truman in his first term was
  * A. inflation.

    B. dropping prices.

    C. a dwindling money supply.

    D. tight credit.

5. The Office of Price Administration

    A. managed to keep prices high through the 1940s.

    B. managed to keep prices low through the 1940s.

    C. was created in 1946 to deal with the economic problems associated with demobilization.

   * D. was phased out shortly after the war.

6. The Taft-Hartley Act of 1947

    A. was passed with Roosevelt's support.

    B. set up a Council of Economic Advisors.

    C. ended discrimination on the basis of race in hiring for defense-related jobs.

   * D. was generally a setback for labor.

7. The National Security Act, which established the National Security Council and the Central Intelligence Agency, was passed as a response to

    A. Hitler's rapid rise to power.

   * B. the success of Japan's attack on Pearl Harbor.

    C. charges that Communists had infiltrated the government.

    D. the launching of Russia's Sputnik I.

8. The Twenty-second Amendment

   * A. limited presidents to two terms.

    B. placed the Speaker of the House next in line for the presidency after the vice-president.

    C. lowered the national voting age to 18.

    D. repealed the Prohibition Amendment.

9. Which of the following was *not* a permanent member of the Security Council of the United Nations?

   * A. Canada

    B. China

    C. the United States

    D. Russia

10. The person usually credited with formulating the first formal statement of America's policy of containment was

   * A. George F. Kennan.

    B. William Fulbright.

    C. James F. Byrnes.

    D. Bernard Baruch.

11. Under the Truman Doctrine, Congress voted for an initial $400 million in economic aid to
    A. Yugoslavia.
    B. Turkey and Yugoslavia.
    C. Albania.
    * D. Greece and Turkey.

12. The Marshall Plan of economic aid
    A. was "to support free peoples who are resisting attempted subjugation by armed minorities or by outside pressures."
    B. set up the so-called Committee of National Liberation.
    * C. was "directed not against country or doctrine, but against hunger, poverty, desperation, and chaos."
    D. prevented a Soviet takeover of Czechoslovakia.

13. East Germany was controlled after World War II by
    A. the United States, France, and Great Britain.
    B. the United States, France, and Italy.
    C. the United States.
    * D. Russia.

14. The North Atlantic Treaty
    A. pledged signers to "consult immediately" in case of attack.
    * B. was ratified by a large margin in the Senate.
    C. was a response to the news that the Soviets had set off an atomic bomb.
    D. was between Britain and the United States.

15. When Jewish leaders proclaimed the independent state of Israel in 1948, the United States
    A. refused to recognize the new state until democratic elections had been held.
    B. broke diplomatic relations with most of the Arab states.
    * C. recognized the new state immediately.
    D. offered military and financial aid to the Arab states.

16. In response to a Soviet blockade of West Berlin in 1948, Truman
    A. used armed convoys to supply the city.
    * B. used a massive airlift to supply the city.
    C. conceded Berlin to the Russians in order to save West Germany.
    D. conceded Berlin to the Russians in order to save East Germany.

17. In the 1948 election, Republicans
    A. saw no hope for victory in the presidential race.

B. campaigned against the New Deal reforms.
* C. nominated Thomas E. Dewey for president.
D. nominated Alben Barkley for vice-president.

18. The presidential candidate of the States' Rights Democratic party was
   A. Earl Warren.
* B. J. Strom Thurmond.
   C. Henry A. Wallace.
   D. Harold E. Stassen.

19. Which of the following statements about the election of 1948 is *not* true?
   A. The split in the Democratic Party helped Truman.
* B. "Dixiecrats" carried all the former Confederate states.
   C. Truman won in a major upset.
   D. Democrats won majorities in both houses of Congress in addition to winning the White House.

20. Following the election of 1948, Truman was able to push through Congress
   A. a civil rights bill and federal aid to education.
   B. national health insurance.
   C. repeal of the Taft-Hartley Act.
* D. farm price supports, a public housing program, and more money for the TVA and rural electrification.

21. "Point Four" of Truman's foreign policy was
   A. the United Nations.
* B. technical aid for underdeveloped nations.
   C. NATO.
   D. the Marshall Plan.

22. In the "China tangle," the United States sent $2 billion in aid to fight
   A. the Chinese nationalists.
   B. the Kuomintang.
* C. Mao Tse-tung.
   D. Ho Chi Minh.

23. The top-secret document prepared by the National Security Council in 1950
   A. was a plan for military aid to the French-supported regime of Bao Dai in Vietnam.
   B. led to the buildup of America's arsenal of atomic weapons.

    * C. called for rebuilding America's conventional military forces.

    D. addressed the problem of Communists in South Korea.

24. The war in Korea
    A. began in 1946, when Mao Tse-tung's forces refused to leave South Korea.
    B. was responsible for almost 1,000,000 American casualties.
    * C. began in 1950, when North Korean forces invaded South Korea.
    D. lasted just five months.

25. The United States entered the Korean War
    A. against the wishes of President Truman.
    * B. without a vote by Congress.
    C. without sanction by the United Nations.
    D. because of its interest in the oil deposits off the southern tip of the Korean peninsula.

26. Truman removed General Douglas MacArthur
    A. because of popular demand.
    B. because MacArthur did not want to fight an all-out war in Korea and China.
    C. after a Senate investigative committee found that MacArthur had held secret negotiations with Chinese officials.
    * D. because MacArthur openly criticized the president for not wanting to fight Red China.

27. Julius and Ethel Rosenberg
    A. were convicted of perjury in a case involving purported espionage activities.
    B. accused Whittaker Chambers of passing secret documents to Soviet agents.
    * C. were executed for supposedly giving the Russians the secret to the atomic bomb.
    D. sued Richard M. Nixon for slander.

28. "To Secure These Rights" was a committee report on
    * A. civil rights for blacks.
    B. rights for workers and labor unions.
    C. the homeless.
    D. victims of McCarthyism.

29. The McCarran Internal Security Act of 1950
    * A. was passed over Truman's veto.

  B. was upheld by the Supreme Court's "clear and present danger" doctrine.

  C. forced over 2,000 civil service employees to resign.

  D. led to the arrest of Alger Hiss.

30. By the end of the Truman years the United States had

  A. returned to its isolationist stance.

  B. repudiated almost all its peacetime alliances.

  * C. become committed to a major and permanent national military establishment.

  D. repudiated the Monroe Doctrine.

Suggested Essay Questions

1. Describe the social and economic effects of demobilization at the end of World War II.

2. Trace the major developments in the Cold War from 1945 to 1948.

3. Why did Truman win the presidential election of 1948? Why was his victory considered a major upset?

4. What did Truman mean by a "Fair Deal"? How did it compare to FDR's New Deal?

5. Describe the Red Scare that followed the end of World War II. What caused it? What were its major results?

Chapter 31

THROUGH THE PICTURE WINDOW: SOCIETY AND CULTURE, 1945–1960

This chapter discusses the growth of the postwar economy, suburban migration, and other factors that led to the so-called corporate life, or conformity, of the 1950s. Various reactions to the corporate life by social critics, artists, and writers are also covered.

Chapter Outline

I. People of plenty
- A. The postwar economy
  1. Growth of the economy
     - a. GNP doubled from 1945 to 1960
     - b. Perpetual economic growth now seen as possible and desirable
  2. Reasons for growth
     - a. Military spending
     - b. American monopoly
     - c. Consumer demand
     - d. "Baby boom"
- B. Consumer culture
  1. Increased production
     - a. Variety
     - b. The television
  2. Increased purchasing
     - a. Dispersion through society
     - b. Role of advertising
     - c. Credit
  3. Cultural effects
     - a. Shopping centers
     - b. Effect on young people
- C. Suburban migration
  1. Urban growth
     - a. Most population growth was urban and suburban
     - b. Rise of "Sunbelt"
     - c. Suburbia

    2. Reasons for suburban growth
      a. Levittown and mass production
      b. Low-cost loans
      c. Automobiles and highways
      d. Other considerations, including race

II. A conforming culture
  A. Corporate life
    1. Growth of the middle class
    2. Growth of big business
  B. Women's place
    1. Conformity emphasized
    2. The cult of domesticity
  C. Religious revival
    1. Americans as joiners
    2. Increase in church membership
    3. Other reasons for religious revival
      a. Patriotism
      b. The marketing of religion
      c. The message of the popular religion
  D. Neo-orthodoxy
    1. Criticism of popular religion
    2. Reinhold Niebuhr

III. Cracks in the picture window
  A. Social criticism
    1. Galbraith's *The Affluent Society*
    2. Keats's *The Cracks in the Picture Window*
    3. Riesman's *The Lonely Crowd*
  B. Alienation on the stage: Miller's *Death of a Salesman*
  C. The novel
    1. Salinger's *Catcher in the Rye*
    2. Other novels
  D. Painting
    1. Edward Hopper
    2. Jackson Pollock
  E. The Beats
    1. Leading figures
      a. Allen Ginsberg
      b. Jack Kerouac
      c. William Burroughs
      d. Neal Cassady
    2. Their philosophy and works

Suggestions for Lecture Topics

David M. Potter's *People of Plenty: Economic Abundance and the American Character* (1954) would support a lecture on the economy and culture of the 1950s.

Dr. Spock's book on child care, discussed in this chapter, might prove a good lecture topic. Begin by looking at Nancy P. Weiss's "Mother, the Invention of Necessity: Dr. Benjamin Spock's *Baby and Child Care"* (*American Quarterly* 29 [1977]: 519–546).

Herbert J. Gans's *The Levittowners: Ways of Life and Politics in a New Suburban Community* (1967) is a lengthy book with plenty of information to draw on for a lecture on one of America's most famous and interesting suburban communities.

For a lecture on the "Beats," the best source is John Tytell's *Naked Angels: The Lives and Literature of the Beat Generation* (1976).

Multiple-Choice Questions

1. Between 1945 and 1960 the Gross National Product
    A. stayed roughly the same, in constant dollars.
    B. actually declined, in constant dollars.
  * C. nearly doubled.
    D. quadrupled.

2. During the 1950s
    A. American leaders realized that sustained economic growth was not necessary for national well-being.
    B. the gap in living standards between the United States and the rest of the world decreased.
    C. President Eisenhower warned that another economic collapse was possible.
  * D. economic safeguards from the New Deal assured most Americans.

3. The largest single stimulant to the post-1945 economy was
  * A. military spending.
    B. high employment.
    C. the movement of women into the workforce.
    D. growth in the computer industry.

4. The baby boom
    A. peaked in 1957.
    B. was a large part of a 30 percent growth in American popu-
       lation between 1945 and 1960.
    C. paralleled a similar boom in consumer demand.
  * D. is correctly represented by all the above.

5. The average real income of Americans in 1955, compared to that
   just before the Crash of 1929, was
    A. about half as much.
    B. about 10 percent less.
    C. slightly more.
  * D. twice as much.

6. Which of the following statistics covering the years 1945 to 1960
   is *not* true?
    A. Advertising expenditures increased over 1,000 percent.
    B. Consumer credit increased 800 percent.
    C. Ownership of television sets increased from 7,000 to 50
       million.
  * D. The portion of income that Americans saved (rather than
       spent) increased from 5 percent to between 10 and 20
       percent.

7. All the following factors promoted the growth of suburbs *except*
    A. low-cost government loans.
    B. expanded road and highway construction.
  * C. laws forbidding residential segregation by races.
    D. increased auto production.

8. According to Adlai Stevenson and articles in *Life* magazine, the
   proper role for women in the 1950s was
  * A. being a good mother and wife.
    B. working.
    C. being active in government and civic affairs.
    D. fighting for women's rights.

9. Which of the following did *not* promote the upbeat and soothing
   popular religion of the 1950s?
    A. Jane Russell
  * B. Reinhold Niebuhr
    C. the Protestant Council of New York City
    D. Norman Vincent Peale

10. The author of *The Power of Positive Thinking* was
    A. Oral Roberts.
    * B. Norman Vincent Peale.
    C. Billy Graham.
    D. Agnes Meyer.

11. Which of the following did not increase between 1945 and 1960?
    * A. substandard housing
    B. worker productivity
    C. the gap in living standards between the United States and the rest of the world
    D. the number of shopping centers

12. Which of the following statements about Long Island's Levittown is *not* true?
    A. It contained over 10,000 homes.
    B. Blacks were not allowed to buy homes there.
    C. Veterans could buy a Levitt house with no down payment and monthly installments of $56.
    * D. Children were not allowed until after 1963.

13. The fastest-growing periodical in the 1950s was
    A. *Business Week*.
    B. *Life*.
    C. *Parents*.
    * D. *TV Guide*.

14. Which of the following statements, all of which cover the period 1945 to 1960, is *not* true?
    A. Suburbs grew six times faster than central cities.
    * B. The so-called "Sunbelt" became the most densely populated area of the country.
    C. Black migration from the rural South to northern and midwestern urban areas increased over pre-World War II levels.
    D. Church membership increased from about 50 percent to over 65 percent of the population.

15. The emphasis of the religious revival of the 1950s was on
    A. personal guilt.
    * B. psychological security and happiness.
    C. social ills (such as poverty and racial segregation).
    D. Calvinism.

16. The author of the neoconservative religious movement was
    * A. Reinhold Niebuhr.
    B. Billy Graham.

    C. Oral Roberts.

    D. Normal Vincent Peale.

17. The book by John Kenneth Galbraith which argued that sustained economic growth would not in itself solve the nation's social problems was

    A. *The Failure of America.*

* B. *The Affluent Society.*

    C. *The Waste Makers.*

    D. *The Other America.*

18. *The Lonely Crowd*, the book that discussed a shift in American personality from "inner-directed" to "outer-directed," was written by

    A. John Keats.

* B. David Riesman.

    C. Joseph Wood Krutch.

    D. Oprah Winfrey.

19. According to David Riesman, Dr. Spock's book on child care

    A. stressed the value of teaching children independence.

    B. emphasized feeding schedules and how to change a diaper rather than social values.

* C. encouraged parents to develop the "gregarious" talents of their children.

    D. had low sales in the 1950s because parents were more interested in their own well-being than in their children's.

20. The "corporate character" of American life, as described in this chapter,

    A. led to an "inner-directed" personality type.

* B. was an increasingly regimented conformity.

    C. concerned primarily the increasing role of business in Americans' lives.

    D. was the focus of Arthur Miller's *The Organization Man.*

21. According to Reinhold Niebuhr,

    A. "each age finds its own [artistic] techniques."

    B. parents should foster in their children qualities that would enhance their chances in the "personality market."

    C. advertisers should take an active role in creating consumer demand.

* D. the popular religion of the 1950s was inadequate to cure the ills of society.

22. *The Crack in the Picture Window*
    A. was written by John Keats.
    B. ridiculed Levittown and similar mass-produced communities.
    C. argued that suburbanites were living in a "homogeneous, postwar Hell."
    * D. is correctly represented by all the above.

23. *Death of a Salesman*, the play whose character Willy Loman typified the loneliness of postwar society, was written by
    * A. Arthur Miller.
    B. Edward Albee.
    C. Tennessee Williams.
    D. Philip Roth.

24. Of the following, which best fits into the category that *Time* magazine called the "dread-despair-and-decay camp of American letters"?
    A. *The Cardinal*
    B. *The Robe*
    * C. *The Victim*
    D. *Exodus*

25. *Catcher in the Rye*, a troubling exploration of a young man's search for meaning and self in a smothering society, was written by
    A. Joseph Heller.
    B. James Baldwin.
    * C. J. D. Salinger.
    D. H. G. Wells.

26. The American painter whose work showed isolated melancholy and anonymous individuals was
    A. Jackson Pollock.
    B. Norman Rockwell.
    * C. Edward Hopper.
    D. Franz Kline.

27. The major proponent of abstract expressionism was
    A. John Updike.
    B. Edward Hopper.
    * C. Jackson Pollock.
    D. Gregory Corso.

28. The Beats
  * A. were, like the abstract expressionists, motivated by a desire to liberate self-expression.
  B. originated in San Francisco.
  C. were ironically themselves conformists, for they each subsumed their own unique personalities to the "Beat" philosophy.
  D. are correctly represented by all the above.

29. All the following were Beats *except*
  A. Neal Cassady.
  B. Allen Ginsberg.
  C. Jack Kerouac.
  * D. George Meany.

30. William Burroughs wrote the book
  A. *Howl.*
  * B. *Naked Lunch.*
  C. *Leaves of Grass.*
  D. *On the Road.*

Suggested Essay Questions

1. What factors account for the growth of the American economy after World War II?

2. What were the main reasons for the growth of suburbs in this period? How did this affect American society?

3. How did the image of women reflect the "corporate life" of the 1950s?

4. How did the religious revival and neo-orthodoxy fit into the culture of the 1950s?

5. Show briefly how playwrights, novelists, painters, and the Beats reacted to the conformist culture of the 1950s.

Chapter 32

CONFLICT AND DEADLOCK:
THE EISENHOWER YEARS

This chapter covers Eisenhower's rise to the presidency and his domestic and foreign policies, including developments in civil rights and the Cold War.

Chapter Outline

I. Eisenhower's rise to the presidency
   A. "Time for a change" from the Truman administration
   B. Republicans in 1952
      1. Robert A. Taft inspired little enthusiasm
      2. Dwight D. Eisenhower won nomination
   C. Democrats in 1952
      1. Truman decided not to run again
      2. Nomination went to Adlai Stevenson
   D. The election of 1952
      1. Eisenhower won landslide victory
      2. Victory for Republicans
      3. Except for presidency, Democrats fared well in 1952
   E. Eisenhower's career before 1952
   F. Eisenhower's approach to the presidency
      1. Methodical staff work
      2. Questionable cabinet appointments

II. Eisenhower's "dynamic conservatism"
   A. Cutbacks in New Deal programs
   B. Endurance of the New Deal

III. The Korean peace talks
   A. Continuing deadlock in early 1953
   B. Aerial bombardment and "secret" threats used to obtain agreement
   C. Negotiations moved quickly to armistice

IV. The end of McCarthyism
   A. McCarthy still strong after 1952
   B. Televised hearings led to McCarthy's downfall

    C. Eisenhower's concern for internal security
       1. Executive order allowed firing of "security risk" government workers
       2. J. Robert Oppenheimer's security clearance removed
    D. The Warren Court and the Red Scare

V. Foreign policy in Eisenhower's first term
    A. John Foster Dulles
       1. Dulles's career
       2. Dulles's foreign policy
          a. Containment was needlessly defensive
          b. Policy of liberation
    B. Covert actions
       1. Role of the Central Intelligence Agency
       2. Foreign governments overthrown
          a. Iran
          b. Guatemala
    C. Dulles and containment
       1. No significant departure from containment
       2. "Massive retaliation"
       3. "Brinksmanship"
    D. Indochina
       1. European colonies in Asia
          a. Independence for British colonies
          b. United States aided Dutch and French efforts to regain colonies from local control
          c. Ho Chi Minh's efforts for Indochinese independence
       2. First Indochina War
          a. Conflict between Ho and French
          b. Increased American aid for French
          c. Eisenhower's "domino theory"
          d. French defeat at Dienbienphu
       3. The Geneva Accords
          a. Proposed to unify Vietnam after 1956 elections
          b. American response—the establishment of the Southeast Asia Treaty Organization (SEATO)
       4. Rise of Ngo Dinh Diem
          a. Installed as Vietnamese premier by the French
          b. Diem's corrupt and oppressive regime
          c. Refused to sanction elections in 1956
          d. Emergence of Vietcong and the National Liberation Front

VI. Civil rights in the 1950s
    A. Eisenhower's ambiguous stance

B. The *Brown* decision (1954)
C. Montgomery bus boycott
1. Rosa Parks arrested for refusing to give up her seat on a bus to a white man
2. Martin Luther King, Jr., organized a bus boycott
3. Federal courts ruled against "separate but equal"
4. Southern Christian Leadership Conference formed
D. Civil Rights Act of 1957
E. Little Rock
1. Arkansas Governor Orval Faubus prevented black students from registering for high school
2. Eisenhower ordered military protection for students

VII. The election of 1956
A. Republicans nominated Eisenhower
B. Democrats chose Stevenson
C. Victory for Eisenhower

VIII. Foreign crises in the election year
A. The Middle East
1. Failure of the Middle East Treaty Organization
2. Suez Canal
a. Israel, France, and Britain began military attacks on Egypt
b. America sided with Nasser
B. Communist repression in Hungary
1. Hungary withdrew from the Warsaw Pact
2. Russian troops forced Hungary back into the Communist fold

IX. Domestic affairs in Eisenhower's second administration
A. The beginning of the space race
1. Russia launched Sputnik I (October 1957)
2. Americans suddenly noted apparent "missile gap"
a. Enlarged defense spending
b. Created NASA
c. National Defense Education Act of 1958 authorized federal grants for training in sciences
B. Domestic problems
1. Public confidence in Eisenhower dropped
2. Corruption in the White House
3. Eisenhower faced three successive Congresses dominated by the opposition party

X. Problems abroad
A. Lebanon

1. Leftist coup in Iraq threw out the pro-Western government
2. Lebanon received American military aid
3. American marines left Beirut when the situation stabilized

B. West Berlin
1. Khrushchev raised possibility of another blockade
2. Khrushchev stressed "peaceful coexistence"

C. The "U-2 summit"
1. Russians shot down American U-2 spy plane
2. Eisenhower's response
3. Khrushchev left the summit meeting

F. Cuba
1. Castro at first had American support
2. Castro crushed the opposition, became a dictator, and welcomed Communist aid
3. Eisenhower's reaction

XI. Assessing Eisenhower's presidency

Suggestions for Lecture Topics

One way to lecture on Eisenhower's administration would be to focus on his presidential style. See Fred I. Greenstein's *The Hidden-Hand Presidency: Eisenhower as Leader* (1982).

For a lecture on McCarthyism, a good source is David Caute's *The Great Fear: The Anti-Communist Purge under Truman and Eisenhower* (1978).

See William H. Chafe's *Civilities and Civil Rights: Greensboro, North Carolina, and the Black Struggle for Freedom* (1980) for a discussion of how one southern community reacted to the *Brown* school desegregation decision.

For a lecture on the cultural origins of the war in Vietnam, see Loren Baritz's *Backfire* (1985).

Multiple-Choice Questions

1. Senator Robert A. Taft
   A. was the Democratic candidate for president in 1952.
   B. was Eisenhower's running mate in 1952.
 * C. was known as "Mr. Republican," although he was a dull public speaker.
   D. led an investigation of corruption in Truman's administration.

2. In the election of 1952
   A. women voters overwhelmingly supported Taft.
   B. Democrats for the first time since 1860 carried every state in the Northeast.
   * C. Eisenhower won five states in the outer South.
   D. Democrats were able to keep their New Deal coalition intact.

3. Eisenhower's "domestic conservatism" included all the following *except*
   A. budget cutting.
   * B. cutting support for the Interstate highways.
   C. ending wage and price controls.
   D. reducing farm subsidies.

4. Eisenhower's administration extended the reach of the New Deal through all the following *except*
   A. extending the coverage of the Social Security Act.
   B. increasing the federal minimum wage.
   C. increasing federal expenditures for public health.
   * D. increasing federal expenditures for health care for the elderly and housing for the poor.

5. The main stumbling block to an armistice in Korea was the issue of
   * A. prisoner return.
   B. reparations.
   C. boundaries.
   D. fishing rights.

6. Joseph Welch was
   * A. the army counsel in the televised McCarthy hearings.
   B. America's chief negotiator in Korea.
   C. Eisenhower's chief advisor on matters of fiscal policy.
   D. chairman of the Permanent Investigation Subcommittee of the Senate Committee on Government Operations.

7. The Warren Court
   * A. overturned or limited several internal security measures.
   B. took the apparently paradoxical position that the states, and not the federal government, were responsible for internal security.
   C. took a broad view of the Smith Act of 1940.
   D. overturned the conviction of Julius and Ethel Rosenberg.

8. John Foster Dulles argued that the policy of containment
   A. should be expanded to include Asia as well as Europe.

* B. was needlessly defensive.
  C. would help free people from "Communist enslavement."
  D. might draw the United States into an unexpected and unwanted war.

9. In order to end the deadlock in the Korean peace talks, Eisenhower
   * A. hinted the the United States might use atomic weapons.
     B. agreed to return all prisoners.
     C. threatened to cut off shipments of food and medicine to North Korea.
     D. suggested that the peace talks be moved to Moscow.

10. "Brinksmanship" is associated with
    A. Kermit Roosevelt.
    * B. John Foster Dulles.
    C. Winston Churchill.
    D. Harry Truman.

11. Concerning the uprisings in the French colonies in Indochina, the Truman and Eisenhower administrations
    * A. sided with the French.
      B. sided with the Vietnamese.
      C. organized summit conferences, like the Bandung Conference in 1955.
      D. tried to remain strictly neutral.

12. The Geneva Accords
    A. were signed in 1959.
    B. left the French in control of North Vietnam.
    * C. called for elections to reunify Vietnam in 1956.
    D. were signed by the Americans.

13. Ho Chi Minh
    A. was a Communist.
    B. was a Vietnamese nationalist.
    C. had received American aid against Japan during World War II.
    * D. is correctly represented by all the above.

14. Who lost at Dienbienphu?
    A. the Americans
    B. the Vietminh
    * C. the French
    D. the Dutch

15. Ngo Dinh Diem
    A. was a Communist.
  * B. at first had Eisenhower's support.
    C. was the French-supported leader of South Vietnam from 1946 to 1955.
    D. is correctly represented by all the above.

16. During the Eisenhower administration, most advances in civil rights came from
  * A. the judicial branch.
    B. the executive branch.
    C. southern senators.
    D. northern senators.

17. In the case of *Brown v. Board of Education of Topeka, Kansas*, the Supreme Court
    A. ruled in favor of the Topeka Board of Education.
    B. outlawed segregation in public schools by a split five to four decision.
    C. agreed with Eisenhower's sentiments toward civil rights.
  * D. cited sociological and psychological findings in support of its decision.

18. "Massive resistance" was a slogan and policy associated with which of the following?
    A. Thurgood Marshall
    B. the NAACP
  * C. Harry F. Byrd
    D. Martin Luther King, Jr.

19. Orval Faubus
  * A. refused to allow black students to enter a previously all-white high school.
    B. was governor of Mississippi.
    C. wrote the so-called "Southern Manifesto" condemning the Supreme Court's decision in the *Brown* case.
    D. is correctly represented by all the above.

20. The name of Rosa Parks is usually identified with
    A. the Citizens' Councils.
    B. the Civil Rights Act of 1957.
  * C. the Montgomery bus boycott.
    D. the school desegregation cases.

21. In the election of 1956
    A. Eisenhower's heart attack of 1955 almost cost him the Republican nomination.

    * B. the Democratic presidential candidate was Adlai Stevenson.

    C. Democrats campaigned mainly on the civil rights issue.

    D. the Republican vice-presidential candidate was Estes Kefauver.

22. When Israeli forces invaded Egypt in October 1956, the United States
    * A. supported the Egyptians.
    B. supported the Israelis.
    C. tried to remain strictly neutral.
    D. opposed the Soviet position.

23. Eisenhower's vice-presidential running mate in 1956 was
    * A. Richard Nixon.
    B. Sherman Adams.
    C. Dean Acheson.
    D. Martin Durkin.

24. Americans suddenly became concerned about the apparent "missile gap" between the United States and the Soviet Union
    A. when the CIA discovered the size of the Russian military budget.
    B. as a direct result of the heavy cuts in defense spending during the budget battle of 1957.
    * C. when Russia launched its Sputnik I.
    D. when Russia exploded its first atomic bomb.

25. The Southeast Asia Treaty Organization (SEATO)
    A. was, like NATO, a common defense organization.
    B. was also called the Baghdad Pact.
    * C. included only three Asian countries.
    D. is correctly represented by all the above.

26. During the first two years of Eisenhower's second administration,
    A. opinion polls showed that confidence in his performance rose almost 40 percent.
    * B. Eisenhower's image was tarnished when congressional investigations revealed scandals in the White House.
    C. Republicans had small but sure majorities in both houses of Congress.
    D. Republicans gained support among farmers and union workers.

27. The Eisenhower Doctrine promised financial and economic aid against Communist aggression in what area?

    * A. the Middle East
    B. East Asia
    C. Berlin
    D. Hungary

28. The 1960 Russian-American summit meeting in Paris failed
    A. when Eisenhower refused to give Russia permission to inspect American military installations.
    B. after Russia offered military aid to the rebel government in Hungary.
    * C. because of the U-2 spy-plane incident.
    D. when Russian troops invaded Iraq just one week before the proposed meeting.

29. Fidel Castro's revolution in Cuba
    A. replaced Fulgencio Batista, who had brought democratic government to Cuba, with a dictatorship.
    B. angered many Russians who had wanted Cuba as a Communist foothold in the western hemisphere.
    * C. initially had the support of many Americans.
    D. ushered in a golden age of Cuban-American trade relations.

30. In his Farewell Address, Eisenhower warned against
    A. increased unemployment.
    * B. the growing military-industrial complex.
    C. moral laxity in foreign affairs.
    D. an overemphasis on looking to the future.

Suggested Essay Questions

1. Compare the achievements of Eisenhower's "dynamic conservatism" to those of the New Deal.

2. How did America become involved in Indochina? How did that involvement escalate during Eisenhower's administration?

3. Discuss the civil rights movement in the 1950s. What civil rights did blacks achieve in that decade?

4. Describe the major trends in American relations with the Soviets in the 1950s.

5. Why did Eisenhower's popularity decline between 1956 and 1958?

Chapter 33

INTO THE MAELSTROM: THE SIXTIES

This chapter covers the administrations of Kennedy and Johnson, including social and economic developments, the civil rights revolution, and developments in Vietnam.

Chapter Outline

I. Kennedy's rise
   A. The election of 1960
      1. Kennedy and Nixon: backgrounds
      2. The campaign
      3. Results
   B. Kennedy's administration
      1. Cabinet appointments emphasized youth and "Eastern Establishment"
      2. The "Kennedy style"

II. The Kennedy record
   A. Congress Democratic but conservative
   B. Legislative successes
   C. Civil rights
      1. Kennedy's stance
      2. The civil rights movement since 1955
         a. Sit-ins
         b. Freedom riders
         c. Integration of the University of Mississippi
         d. Demonstrations in Birmingham
         e. March on Washington
      3. Kennedy called for new civil rights legislation
   D. The Warren Court
      1. School prayer
      2. Criminal rights
         a. *Gideon v. Wainwright*
         b. *Miranda v. Arizona*

III. Foreign frontiers
   A. Bay of Pigs disaster
      1. 1,500 anti-Castro Cubans prepared by CIA

        2. Failure of invasion
- B. Berlin Wall
    1. Khrushchev threatened to limit access to Berlin
    2. Kennedy asked Congress for more defense funds
    3. Soviets constructed Berlin Wall
- C. Cuban missile crisis
    1. Discovery of missiles in Cuba
    2. Kennedy's reaction: blockade of Cuba
    3. Soviet response
        a. Soviet ships did not try to cross blockade
        b. Two messages from Khrushchev
    4. Aftereffects
- D. Vietnam
    1. Neutrality for Laos
    2. Kennedy's reluctance to escalate
    3. Premier Ngo Dinh Diem
        a. Lack of economic and social reform
        b. Opposition to Diem
        c. Increase in number of American military advisors
        d. Overthrow of Diem and later military regimes

IV. The end of Kennedy's administration
- A. Assassination in Dallas
- B. Images of Camelot

V. Lyndon Johnson and the Great Society
- A. Johnson's background and style
    1. Comparisons to other leaders
    2. Admiration for FDR
    3. Mastery of politics and Congress
- B. The war on poverty
    1. Michael Harrington's *The Other America*
    2. Economic opportunity bill
- C. The election of 1964
    1. Republicans
        a. Sought "a choice, not an echo"
        b. Nominated Barry Goldwater
        c. Goldwater's weaknesses
    2. Johnson's appeal for consensus
    3. Landslide victory for Johnson
- D. Landmark legislation
    1. Health insurance
        a. Medicare for the aged
        b. Medicaid for the indigent
    2. Federal aid to education

3. Appalachian redevelopment
4. Housing and urban development
5. Failure: the Great Society

VI. The civil rights to Black Power
    A. Civil rights legislation
        1. Civil Rights Act of 1964
        2. Voting Rights Act of 1965
            a. The march to Montgomery
            b. Provisions of the act
    B. Rise of the Black Power movement
        1. Riots in 1965 and 1966
        2. Condition of urban blacks
        3. Philosophy of the Black Power movement
        4. Leaders of the movement
        5. Assessment of the Black Power movement

VII. The tragedy of Vietnam
    A. Efforts to avoid defeat
        1. Escalation
        2. The cost of the war
    B. The Tonkin Gulf Resolution
        1. Response to attack on American destroyers
        2. Interpreted as congressional approval for war
    C. Escalation in 1965
        1. Attack at Pleiku
        2. "Operation Rolling Thunder"
        3. Combat troops to Vietnam
    D. The context for policy
        1. Consistent with earlier foreign policy goals
        2. Goal of American involvement
        3. Erosion of support
    E. The turning point
        1. The Tet Offensive
        2. Further erosion of support
        3. Presidential primaries became referendums on Johnson's Vietnam policy
        4. Johnson announced that he would not seek another term

VIII. The crescendo of the sixties
    A. Tragedies of 1968
        1. Assassination of Martin Luther King, Jr.
        2. Assassination of Robert Kennedy
    B. The election of 1968
        1. Democrats

           a. Nominated Hubert Humphrey
           b. Party in disarray
        2. Republicans
           a. Quiet convention in Miami
           c. Nixon represented stability and order
        3. George Wallace
           a. Candidate of the American Independent party
           b. Could have thrown the election into the House
              of Representatives
        4. Results
           a. Narrow victory for Nixon
           b. Wallace received 10,000,000 votes

Suggestions for Lecture Topics

For a lecture on the civil rights movement in the Kennedy and Johnson
years, Harvard Sitkoff's *The Struggle for Black Equality, 1954–1980*
(1981) would be a good source.

A lecture on the domestic policies of JFK and LBJ could make use of
James L. Sundquist's *Politics and Policy: The Eisenhower, Kennedy, and
Johnson Years* (1968).

George C. Herring's *America's Longest War: The United States and
Vietnam, 1950–1975* (2nd ed., 1986) would be good for a discussion of
developments in the Vietnam War.

James David Barber's analysis in *The Presidential Character* (3rd ed.,
1985) is interesting and often useful. The section on Kennedy could provide the basis for a good lecture.

Multiple-Choice Questions

  1. Which of the following statements about Richard Nixon is *not*
     true?
       A. He attended Whittier College and Duke University Law
          School.
       B. He practiced law in California.
       C. By 1950 he was a nationally known Republican politician.
     * D. He wrote *Profiles in Courage,* a book about political
          leaders who "made the tough decisions."

  2. Which of the following statements about John F. Kennedy is *not*
     true?
       A. He attended Harvard University.
     * B. His family was poorer than Richard Nixon's.

C. He was not an outspoken opponent of McCarthyism.

D. He was the first Catholic to run for the presidency since Al Smith.

3. In the 1960 presidential election,

A. Kennedy's margin in the electoral college was small: 268 to 254.

* B. Kennedy's margin in the popular vote was small: under 120,000.

C. Nixon lost in the electoral college, but actually had more popular votes than Kennedy.

D. Nixon failed to carry a single southern state.

4. Robert Kennedy, the president's younger brother, served as JFK's

A. secretary of defense.

B. secretary of state.

* C. attorney-general.

D. special assistant for national security affairs.

5. Kennedy's cabinet appointments

* A. emphasized youth and the "Eastern Establishment."

B. were mostly politicians who had been especially helpful to the Democratic Party.

C. included the first black secretary of the treasury.

D. indicated a decentralization of control over both domestic and foreign affairs.

6. One of the biggest legislative accomplishment of the Kennedy administration came in the field of

* A. tariff reduction.

B. civil rights for blacks.

C. federal aid to education.

D. corrupt practices reforms.

7. Which of the following was Kennedy unable to persuade Congress to pass?

A. support for a space program to reach the moon by the end of the decade

B. a new housing act

C. "Alliance for Progress" foreign aid programs to help Latin American nations

* D. health insurance for the aged

8. The Bay of Pigs incident

A. freed 154 American prisoners-of-war still being held by the North Koreans.

B. was a limited success.
* C. resulted in the capture of 1,200 men.
D. forced Cuba to grant certain trade concessions.

9. The Berlin Wall
   A. was a response to, among other things, JFK's request for an additional $3 billion for defense.
   B. cut off movement between East and West Berlin.
   C. increased tensions between the Soviet Union and the United States.
   * D. is correctly represented by all the above.

10. Faced with the presence of Soviet missiles in Cuba, Kennedy
   A. ordered a "surgical" air strike.
   B. waited to see what the Russians would do.
   * C. ordered a naval blockade of Cuba.
   D. broke off diplomatic relations with Cuba.

11. Concerning Vietnam, Kennedy
   A. continued to support Premier Diem.
   * B. increased the number of American "advisors" from 2,000 to 16,000.
   C. asked Congress to send American combat troops to force the surrender of Diem's pro-Communist regime.
   D. reduced the number of American troops there by half.

12. Following the Cuban missile crisis, several steps were taken that eased Russian-American tensions. These included all the following *except*
   A. a nuclear test ban treaty.
   B. installation of a "hot line" between Moscow and Washington.
   * C. the halting of construction on the Berlin Wall for several years.
   D. the removal of obsolete missiles from Turkey, Italy, and Britain.

13. Lyndon Johnson
   A. was unfamiliar with Washington politics.
   * B. proved to be more able in domestic politics than in foreign affairs.
   C. was intimidated by most congressmen.
   D. was closer to Herbert Hoover in temperament and character than he was to Franklin Roosevelt.

14. The author of *The Other America*, the book that opened many Americans' eyes to the problem of poverty, was

* A. Michael Harrington.
  B. Averell Harriman.
  C. Hubert H. Humphrey.
  D. Robert C. Weaver.

15. Johnson's Economic Opportunity Bill included all the following *except*
    A. a Job Corps for youth.
    B. Volunteers in Service to America (VISTA).
    C. job-training programs.
  * D. a relief program of make-work jobs.

16. In the early 1960s many Republicans felt that their party in the previous two decades had
    A. been too conservative.
  * B. merely echoed the Democratic party.
    C. strayed too far from the principles of Franklin Roosevelt.
    D. been too ideological.

17. In the election of 1964
    A. Republicans increased their majorities in Congress.
  * B. Johnson won by a landslide.
    C. the race issue helped Johnson win the states of the Deep South.
    D. Barry Goldwater campaigned on a platform of "Peace in Vietnam and civil rights at home."

18. The health insurance bill passed by Congress in 1965
  * A. created Medicaid, to help cover medical payments for the indigent.
    B. was opposed by the American Medical Association.
    C. was vetoed by Johnson because Congress refused to raise taxes to pay for it.
    D. was ruled unconstitutional by the Supreme Court two years later.

19. James H. Meredith
  * A. was a black student who needed the help of federal troops to enroll at the University of Mississippi.
    B. led the "sit-in" at the Woolworth's lunch counter in Greensboro, North Carolina.
    C. defied a court order by refusing to allow black students to enroll at the University of Alabama.
    D. was the Birmingham police commissioner who used attack dogs and electric cattle prods on black protestors.

20. The Civil Rights Act of 1964
    A. was the most far-reaching civil rights measure ever enacted by Congress.
    B. outlaw discrimination in public accommodations.
    C. empowered the attorney-general to bring suits for school desegregation.
    *   D. is correctly represented by all the above.

21. The Watts riot in 1965
    A. led to passage the following year of the Voting Rights Act.
    *   B. signaled a new phase in the civil rights movement.
    C. began with the assassination of Malcolm X.
    D. is correctly represented by all the above.

22. The philosophy of "militant nonviolence" was best seen in the work of
    A. Stokely Carmichael.
    *   B. Martin Luther King, Jr.
    C. the "Black Power" movement.
    D. Huey P. Newton.

23. The Tonkin Gulf Resolution
    A. was the declaration by the United Nations that condemned Communist aggression in South Vietnam.
    *   B. authorized the president to use whatever means were necessary to defend American forces and prevent further Communist aggression.
    C. was the result of a North Vietnamese attack on a camp of U.S. military advisors.
    D. was vetoed by Johnson.

24. Operation "Rolling Thunder"
    A. began in 1963.
    B. began in 1967.
    C. was the first major "search and destroy" operation carried out under General William C. Westmoreland.
    *   D. was the first sustained bombing of North Vietnam.

25. America's goal in Vietnam was to
    A. provoke Red China to enter the war.
    *   B. keep the North Vietnamese and Vietcong from winning.
    C. force the Communists from North Vietnam.
    D. reopen vital Asian trade routes.

26. All the following happened in 1968 *except*
    *   A. Congress passed the nation's most comprehensive voting rights acts.
    B. Johnson announced that he would not seek reelection.

    C. the Vietcong and the North Vietnamese carried out the Tet Offensive.

    D. Martin Luther King, Jr., was killed.

27. All the following were liberal Democrats who promised to seek peace in Vietnam *except*
    - A. Hubert H. Humphrey.
    - B. Robert Kennedy.
    - * C. Curtis LeMay.
    - D. Eugene McCarthy.

28. The 1968 Republican convention
    - * A. was held in Miami.
    - B. was held in Chicago.
    - C. was marred by riots and antiwar demonstrations.
    - D. named Dean Rusk as its vice-presidential candidate.

29. The candidate of the American Independent Party in 1968 was
    - A. Eugene McCarthy.
    - B. Clark Clifford.
    - * C. George Wallace.
    - D. Spiro Agnew.

30. In the election of 1968,
    - A. Nixon won by a landslide.
    - * B. Nixon won by fewer than a million votes.
    - C. the American Independent candidate carried four states in the Northeast.
    - D. the American Independent candidate carried four states in the Midwest.

Suggested Essay Questions

1. What were the main goals of the civil rights movement in the 1960s? Which of these goals did it accomplish?

2. What were the main domestic achievements of JFK's New Frontier? of LBJ's Great Society? Why was Johnson able to accomplish more?

3. Describe the major trends in the Cold War in the 1960s.

4. "American military intervention in Vietnam was . . . a logical culmination of the assumptions widely shared by the foreign policy establishment and leaders of both political parties since the early days of the Cold War." Explain this statement.

5. Describe the candidates, issues, and results of the presidential elections of 1960, 1964, and 1968.

Chapter 34

REBELLION AND REACTION: THE NIXON YEARS

This chapter describes the youth revolt of the late 1960s, including the New Left and the counterculture, and traces the gains made by women and ethnic minorities. It also covers Nixon's foreign and domestic affairs, stressing Vietnam, stagflation, and Watergate.

Chapter Outline

I. Attacks on traditional institutions
    A. Youth revolt
        1. The maturing baby-boom generation
        2. The beginnings of the youth revolt
    B. The New Left
        1. Students for a Democratic Society
            a. Founded by Tom Hayden and Al Haber
            b. The Port Huron statement
        2. Free Speech Movement
            a. Origins at Berkeley
            b. Program and tactics
        3. Role of Vietnam war in radicalizing youth
        4. Increased college protests
        5. The 1968 Democratic convention
        6. The breakup of the New Left
    C. The counterculture
        1. Origins and philosophy
        2. Communal living
        3. Rock music concerts
        4. Downfall of the counterculture
    D. Feminism
        1. Betty Friedan's *The Feminine Mystique*
        2. National Organization for Women
        3. Legal gains
        4. Divisions within the movement
        5. Changes in traditional sex roles

E. Minorities
   1. Hispanics
   2. American Indians
      a. Conditions that fostered concern
      b. Tactics

II. Nixon and Vietnam
   A. Gradual withdrawal
      1. Immediate withdrawal of troops rejected
      2. Nixon's Vietnam policy
         a. Paris peace talks
         b. "Vietnamization" of war
         c. Expansion of air war
   B. Divisions at home
      1. My Lai massacre
      2. Nixon's Cambodian "incursion"
         a. Kent State
         b. Jackson State College
      3. Publication of *Pentagon Papers*
   C. War without end
      1. Peace talks
         a. Shifts in American negotiating position
         b. "Christmas bombings"
         c. Peace agreement signed
      2. Effects of American withdrawal
      3. The legacy of Vietnam

III. Nixon and Middle America
   A. Domestic affairs
      1. Civil rights
         a. Nixon's stance
         b. Supreme Court decisions
      2. The Warren Court characterized
      3. Nixon's domestic program characterized
      4. Social legislation of the Democratic Congress
   B. Economic malaise
      1. Effects
      2. Causes
         a. Holdover problems from Johnson's administration
         b. International competition
         c. Oil embargo
         d. Increasing workforce

       3. Efforts to cure stagflation
    C. Environmental protection
       1. Creation of Environmental Protection Agency
       2. Increased understanding of limited nature of resources
       3. Few people willing to sacrifice

 IV. Nixon triumphant
    A. Official recognition of China
    B. SALT agreement with Russia
    C. Shuttle diplomacy
       1. Problems in Middle East
       2. Kissinger's role in seeking peace
    D. 1972 election
       1. Republicans nominate Nixon
       2. Democrats nominate McGovern
       3. Landslide victory for Nixon

  V. Watergate
    A. Uncovering the coverup
       1. Previous incidents of "dirty tricks"
       2. Developments in the Senate committee hearings
       3. Nixon's resignation
    B. Effects of Watergate
       1. Cynicism over Ford's pardoning of Nixon
       2. Legislative responses to Watergate
       3. Disillusionment with national leaders
       4. Crisis of confidence

Suggestions for Lecture Topics

For a lecture on a particularly controversial aspect of Nixon's Vietnam policy, see William Shawcross's *Sideshow: Kissinger, Nixon, and the Destruction of Cambodia* (1979).

Good sources for a lecture on American culture in the 1960s include Theodore Roszak's *The Making of a Counter Culture* (1968) and Morris Dickstein's *Gates of Eden* (1977).

For a lecture on the feminist movement, see Gayle Graham Yate's *What Women Want: The Ideas of the Movement* (1975). William H. Chafe's *The American Women* (1972) is good for background.

There are numerous sources for a lecture on Watergate. Carl Bernstein and Robert Woodward's *All the President's Men* (1974) is a detailed account of how these two reporters uncovered much of the Watergate story. Useful for putting the incident in historical perspective are Theodore White's *Breach of Faith* (1975) and Arthur M. Schlesinger, Jr.'s *The Imperial Presidency* (1973).

Multiple-Choice Questions

1. The downfall of the counterculture can be traced to all the following *except*
    A. the Rolling Stones' concert at Altamont, California.
    B. increased commercialization.
    C. the naïveté of its members.
  * D. increased political involvement.

2. The leading force behind the formation of the United Farm Workers was
  * A. Cesar Chavez.
    B. Francisco Ramirez.
    C. Agapito Gomez.
    D. Henry B. Gonzalez.

3. The author of *The Feminine Mystique*
    A. was Alice Paul.
    B. was Jane Fonda.
    C. focused on the many gains women had made in the twentieth century.
  * D. protested against the idealization of blissful domesticity for American women after World War II.

4. Which of the following is the fastest-growing minority group in America?
  * A. Hispanics
    B. blacks
    C. women
    D. American Indians

5. Leaders of the Native American movement were most successful when they
    A. copied the tactics of the civil rights movement.
    B. mounted mass protests at sites of former injustices to Indians.
  * C. showed how the old treaties signed by officials of the American government in the nineteenth century had been violated.
    D. used their political power to elect Indians to Congress.

6. Rachel Carson's *Silent Spring* concerned
   A. civil rights for blacks.
   * B. the ecology.
   C. the My Lai massacre.
   D. civil rights for American Indians.

7. "We are the people of this generation, bred in at least moderate comfort, housed in universities, looking uncomfortably to the world we inherit." This statement
   A. was written by Al Haber.
   * B. was the 1962 ideology of the Students for a Democratic Society.
   C. was called by Theodore Roszak "the hippie's creed."
   D. is correctly represented by all the above statements.

8. The leader of Berkeley's Free Speech Movement was
   A. Al Haber.
   B. Tom Hayden.
   * C. Mario Savio
   D. Clark Kerr.

9. The major factor in radicalizing the youth revolt was
   * A. the war in Vietnam.
   B. the civil rights movement.
   C. restrictive college curricula.
   D. restrictions on freedom of speech.

10. The phrase "Tune in, turn on, drop out"
    A. captures the spirit of the New Left.
    * B. was coined by Timothy Leary.
    C. was a parody of a Zenith television advertisement.
    D. is correctly represented by all the above statements.

11. The economic malaise during Nixon's administration was caused by all the following *except*
    * A. a sharp decrease in the number of new workers.
    B. increased government spending through the 1960s without a major tax increase.
    C. the stiff competition American goods faced on the international market.
    D. the oil shortage.

12. The so-called *Pentagon Papers*
    A. were published in defiance of a Supreme Court decision prohibiting such publication.

    B. quieted many critics of the Vietnam War.

    C. broke the story of the My Lai massacre.

* D. revealed that Congress and the American people had not been told the full story of the Tonkin Gulf incident.

13. Which American diplomat was known for his "shuttle diplomacy" in the Middle East?

    A. Maxwell Taylor

    B. Clark Clifford

* C. Henry Kissinger

    D. Robert McNamara

14. The "silent majority" referred to

* A. conservative working- and middle-class citizens.

    B. women.

    C. the coalition of ethnic minorities, youth, the aged, women, and the poor.

    D. the nation's youth, defined by Abbie Hoffman to be anyone under thirty.

15. The SALT agreement

    A. ended the arms race.

    B. greatly limited the development of new weapons systems.

* C. set limits on certain types of nuclear weapons.

    D. prohibited either side from producing or possessing intercontinental ballistic missiles.

16. The only army officer convicted as a result of the My Lai massacre was

    A. Peter Cooper.

    B. William Edward Preston.

* C. William Calley.

    D. Franklin Alexander.

17. George McGovern's problems in the 1972 election included all the following *except*

    A. the revelation that his running mate had undergone psychiatric treatment.

* B. George Wallace's strong showing at the Democratic convention.

    C. reforms in the Democratic Party that alienated the party regulars.

    D. his support for values associated with the turbulence of the 1960s.

18. The Supreme Court case of *Bakke v. Board of Regents of California* (1978)
    A. was a clear victory for liberals and blacks.
    B. cut off federal aid to colleges that discriminated against women.
    C. overturned the conviction of an antiwar protester.
    * D. restricted the use of quotas to achieve racial balance.

19. In response to the Watergate revelations, Congress passed several pieces legislation designed to curb executive power. This legislation included all the following *except*
    A. the War Powers Act.
    B. an act that set new limits on campaign contributions and expenditures.
    C. an act strengthening the Freedom of Information Act.
    * D. the Presidential Pardon Act.

20. Nixon's involvement in the Watergate affair
    A. included planning the break-in at the Democratic National Committee headquarters.
    B. led to his impeachment.
    * C. led to a very serious constitutional crisis.
    D. was an isolated incident in an otherwise scandal-free administration.

21. Each of the following resigned from office as a result of the Watergate affair *except*
    * A. John J. Sirica.
    B. L. Patrick Gray.
    C. Elliot Richardson.
    D. John Ehrlichman.

22. Victories for the women's movement in the 1970s included all the following *except*
    A. Title IX of the Educational Amendment Act of 1972.
    B. *Roe v. Wade.*
    * C. ratification of the Equal Rights Amendment.
    D. increased economic and political influence.

23. When the United States signed peace terms in January 1973 ending the war in Vietnam,
    * A. the North Vietnamese kept regular army troops in South Vietnam.
    B. the war-torn country of Vietnam was finally reunited.

    C. South Vietnam agreed to a Communist government.

    D. America could justly claim both victory and "peace with honor."

24. Nixon's policies on civil rights
* A. led to a letter of protest signed by 65 lawyers in the Justice Department.
  B. had the support of liberal congressmen.
  C. included strong efforts to desegregate the nation's public schools.
  D. included support for a renewed Voting Rights Act.

25. The Supreme Court ruled in 1971 that cities must bus students out of their neighborhoods if necessary to achieve racial integration in the case of
* A. *Swann v. Charlotte-Mecklenburg Board of Education.*
  B. *Alexander v. Holmes County Board of Education.*
  C. *Milliken v. Bradley.*
  D. *Engel v. Vitale.*

26. Nixon's domestic program
  A. was at one time called the "New Federalism."
  B. included a revenue-sharing plan to return money to the states.
  C. was in part an attempt to revive traditional values, such as free enterprise and individual initiative.
* D. is correctly described by all the above.

27. The Weathermen
  A. made up the pacifist faction of the SDS.
* B. followed the strategy of revolutionary terrorism.
  C. were led by Clark Kerr.
  D. broke from the SDS over the issue of civil rights.

28. Nixon's Vietnam policy included all the following *except*
  A. demands at the Paris peace talks for the withdrawal of Communist forces from South Vietnam.
* B. continued buildup of American armed forces in Vietnam.
  C. reduction of domestic unrest over the war.
  D. expansion of the air war in Vietnam.

29. The student demonstrators at Kent University on May 4, 1970, were protesting
  A. new of the My Lai massacre.
  B. passage of the Gulf of Tonkin resolution.

    C. Nixon's announcement of his planned "Vietnamization" of the war.
* D. Nixon's announcement of his "incursion" into Cambodia.

30. Nixon's triumph concerning China was
* A. American diplomatic recognition of the People's Republic of China.
    B. the signing of reciprocal trade agreements.
    C. the successful conclusion of negotiations for nuclear arms reduction.
    D. the signing of a mutual defense treaty.

Suggested Essay Questions

1. Discuss the various aspects of President Nixon's Vietnam policy. How was Nixon's policy different from that of his predecessors?

2. Briefly describe the major events of the Watergate affair, and assess its impact on America.

3. How did the New Left and the counterculture differ? What led to the downfall of each?

4. Assess the domestic policies of the Nixon administration.

5. Describe the gains made by women and ethnic minorities in the 1960s and early 1970s. In each case, what accounted for the gains?

Chapter 35

RETRENCHMENT: FORD TO REAGAN

This chapter discusses the domestic and foreign policies of the Ford, Carter, and Reagan administrations, paying particular attention to the Reagan years.

Chapter Outline

I. Drifting: Ford and Carter
   A. The Ford years
      1. Conservative domestic philosophy
      2. Foreign policy
         a. Arms talks
         b. Middle East
         c. Cambodian communists
   B. The 1976 election
      1. Republicans nominated Ford
      2. Democrats nominated Carter
      3. Carter won
         a. New Deal coalition
         b. Low voter turnout
   C. Domestic affairs
      1. Liberal successes
      2. Energy policy
   D. Panama Canal treaty
   E. The Camp David accords
   F. Mounting troubles
      1. The economy
      2. SALT II
      3. Soviet invasion of Afghanistan
   G. Iran
      1. Background to problem
      2. Hostages taken
      3. Rescue attempt failed

II. The Reagan restoration
   A. The making of a president

      1. Reagan's background
      2. Influence of FDR
      3. Conservative transformation
      4. Reagan's attraction
      5. Reagan as California governor

B. The move to Reagan
    1. Factors favoring Reagan
      a. Demographic
      b. Rise of new fundamentalism
      c. Carter's misfortunes
    2. The 1980 election
      a. Reagan's campaign
      b. Results of the election

C. Inauguration

D. Reaganomics
    1. Reagan's style
    2. Reagan's "supply-side" economics
    3. Economic program passed by Congress
      a. Social programs cut
      b. Deficit increased
      c. Taxes increased

E. Wayward appointees
    1. James Watt
    2. Scandals in the administration
    3. The "sleaze factor" and the "Teflon presidency"

F. Union, women, and minorities
    1. Reagan's stance on unions
      a. Pro-management
      b. Air traffic controllers' strike
    2. Reagan's stance on women
      a. Antifeminist position
      b. Appointment of first woman to Supreme Court

III. America and the world in the 1980s
  A. The defense buildup
    1. Defense spending increased
    2. Cold War rhetoric
  B. The Americas
    1. El Salvador
    2. Nicaragua
      a. Background
      b. Reagan's policy
  C. The Middle East
    1. Reasons for tensions
    2. America's position

3. Tragedy in Lebanon
D. Grenada
1. Reasons for concern
2. American invasion
3. Effects of invasion

IV. Reagan's second term
  A. The election of 1984
    1. Republicans
      a. Helped by economic recovery
      b. Nominated Reagan
    2. Democrats
      a. Nominated Walter Mondale
      b. Geraldine Ferraro for vice-president
      c. Mondale's acceptance speech
    3. Election results
  B. The landslide syndrome
    1. Reagan's problems
    2. Reshuffling of administration positions
    3. Reagan's luck held out
  C. Tax reforms
    1. Reagan's proposed "tax simplification"
    2. Passage of Tax Reform Law of 1986
  D. Arms control
    1. Geneva summit
      a. Limited success of summit
      b. Refused to compromise on SDI
    2. Reykjavik meeting
      a. Far-reaching proposals
      b. Again, SDI got in way
  E. Twilight of a presidency
    1. Space shuttle disaster
    2. Surges in Reagan's popularity
    3. Republicans lost midterm elections
    4. Iran-Contra affair
      a. Story uncovered
      b. Role of Oliver North
      c. The Tower Commission
    5. Conservative critics
    6. Other crises
      a. AIDS
      b. Materialism
      c. Wall Street crash
    7. The INF treaty
  F. The Reagan legacy

Suggestions for Lecture Topics

Perhaps the most useful book for a lecture on Carter is Betty Glad's *Jimmy Carter: In Search of the Great White House* (1980).

There are several good works to draw on for a lecture on Reagan. Lou Cannon's *Reagan* (1982) is probably the best account of Reagan's career through his first year as president. Robert Dallek's *Ronald Reagan: The Politics of Symbolism* (1984) carries the analysis of his leadership, as discussed in this chapter, much further. *The Reagan Record*, edited by John L. Palmer and Isabel V. Sawhill (1984), analyzes various aspects of Reagan's domestic policy. Colin Campbell's *Managing the Presidency* (1986) compares the Carter and Reagan administrations.

Multiple-Choice Questions

1. As president, Gerald Ford
    A. thought that the federal government should be active in domestic affairs.
    B. was more liberal than Lyndon B. Johnson in domestic affairs.
    C. favored wage and price controls to curb inflation.
  * D. lost popularity following the fall of South Vietnam in May 1975.

2. In the presidential election of 1976
  * A. Carter won most of the black vote in the South.
    B. Jimmy Carter beat Ronald Reagan by a small margin.
    C. the Democratic win was attributed to the area west of the Mississippi, where Carter won all the states but one.
    D. voter turnout was over 60 percent, reflecting a greatly increased political awareness following the Watergate affair.

3. As president, Carter
    A. pushed important environmental bills through Congress.
    B. turned control of the Panama Canal over to the government of Panama.
    C. offered amnesty to draft evaders who had fled the country rather than go to Vietnam.
  * D. accomplished all the above.

4. The Camp David accords concerned
    A. Iran and Iraq.

    B. Israel and Syria.
    C. Egypt and Iran.
 * D. Israel and Egypt.

5. Jimmy Carter
    A. was, like Lyndon Johnson, an expert at manipulating Congress.
    B. was one of the few presidents to show a sustained increase in popularity after entering the White House.
 * C. chose Walter Mondale as his vice-presidential running mate.
    D. was the first president to appoint a woman to the Supreme Court.

6. Faced with the Soviet invasion of Afghanistan, Carter did all the following *except*
    A. suspend shipments of grain to Russia.
    B. shelve the SALT II agreements.
    C. urge an international boycott of the 1980 Olympics in Moscow.
 * D. persuade Congress to pass a law that greatly reduced the number of Russians who could immigrate to the United States.

7. The American hostages held in Iran
    A. were rescued in a daring commando raid.
 * B. were symbols of Iranian displeasure with American foreign policy.
    C. were captured during CIA covert operations in Beirut.
    D. allowed the United States to increase its stature in the international sphere.

8. Ronald Reagan
    A. turned to politics after a successful career as a lawyer.
 * B. had at one time supported FDR's New Deal.
    C. pushed for a stronger defense during his three terms in the U.S. Senate.
    D. resigned from Nixon's cabinet during the Senate Watergate hearings.

9. James Watt
    A. was Carter's secretary of state.
    B. was Carter's secretary of labor.
 * C. was Reagan's secretary of the interior.
    D. was Reagan's secretary of state.

10. The Tower Commission
    A. recommended that NASA scrap its space shuttle flights.
    B. condemned President Ford for pardoning Nixon.
    C. recommended that Reagan do away with wage and price controls.
  * D. investigated the Iran-Contra affair.

11. In the election of 1980, Reagan profited from all the following *except*
    A. demographic trends.
    B. a revival of evangelical religion.
    C. the Iranian crisis.
  * D. a growing mood of liberalism in the nation.

12. Walter Mondale
    A. was the Democratic vice-presidential candidate in 1984.
    B. promised he would not raise taxes.
    C. ran for president in 1980 as an independent candidate.
  * D. won only Minnesota and the District of Columbia when he ran for president.

13. John Anderson
    A. was Carter's secretary of energy.
    B. was Ford's secretary of state.
    C. tried to assassinate Reagan in 1981.
  * D. ran as an independent candidate in the 1980 presidential election.

14. Democrats won control of both houses of Congress in the election of
    A. 1980.
    B. 1982.
    C. 1984.
  * D. 1986.

15. Before he became governor of California, Reagan
    A. was a Democrat.
    B. was president of the Screen Actors Guild.
    C. served as a spokesman for General Electric.
  * D. is correctly described by all the above statements.

16. Reagan's economic policy most closely resembled that of
  * A. Andrew Mellon.
    B. Franklin D. Roosevelt.

    C. John F. Kennedy.
    D. Dwight D. Eisenhower.

17. What was David A. Stockman's role in the Reagan administration?
  * A. budget director
    B. chief of staff
    C. secretary of state
    D. secretary of the interior

18. As president, Reagan opposed
    A. cutting funds for civil-rights enforcement.
  * B. abortion on demand.
    C. budget cuts for food stamps and school meals.
    D. all the above.

19. The term "Teflon presidency"
    A. was coined by Gary Hart.
    B. was coined by Richard Nixon.
  * C. refers to Ronald Reagan.
    D. refers to Gerald Ford.

20. As president, Reagan supported
    A. the Equal Rights Amendment.
    B. synthetic fuels projects.
  * C. the firing of striking air traffic controllers.
    D. all the above.

21. Geraldine Ferraro
    A. was fired from her position as chief of toxic waste cleanup at the EPA for favoritism to polluters.
    B. was the first woman to sit on the Supreme Court.
  * C. was the Democratic vice-presidential candidate in 1984.
    D. was Jimmy Carter's press secretary.

22. The Wall Street crash of October 19, 1987,
    A. was the worst one-day drop in history.
    B. was caused in part by the size of the national debt and the high trade deficit.
    C. occurred partly because foreign investors were less willing to invest in the United States.
  * D. is correctly represented by all the above.

23. The INF treaty
  * A. would eliminate intermediate-range nuclear missiles.
    B. was between England, France, and the United States.

    C. doubled the amount of wheat sold annually to the Soviet Union.

    D. concerned whaling off the coast of Norway.

24. The fifty-three American hostages held in Iran were released after

  * A. 444 days.

    B. 7 months.

    C. 3 months.

    D. 17 days.

25. The comprehensive Tax Reform Law passed in 1986

    A. was vetoed by Reagan.

    B. increase tax shelters for businesses.

    C. raised the maximum rate to 50 percent.

  * D. reduced the number of tax brackets.

26. The major stumbling block to agreement on arms limitations in 1985 and 1986 was

    A. the Soviet presence in Afghanistan.

  * B. Reagan's Strategic Defense Initiative.

    C. the issue of nuclear submarines.

    D. Soviet missiles in Turkey.

27. Over 200 American Marines were killed when a truck loaded with explosives blew up at their quarters in

    A. Jerusalem.

  * B. Beirut.

    C. San Salvador.

    D. Teheran.

28. All the following statements about supply-side economics are true *except*

    A. it is also called "trickle-down" economics.

  * B. it favors a more progressive income tax.

    C. it favors tax breaks for the wealthy.

    D. it is similar in many ways to the government's economic program of the 1920s.

29. American troops were sent to Lebanon

    A. to retaliate for an air strike against Israel.

    B. to prepare for the invasion of Grenada.

  * C. to protect the peace in that volatile area.

    D. over Reagan's veto.

30. In Nicaragua, Reagan supported
   A. followers of President José Napoleon Duarte.
 * B. the Contras.
   C. the Sandinistas.
   D. the National Liberation Front.

Suggested Essay Questions

1. What were the main foreign-policy achievements of the Carter administration? Where did Carter fail?

2. What economic problems did Presidents Ford and Carter face? How did they try to solve these problems, and how successful were they?

3. Describe the main features of Reaganomics.

4. According to some commentators, Reagan's administration may prove to be one of the most corrupt in history. Is this assertion true? Why or why not?

5. Describe America's role in world affairs in the 1980s.

APPENDIX: SAMPLE FINAL EXAMINATIONS

The following sample final examinations may be of use to instructors using the Tindall/Shi text. These four samples (two covering American history through Reconstruction, two from Reconstruction to the present) are designed as three-hour exams. Instructors should use these samples only as guides; they are based on the textbook and cannot reflect the emphasis or additional information that an instructor adds in lectures. Instructors are therefore encouraged to modify these tests to suit their particular courses.

Instructors can, of course, make up a final examination consisting entirely of multiple-choice questions selected from the chapter tests, and in large classes this may be the only practical course. The exams that follow, however, are meant to allow students to show their mastery of the material by synthesizing facts, analyzing a large body of knowledge, and discerning trends over a long period of time. At this stage in a course, students should be prepared to use the facts they have learned to write historical essays.

Instructors may wish to remind students that, unless a narrative is specifically requested in an essay, they should concentrate instead on explanation—that is, they should analyze rather than retell the story. Students should be encouraged to write coherent, organized essays. (You may wish to suggest that your students purchase and read a copy of Strunk and White's *Elements of Style* or another good style manual.) On the "short answer" sections, organization and careful thought are again needed, perhaps even more so than in the longer essays. Finally, the "identifications" are useful for testing more specific knowledge, but even here students should be reminded that facts do not exist in isolation. Suggest that students include a short sentence explaining the significance of each particular term or person.

American History Final Examination—Through Reconstruction

Example 1

Part I. *Essay.* Answer any one of the following. 40 points.

1. Trace the course of American two-party politics from 1790 to 1860. What accounted for the rise of the major parties? What were the main issues and constituencies involved in each?

2. On the eve of the Civil War, had America grown into two different civilizations, North and South? What were the main factors that contributed to the growth of sectional tensions?

Part II. *Short answer.* Write full paragraphs on three (3) of the following. 30 points (10 points each).

1. At what point did it become clear that England, and not Spain, France, the Netherlands, or some other country, would control most of North America? Why?

2. What arguments might the English have advanced in favor of the Stamp Act? What arguments did the colonists use against it?

3. What problems arose under the Articles of Confederation, and how did the Constitution address these problems?

4. What were the causes of the War of 1812? How did the Treaty of Ghent address these issues?

5. What advantages did the North have at the outbreak of the Civil War? What advantages did the South have?

Part III. *Identifications.* Identify and explain the significant of ten (10) of the following. 30 points (3 points each).

1. the "great biological exchange"
2. Capt. John Smith
3. Olive Branch Petition
4. Battle of Yorktown
5. Report on Manufactures
6. Jay's Treaty
7. Battle of New Orleans
8. "pet banks"
9. cotton gin
10. Ralph Waldo Emerson
11. Nat Turner
12. "anaconda strategy"
13. Wade-Davis Bill

American History Final Examination —Through Reconstruction

Example 2

Part I. *Essay.* Answer any one (1) of the following. 40 points.

1. What three American presidents, from Washington to Grant, were most important in shaping American history? Your answer should show not only the contributions the three made, but also how these contributions changed the course of history, either for better or for worse.

2. "From colonial times onward, American history has been marked more by division than by unity." Is this statement true for the period up to 1870? What factors united Americans? What factors were more divisive?

Part II. *Short answer.* Write full paragraphs on three (3) of the following. 30 points (10 points each).

1. Which of the English colonies in America was most successful? Why?

2. Assess the social effects of the American Revolution.

3. Compare Thomas Jefferson's view of American society to that of Alexander Hamilton. Which had more influence through the middle of the nineteenth century?

4. Describe the Compromise of 1850. How was it designed to ease sectional tensions? What were its effects?

5. Describe the plans of Reconstruction proposed by Andrew Johnson and the Radicals. What philosophies motivated these plans?

Part III. *Identifications*. Identify and explain the significance of ten (10) of the following. 30 points (3 points each).

1. Roger Williams
2. Albany Congress
3. virtual representation
4. Shays's rebellion
5. *The Federalist*
6. *Marbury v. Madison*
7. John Marshall
8. Webster-Hayne debate
9. Seneca Falls Convention
10. manifest destiny
11. George Fitzhugh
12. Wilmot Proviso
13. George B. McClellan

American History Final Examination—Reconstruction to the Present

Example 1

Part I. *Essay*. Answer any one (1) of the following. 40 points.

1. Describe the goals, methods, and achievements of Progressivism, the New Deal, and the Great Society.

2. What five periods have witnessed the most change (advancement or otherwise) in the status of blacks from 1865 to the present? Be sure to explain the changes involved.

Part II. *Short answer*. Write full paragraphs on three (3) of the following. 30 points (10 points each).

1. What did Reconstruction accomplish (and fail to accomplish) in the South?

2. What factors promoted the growth of industry in late-nineteenth-century America?

3. What were the arguments for and against America's annexation of the Philippines?

4. Describe the cultural paradox of the 1920s.

5. Explain the main features of Reaganomics.

Part III. *Identifications*. Identify and tell the significance of ten (10) of the following. 30 points (3 points each).

1. Crédit Mobilier
2. Dawes Severalty Act
3. the "new immigration"
4. John Dewey
5. Roosevelt Corollary
6. New Freedom
7. "the Sahara of the Bozart"
8. "Normalcy"
9. Agricultural Adjustment Administration
10. Washington Armaments Conference
11. George F. Kennan
12. "dynamic conservatism"
13. Betty Friedan

American History Final Examination—Reconstruction to the Present

Example 2

Part I. *Essay.* Answer any one (1) of the following. 40 points.

1. The major thrust of American foreign policy since the Civil War has vacillated between interventionist and isolationist. What factors have led to these shifts?

2. What three American presidents in the period since Reconstruction have been most important in shaping American history? Your answer should show not only the contributions the three made, but also how these contributions changed the course of history, either for better or for worse.

Part II. *Short answer.* Write full paragraphs on three (3) of the following. 30 points (10 points each).

1. Compare the racial philosophies of Booker T. Washington and W.E.B. Du Bois. Which approach has been more effective in advancing the cause of civil rights?

2. What were the main provisions of the platform of the Populist Party? Have these had practical effect since?

3. What were the main themes of progressivism?

4. Was the New Deal fundamentally conservative or liberal? Explain.

5. What caused the Cold War?

Part III. *Identifications.* Identify and tell the significance of ten (10) of the following. 30 points (3 points each).

1. Henry W. Grady
2. *Gospel of Wealth*
3. American Protective Association
4. *Plessy v. Ferguson*
5. Upton Sinclair
6. Zimmerman telegram
7. Sacco and Vanzetti
8. Huey Long
9. Operation "Overlord"
10. Yalta
11. Marshall Plan
12. Ngo Dinh Diem
13. counterculture